Using Image and Narrative in Therapy for Trauma, Addiction and Recovery

Using Image and Narrative in
Therapy *for* Trauma, Addiction *and* Recovery

Edited by James D. West

Foreword by Martin Weegmann

Jessica Kingsley Publishers
London and Philadelphia

First published in Great Britain in 2021 by Jessica Kingsley Publishers
An Hachette Company

3

A CIP catalogue record for this title is available from the
British Library and the Library of Congress

ISBN 978 1 78775 051 7
eISBN 978 1 78775 052 4

Printed and bound by CPI Group (UK) Ltd, Croydon, CR0 4YY

Jessica Kingsley Publishers' policy is to use papers that are natural,
renewable and recyclable products and made from wood grown in
sustainable forests. The logging and manufacturing processes are expected
to conform to the environmental regulations of the country of origin.

Jessica Kingsley Publishers
Carmelite House
50 Victoria Embankment
London EC4Y 0DZ

www.jkp.com

Dedicated with love to my father, Barry West (1928–1987)

An attempt to enunciate unspoken pain

The online colour plate is available to download from
www.jkp.com/catalogue/book/9781787750517

Contents

Post-traumatic Growth, Recovery and Community

To Be Continued…The Wider Context and the Return

Foreword

If a picture can paint a thousand words, then words, be they spoken or written, can conjure up whole pictures. As literary animals, we respond, understand and participate by means of stories, almost from the start of life. Our cognitive equipment relies on models and imagery, we drop metaphors and analogies into everyday conversations and want to feel satisfied that we can make our points effectively. Language is a uniquely crafted affair and life, as Wilde so ably put it, really does imitate art.

All that this amounts to is to say that the human mind develops with images, models and narratives that are woven so closely it is artificial to separate them. So, for example, an image can be expressed in terms of a 'story about something' whilst the telling of a narrative stimulates our imaginations and ability to 'see something'. We think with and by such resources, from morning to nightfall, not forgetting the dreams that populate our sleep-time. To understand this fully, we require all the insights that literature *and* neuroscience have on offer – as literary critic A.I. Richards once suggested, we need to draw upon both the Shelleys and Sheringhams of this world. Likewise, scientist Giovanni Frazzetto comments that we need to draw upon knowledge of both 'sonnets and synapses' if we are to properly understand human emotions.

This book offers richly rewarding journeys into the areas of image and narrative with respect to two of the most prevalent disorders of our times: addiction and trauma. I have learned so much from the chapters and the varied ways in which they tell the story of these twin disorders. It is not for academic reasons that this is important, as people recover from addiction and trauma when they can visualize a way forward, imagine a better future, and envisage hope, and can narrate their steps in so doing.

In his introductory chapter, our editor James D. West draws attention to the many therapeutic tales told throughout this book and how in our work the fragments of meaning are brought together – into better combination and conversation, as it were – and how in the act of retelling, progress can be made. I cannot begin to summarize the chapters and leave it to the authors themselves. But, as James remarks – and as I restate – enjoy where reading them takes you...

Martin Weegmann
Clinical Psychologist, Psychotherapist and Author
NHS and Independent Practice, London, UK

Acknowledgements

It is inevitable in a practitioner research such as this that authors must draw on their own resources in completing the project, and so for me enormous thanks are due again to my family: my partner Pauline Johnson, my son Søren, my daughter Eve and my step-daughter Nadine Thomas, who have supported me in this project during these strange and isolating times. Particular thanks are also due to my friend the writer David Spicer, who through our socially distanced conversations about stories and writing provided a good-humoured backdrop for discussion that has helped me maintain my sanity through this time.

Thank you also to my 21 co-authors who offered helpful feedback throughout the project, gave the book its direction and have made it a truly collective and collaborative work.

Joan Woddis, art therapist, group analyst and supervisor, with the wisdom of longevity, has guided me over many years in my practice and on this occasion has also offered anonymized peer review alongside Julie Watson, who coordinated it and encouraged a service-user perspective. They offered a vital service to the book and have ensured the clients' voice is emphatic throughout the book.

Our gratitude is due again to Hephzibah Kaplan for offering us a venue at London Art Therapy Centre for our authors' meetings.

I wish to express gratitude to the editors, the production and marketing team at Jessica Kingsley Publishers who entrusted us with this project, but particularly the commissioning editors Jane Evans and Simeon Hance who have guided, supported and encouraged me as editor and offered support and practical advice to the authors over the last two years.

I also thank all the clients and the supervisees, whose experiences of trauma and addiction in their lives and in their work have aided us in our inquiry. It is in their service that we exist as therapists and supervisors and *for this* I offer a heartfelt 'Thank you!' and hope that these dialogues drawn from practice can help us find a future we can all wish for in these riven and conflictual times. Special thanks are due to the Arts Therapy Team at Homerton Hospital for all the learning that occurred there.

This manuscript was submitted prior to the global Black Lives Matter (BLM) protests triggered by the murder of George Floyd. The chapters of this book point to inequalities and accumulated traumas within communities that often lead to psychological and physical ill health in individuals. Racism and economic inequality, past and present, are major contributors to these global phenomena. I hope that the reader will appreciate our implicit and explicit critique of the historic injustices that are highlighted by the following three recent global events; the climate change protests, the current pandemic and the ongoing BLM protests. Trauma images and narratives provide a reliable guide for radical change if we can listen, see, feel and unfold their layered messages…together.

Note: Throughout the book, all identifying features, locations and the names of clients have been anonymized, unless specific consent has been granted to do otherwise.

James D. West
Blackheath, London

1

Introduction

James D. West

Setting the scene

It is difficult to believe that I am writing this, separated from family members, in a 14-day isolation due to the Covid-19 pandemic. The economy has gone into a sharp reverse and many therapist colleagues are now considering how to proceed with their clients 'online', at a time when the importance of embodied practice has never been clearer. Our worlds and many of the stable norms and expectations, 'our realities', have suddenly collapsed, and the mass of the population across the globe have suddenly been cast into 'chaos narratives', struggling to make sense of what now confronts us. It is fitting to think about trauma, its effects and the way meaning can be brought to it, and to inform ourselves of 'other' and 'possible worlds'[1] we may not have considered until now.

The Persian poet Rumi (1207–1273) gives a sense of the eternal human struggle of reflective beings cast into this changing world; its purpose and pain:

> *The human shape is a ghost*
> *made of distraction and pain*
> *sometimes pure light, sometimes cruel,*
> *trying wildly to open,*
> *this image tightly held within itself*
> (Rumi 1984)

---

1 Both Umberto Eco (1979) and Jerome Bruner (1986a) use the term *possible worlds* to represent the potentiality of narrative, not setting fact against fiction but mediating the past and the future imaginatively.

It is a convulsive and transitory view of our human fate which meets this time and acknowledges the proximity of death and suffering, grief and the struggle with hopelessness that accompany us in our pivoting dance with 'the news', its meaning and interpretation.

The chapters of this book have many 'takes' on how to build meaning from 'disaster' and so make use of vulnerability to become more fully ourselves together, creating and unfolding images and stories. Images, 'trying wildly to open', drawing us back to the wholehearted meaning and purpose of our lives, always potential and always incomplete. How do images and stories help us to inquire, be and become? An exploration of some possible answers to these questions is held in the pages of this book.

Images

Images are simultaneously found and made as we create worlds within this world. In the chapter that immediately follows this Introduction I discuss how imagery gives us perspective and aids in the exploration of our 'takes' on the world. All the authors reveal the possibilities and the value of image and story-making processes (through the use of mental imagery, memories, painting, drawing, diagrams, maps, film, myth and metaphors) and consider why we recognize them as vital resources in supporting the emergent agencies of recovery. Trauma comes with strong and affecting imagery, which therapy aims to process. The combination of therapy and the arts offers collaborative reflections into 'the act[s] of perceiving, feeling, thinking, remembering, and judging – all of which are embedded with meanings that are concealed and hidden from consciousness' (Moustakas 1994, p.69).

Image and narrative reimport agency into traumatic 'events' and invite us to explore questions of Who? What? How? When? Where? and even the profoundly existential and value-laden question of Why? These explorations can be both painful and tragic, but they can at the same time initiate a sense of emergent agency, which can re-instil hope and initiate actions for justice and bring wisdom and understanding to individuals and thereby offer community resources. They can interrupt transgenerational transmission of destructive routines, bringing insight and helping integrate marginalized (hi)stories of conflict.

Narrative

Images evoke exploratory spaces while narrative evokes purposive time and action. Stories sequence the figures and images we find within them in space-time. Listing events is mere chronology and provides no story. Story requires a plot. Jonathon Culler (2000, p.84) states:

> ...plot requires a transformation. There must be an initial situation, a change involving some sort of reversal, and a resolution that marks the change as significant.

In this definition, if the word *plot* is replaced by *therapy*, it comes close to the aims of therapy in providing the client with a dynamic transformation and, while we must be aware of the risks of the narrative pressure for a 'good story', and make sure the therapist and client check that the change driving the re-storying is in the client's interests, it is important that this active and reflexive re-storying, which occurs both prospectively (towards a future) and retrospectively (in relation to the past), has permission to extend long after the therapy itself has ended. The ending of the story of therapy is always provisional and is therefore always ultimately withheld while we live.

According to Chron (2012), an engaging story requires a plot (What happens?), a protagonist (Whose story is it?) and a sense of what the story is about, its goal and question (What is at stake?). She gives neurological evidence to show we are 'wired for stories' that then help us to explore the fundamental questions of 'Will it help me?' and 'Will it hurt me?' that are basic to our survival.

Robert Moss (2011) eloquently summarizes the virtues of story as 'the shortest route to the meaning of things and our easiest way to remember and carry the meaning we discover. A good story lives inside and outside time and gives us keys to a world of truth beyond fact' (p.121). He captures the dual nature of story as a form of inquiry providing a useful and memorable deposit of learning, but also a route to larger meanings and purpose. If we replace the word *story* with *image* in Moss's statement, we find that this reveals the deep relationship of image to narrative as basic at-hand equipment for the making and remembering of the meaning of experience from birth to death across the ages. The chapters of this book illustrate the process of image and story-making in the collaborative actions of therapy within the contexts of one-to-one and group therapy, supervision, exhibition spaces and other therapeutic community activities.

One of the challenges of this project has been in recognizing the ubiquity of images and narratives across our lives. As Greimas and Courtés (1979, p.210) say: 'Narrativity is the organising principle of all discourse.' Roland Barthes (1989, pp.251–2) spells it out:

> The narratives of the world are numberless. Narrative is first and foremost a prodigious variety of genres, themselves distributed amongst different substances – as though any material were fit to receive man's stories. Able to be carried by articulated language, spoken or written, fixed or moving images, gestures and the ordered mixtures of all these substances… Moreover under this almost infinite diversity of forms narrative is present in every age, in every place, in every society; it begins with the very history of mankind and there nowhere is nor has been a people without narrative. All classes, all human groups, have their narratives… Caring nothing for the division between good and bad literature, narrative is international, transhistorical, transcultural: it is simply there, like life itself.

Images and stories are second, or possibly our first, nature from birth to death. It may be that our first experience of sequenced images and our own image/narrative productions occur in dreams. Dreams, like the imagery of trauma memory, present sequenced images and events, sometimes uncanny, sometimes prosaic, puzzling pictures and plot lines that surround us like amniotic fluid, we barely recognize them as the context to all we do. They invite interpretation.

The origin story of the book

The origin of this book is rooted in another, *Art Therapy in Private Practice* (West 2018). Five years ago a group of art therapists met in a similar collaborative writing project and raised the question with me as editor of whether stories could be legitimately included in their chapters. I was taken aback by the fear that storytelling would be seen as 'subjective' and therefore 'invalid'. I realized that if we consider the dual foundations of therapy in the storytelling of clients and the storytelling of therapists, this question represented a crisis of therapeutic representation that needed to be urgently addressed, especially within the arts therapies, where imaginative means must always be central.

One of the authors had used Mattingly's anthropological study of 'emplotment' (2001) in considering the ways practitioners use story collaboratively with clients but also raised questions around power and authorship in these clinical encounters. In writing up the chapter on practitioner research I wrote a section on 'Pictured and Storied Lives: Art and Narrative Therapy and Research' exploring the native forms of inquiry that evolve from the arts, curating and art history, to encourage art therapists to 're-own' the practice of therapy and the process of art as valid and valuable forms of inquiry.

This growing curiosity about the place of stories and pictures in therapy led me to attend a workshop called 'Narrative Therapy: Integrating Narrative and Psychodynamic Practice' co-run by Martin Weegmann, co-editor of *The Psychodynamics of Addiction*, which had been an inspiration to many art therapists working in the field of addiction. Later on I chaired a workshop with him called '...and thereby hangs a tale', focusing on narrative therapy, narrative psychology and its application for art therapists working with people with addictions. Martin's chapter (13) on mapping and addiction, and his etymological exploration of the terms *trauma* and *addiction*, plumbs deeper resonances uncovering the social and historical roots of our terms and places our work in a historical context while at the same time showing how etymology can be used to reveal the metaphorical roots of our concepts, intentions and values.

In a meeting with JKP editors towards the end of the editing journey of *Art Therapy in Private Practice*, I was asked to suggest titles I felt would be useful for art therapy in practice. One of my suggestions was for a book on trauma and addiction. In professional discussions the question had often been raised why these closely related areas of practice were rarely considered jointly in 'the literature' and having worked in 'rehab' for 34 years I was also aware of the centrality of life story work in the treatment of addiction and the reparative narrative traditions of Alcoholics Anonymous (AA).

Some years ago I had also presented a series of lectures with a colleague where I explored Freud's (1920/2001) elaboration on his earlier notion of the two principles of mental functioning (the pleasure and reality principles). In pondering the function of repetition in what would now be called PTSD in First World War veterans, he asked why the soldiers repeatedly regurgitated traumatic events, replaying them again and again in dream and in memory. With this question in mind he observed his grandson playing with a cotton reel in his mother's absence and noted the child repeatedly hiding and finding the reel and symbolizing this with the words 'gone' and 'here'. He realized that the link between the soldier trying to master his trauma and a child coming to terms with his mother's absence through play was that both were ongoing attempts at mastery. I put forward the notion that addiction and trauma responses can also be seen as attempts to master the pleasure/reality equation from different sides both leading to altered states and challenges to reality testing.

With the intention of taking my inquiry into pictures and stories further, I attended Narativ's 'What's your story?' workshop. I had intended to develop the story of editing a book for its promotion, but I suddenly felt compelled to tell another story about my experience of the bombing of Madrid airport 1986. I immediately faced a steep learning curve about the value and hazards of telling a personal trauma story in a public forum. The powerful revivification of the events it entailed were simultaneously troubling and yet offered significant insights into the nature of trauma, its telling, memory and integration. I learnt on the day of the workshop the meaning of the silence that followed the explosion, thirty years after the event. It was not my loss of hearing but the shocked silence before the cries for help began. Chapter 16 outlines the origin story of Narativ by its founder and lays out their storytelling method.

In the course of editing the book I have done additional training in eye movement desensitization reprocessing (EMDR) and note that five of the authors are also qualified EMDR practitioners. In the course of this experiential training, which involved selecting 'target images' representative of traumatic events, I learnt how a response to a trauma, experienced as an adult, in my case the Madrid airport bombing, can be underpinned by an earlier traumatic scene which for me had remained 'unprocessed'. An image from one traumatic scenario became a gateway to another more troubling image from my experience of boarding school.

The human mind-body system craves a future liberated from negative past experiences and yet it inevitably trawls past experience for survival resources that can offer resilience. Tragically, however, these same experiences often produce distorted and limiting horizons, which can then invite compounding traumas in terms of addiction, relationship difficulties and other forms of acting out. The studies of adverse childhood experience (Merrick et al. 2019) show that trauma can lead to significant long-term negative effects (physiological, psychological and relational). There is therefore a growing recognition that we must urgently address these at source. The chapters of this book represent the many faces of trauma (single, chronic and complex), some of which can lead to an addictive response, but all point to the complex relationship of contemporary actions and deeper pasts, both individual and collective, that can provide opportunities to heal the riven multidimensional worlds of the client and society as a whole. The structure of the book invites a systemic movement between these many and complex levels of interaction and integration of these multiple storied and imagined worlds. The four sections of the book move in a cyclical fashion through the human lifespan and reveal necessary interdependencies of family, schooling, culture, healthcare, environment and nature, encouraging a holistic and systemic understanding of multiple and multilayered systems across time, moving in cycles of renewal and/or repetition. The sections of the book are as follows:

In The Beginning...: Complex Trauma, Embodiment and the Supervisorial Holding of the Work

Meeting Trauma and Addiction in Practice

Post-traumatic Growth, Recovery and Community

To Be Continued...The Wider Context and the Return

The Vortex of the Real

When I started to think about writing the Introduction I decided to let meaning emerge as the chapter submissions came through, deciding not to attempt it until the end. I was on holiday at the time and found myself reflecting on the project as a whole after overhearing my five-year-old daughter's frantic appeal to my son on a six-hour train journey to Marseille. She had pleaded with him 'Is it real?... Is it really real??... Is it actually real???', and although I have since forgotten the topic of their discussion I spent the rest of the journey and much of the holiday mulling over questions about the problem of verification she had raised. I began to realize that this would become a central theme of this book and the nature of inquiry itself. How *do* we know what is real?

I kept coming back to three interrelated areas that together give an ongoing sense of what is real and yet remain unstable, preliminary and incomplete. Our appeals to *experience*, *the facts* and *the law* sometimes reveal our vain attempts to settle matters, which in many ways must remain dynamic. I have called these 'zones of verification' and labelled them *the actual, the factual* and *the normative* (Figure 1.1), relating respectively to *lived experience, generalized knowledge* and *social norms*.

Figure 1.1: The Vortex of the Real represents the interdependent and dynamic nature of the interactive zones of assessment troubled in the experience of trauma and addiction

Trauma and addiction disrupt, disavow and trouble the zones of assessment in different ways and in different phases of their processes, and each has implications for knowledge acquisition, in and through time. *Factual knowledge* is acquired retrospectively and evolves from the past but provides guides for future action until some present encounter contradicts its thesis. It aims to be neutral, objective and true. *Lived experience* is a sequence of embodied presents. It can be recorded or storied and looked at retrospectively as open texts, images or narratives. *The normative* relates to social conventions, codes and values and is set out in relation to past and future actions. The zones are interdependent and evolve from our holistic capacities of being in the world and the collaborative and social sense-making that pervades our lives. This book shows the value of using mixed methodologies and exemplifies how we can traverse and triangulate our means of sense-making through science, art, personal experience and law without the need for a hierarchy of modes. Bruner (1986b), Geertz (1993) and Lévi-Strauss (1973) all point to the value of recognizing different kinds of knowing in the provision of thick, granular, local and embodied quality information. My sense from the chapters is that when we affirm mixed methods and methodologies, we invite our various capabilities to the reunification party of art and science that occurs through practice.

Trauma disrupts and fragments our sense of what is real in similar, but inverse, ways to substance use, which may aim to step aside from it. We have many reasons to gain and 'lose the plot' at different times, and not all of these are destructive. The arts show the value of occasionally being 'out of your head' and potentially moving into your heart, your body and into the experience of others. I wrote a memo after one of the three authors' meetings that 'the arts lubricate the hinges of the contesting domains of the reality assessment in the Vortex of the Real'. I hope the reader will test this thesis as they read.

The problematization of the real represented by the Vortex of the Real promotes a softer and less binary view of fact and fiction. On the same holiday mentioned earlier, I got on everybody's nerves by testing a related theory, challenging the boundary of fact/fiction, by repeatedly asking 'Do you mean that literally or figuratively?' to any statement made. It becomes clear after a while that everything stated literally inevitably has to be stated figuratively to be intelligible, useful (and exemplified).

Reflexivity and personal motivations

At the first authors' meeting we considered adding a joint chapter on our motivations as authors to do what can be considered 'dangerous work' in practice and in our representing it here. Although this idea was dropped, the question of reflexivity has necessarily become part of this inquiry. When and where can practitioners reflect on and represent their own experiences?

As editor, I have inevitably reflected on my motivations in offering trauma work as a practitioner and also in editing this inquiry into trauma, addiction and recovery with clients and colleagues. If I consider the deeper motivations, I find it relevant that I was born in a post-war post-colonial country whose culture was in many ways formed by attitudes to self-expression and denial that developed in coping with a devastating war and in the justifications for imperialism. My father was a shy but occasionally explosive man whose curriculum vitae announced to me after his death that he had been a 'senior police officer' during the Mau Mau Uprising in Kenya. Little was ever said to us of this experience and the carnage he would have witnessed, that abruptly ended for him in a motorcycle accident, major surgery and nearly losing his leg. My mother was a nurse in the hospital where he found himself after being airlifted back the UK to avoid amputation. There were also deeper attachment traumas he had endured in his early life, including surgery for childhood osteomyelitis, the divorce of his parents, parental alcoholism and even being kidnapped in custody battles. He was a loving and sensitive man but prone to explosive rages when he felt slighted. He was deeply hurt in so many ways in his life, and sometimes his injuries would yield the internalized detritus of those experiences. The red laterite of the Kenyan road that had entered his body in the accident literally emerged from his skin in the form of ulcers one Christmas, and likewise the pain of the emotional wounds he had endured as a child often returned. Despite all this, and many other traumatic wounds, he retained a capacity to love and a very active sense of humour. I have therefore relished the moments of defiant and dark humour represented here in these chapters as an accidental resource that recovery often demands.

I have now been a qualified art psychotherapist for 26 years and have done additional training in integrative counselling and psychotherapy, hypnotherapy and neurolinguistic programming (NLP). Over the years I have seen the way that trauma impacts on clients' lives as I have often tried understanding my own in tandem. I agree with Alice Miller (1990) that trauma potentially provides an untouched key to both creativity and destructiveness. It can go either way or evolve in elaborate combinations. In the course of these years as a practitioner it has become clear to me that very many adults, while able to work, struggle with unprocessed and impinging trauma images and memories. Kessler et al. (2017) present the evidence of the prevalence of trauma from the WHO surveys. Studies into the impact of adverse childhood experiences (ACEs) identify psychological, physiological and relational damage consequent on childhood trauma (Merrick et al. 2019). Johnstone and Boyle (2018) represent how the culture and discourses of treatment are changing. Trauma and addictions have previously been seen as symptoms allowing patients to be placed in convenient diagnostic categories with allocated medications. We are now turning more towards listening to the origin stories of trauma and their accompanying legends of survival. This book aims to support this ongoing cultural change.

In the spirit of Ortega y Gasset's statement 'I am I and my circumstance' (1914/2004), I feel all these circumstances outlined above, rather than my active choice, have invited me into the role of editor. If someone were to ask me how to become an editor of such a book, you would not usually respond by pointing to inter- or transgenerational trauma as a qualification (how would you teach and accredit it?), nonetheless

22

maybe it is true here. I know this territory, and I want to explore it further with compassion, good humour and with friends, for my own sake and for others.

The editing process
Editing a book as a form of research

The approach of this inquiry has been to provide practice-based evidence that respects and acknowledges the local contexts of this collaborative investigation into clients' dilemmas and to discover the common ground that exists across these practices. Following an agenda first represented in another context (West 2018), there is an aim to bridge the practice–research gap and give practitioners and clients a direct voice about topics of great importance to them and create a bottom-up approach that parallels the practice of trauma treatment, which must first engage actual embodied experience.

I presented the diagram in Figure 1.2 last year at a meeting of the United Kingdom Council for Psychotherapy's Practice Research Network with the aim of outlining a process of inquiry that began to be developed in the previous book (West 2018, p.23), where I had credited the work of Kim Etherington (2002), who had written about the process of editing a book as a form of research and inquiry.

In the meeting I outlined the use of the adaptable tool of 'mind mapping' to hold the vision of the whole project together through the editing and research process, and also the use of a timeline to gather the important historical developments and dates that we became aware of in the course of the inquiry:

- The timeline (Table 1.1) references key ideas within the chapters and the historical events that have necessitated the development of practitioners' ideas about trauma and that represent cultural responses to tragedies both at the time and in their unfolding consequences.

- The mind map (Figure 1.3) on this occasion evolved from a simple invitation for us to think of the title with the branches initially marked with Who? What? Where? When? How much? How? and Why? but soon replaced by other categories, resulting in the final version represented here where it now summarizes some of our central concerns.

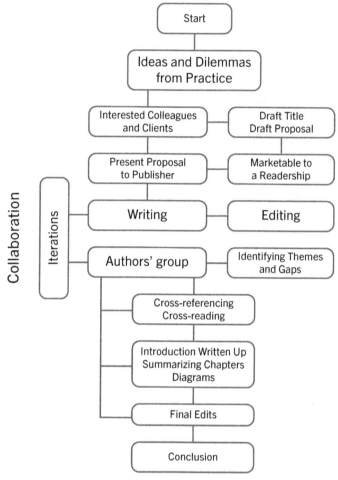

Figure 1.2: Editing a book as a form of research

Table 1.1: Timeline*

Date	Developing Concepts
1867	'On a New List of Categories' published by the founder of semiotics Charles Sanders Peirce where he gives an early account of his categories of signs and outlines the iconic sign with its particular characteristics as one of his three types of sign
1872	Charles Darwin publishes 'The Expression of the Emotions in Man and Animals'
1911	Sigmund Freud publishes 'Formulation on the Two Principles of Mental Functioning' where he separates 'reality testing' and 'pleasure' principles and their related cognitive functions
1914–18	**First World War**

1916–19	Craiglockhart Hydropathic became The Craiglockhart War Hospital. It featured in Pat Barker's Regeneration Trilogy, which represents the work of the hospital and its treatment of shell-shock and neurasthenia in war veterans, including Siegfried Sassoon, Wilfred Owen and Robert Graves, by the anthropologist, neurologist, ethnologist and psychiatrist W.H.R. Rivers
1919	**Founding of Combat Stress**, the veterans' mental health charity. Originally called the Ex-services Welfare Society, its name was changed 35 years later to the Ex-services Mental Welfare Society
1920	S. Freud publishes 'Beyond the Pleasure Principle' where he considers the repetitive dreams of veterans and repetitive play in child development and consolidates his thoughts of earlier papers on repetition and the two principles of mental functioning (the pleasure and the reality principles)
1937	S. Freud publishes 'Moses and Monotheism' where he elaborates on the effects of trauma
1939–45	**Second World War**
1940	John Bowlby publishes 'The Influence of Early Environment in the Development of Neurosis and Neurotic Character'
1942	At the Northfield Military Hospital, psychoanalysts **Wilfred Bion and John Rickman set up The Northfield Experiments** to treat soldiers suffering from shell-shock and war neuroses after the Second World War in the army psychiatric unit run along group lines. The leaders of the experiments were psychoanalysts who were later involved in treatment programmes at the Tavistock Clinic and the Cassel Hospital, and had considerable international influence on psychoanalysis and group therapy. From that time on, the term *therapeutic community* (TC) has been linked to a range of treatment traditions that share the idea of using all the relationships and activities of a residential psychiatric centre to aid the therapeutic task. Maxwell Jones, psychiatrist and pioneer of the TC, started to employ group methods at the Mill Hill Emergency Hospital and soon began to experiment with plays for therapeutic purposes. The Mill Hill Programme, for battle-shocked soldiers, later led to the founding of Henderson Hospital and a worldwide 'social psychiatry' movement. The number of specific TC units peaked in the 1970s and fell in the following decades – although a new variant of TC, working with day treatment programmes instead of residential ones, has grown since the 1990s and is now finding a specific place in the treatment of 'personality disorders'
1946	The term *therapeutic community* was first coined by British psychiatrist Thomas Main in his paper 'The Hospital as a Therapeutic Institution' and subsequently developed by others including Maxwell Jones, R.D. Laing at the Philadelphia Association, David Cooper at Villa 21, and Joshua Bierer at the Marlborough Day Hospital
1946	Viktor Frankl publishes 'Man's Search for Meaning' where he chronicles his experience as a prisoner in Nazi concentration camps during World War II and describes the psychotherapeutic method he developed from his experiences

1947	The Henderson Hospital was founded following Second World War as a Social Rehabilitation Unit established by Maxwell Jones on a corner of the Belmont Hospital site for soldiers suffering from war neuroses. The unit progressed to treating adults who had experienced extreme neglect or abuse in childhood, to help them overcome their difficulties. In 1959 it was renamed the Henderson Hospital, after the Scottish psychiatrist Professor Sir David Henderson, and ran on the basis of 'permissiveness, reality-confrontation, democracy and communalism'. Under the influence of Maxwell Jones, Main, Wilmer and others, combined with the publication of critiques of the existing mental health system and the socio-political influences that permeated the psychiatric world towards the end of and following the Second World War, the concept of the therapeutic community dominated the field of inpatient psychiatry throughout the 1960s
1947	**Partition of British India.** Mass displacement of individuals and children
1951	John Bowlby publishes *Maternal Care & Mental Health*
1952	APA publishes the first version of the DSM that includes 'gross stress reaction', highlighting psychological issues stemming from traumatic events
1952–60	**The Mau Mau Uprising** against British Colonial Rule in Kenya
1955	**The first development of a therapeutic community in a large institution** took place at Claybury Hospital under the guidance of Denis Martin and John Pippard. It involved over 2,000 patients and hundreds of staff. The aim of therapeutic communities was a more democratic, user-led form of therapeutic environment, avoiding the authoritarian and demeaning practices of many psychiatric establishments of the time
1960s	Maxwell Jones was instrumental in amplifying his practice of democratic therapeutic communities to community mental health on a broad scale, beginning in the US in the early 1960s and then applying it to a rural setting in Scotland
1963	Mary Ainsworth began work at the Tavistock Clinic on a research project investigating the effects of early maternal separation under Bowlby's tenure as Director
1965	**R.D. Laing opened the therapeutic community Kingsley Hall** which became home to one the most radical experiments in psychology of the time. The aim of the experiment by the Philadelphia Association was to create a model for non-restraining, non-drug therapies for those people seriously affected by schizophrenia. The idea of starting this type of community was suggested by Mary Barnes, first resident as a patient
1965–74	**The Vietnam War**
1969	Mary Ainsworth publishes *Infancy in Uganda: Infant Care and the Growth of Love*
1969–80	John Bowlby publishes the three volumes of 'Attachment and Loss'

1970	Mary Ainsworth publishes *Strange Situation*
1972	H.F. Searles's Unconscious Processes in Relation to the Environmental Crisis, makes an early connection between the capacity to recover from trauma and our split from the natural world
1972	**Idi Amin orders expulsion of South Asians from Uganda** leading to a mass migration of (African) South Asians to the UK and Canada
1978	Ainsworth et al. publish 'Patterns of Attachment: A Psychological Study of the Strange Situation', which relates to the Strange Situation Procedure
1980	John Bowlby publishes 'A Secure Base'
1980	APA publishes DSM-III that includes PTSD as a distinct disorder
1981	**The AIDs Epidemic.** The first reported case was in the US. The height of the epidemic in New York is considered to be from the mid-80s to the early 90s. Through Murray Nossel's work at the AIDS Day Program, we see the origin of Narativ and storytelling as an advocacy tool. This epidemic is the 'trauma' that Murray was working with, and it was to counter this that he used storytelling as a means for people to witness each other finding their voice and claiming their experience
1985	Main et al.'s first publication relating to the Adult Attachment Interview
1986	**Madrid Airport Bombing**
1988	**The Studio Upstairs was formed** by two art psychotherapists, Douglas Gill and Claire Manson, as a therapeutic arts community, connected to the Philadelphia Association and influenced by the ideas of R.D. Laing
1989	F. Shapiro publishes 'Efficacy of the Eye Movement Desensitization Procedure in the Treatment of Traumatic Memories', which details EMDR therapy
1990	Michael White and David Epston publish 'Narrative Means to Therapeutic Ends'
1991	**The First Gulf War**
1992	J. Herman publishes 'Trauma and Recovery' in which she proposes Complex PTSD as a distinct psychological disorder
1994	DSM-IV published with substantial revision of PTSD classification
1994	A.N. Schore publishes 'Affect Regulation and the Origin of the Self'
1994	**The Rwandan Genocide**
1999	**Creation of UK National Institute for Clinical Excellence (NICE)**
2001	**The Attacks on the World Trade Center, New York** with international repercussions. The 'War on Terror' certainly shaped British military operations over the following years
2001	S.W. Porges publishes 'The Polyvagal Theory: Phylogenetic Substrates of a Social Nervous System'

2002	The Studio Upstairs was approached by Diana Brandenburger who was then working as an art therapist at The Medical Foundation (later to become Freedom From Torture). She was impressed with the combination of serious art practice and authentic relatedness between client and therapist, and took this model to The Medical Foundation and created a similar studio for asylum seekers called The Open Art Studio, which was run by Tania Kaczynski from 2008 to 2014
2003	**The Invasion of Iraq**
2005	NICE generates guidelines for PTSD
2006	A. Bateman and P. Fonagy publish 'Mentalization-based Treatment for Borderline Personality Disorder: A Practical Guide'
2007	Michael White publishes 'Maps of Narrative Practice'
2007	Emily Holmes et al. publish 'Imagery Rescripting in Cognitive Behaviour Therapy: Images, Treatment Techniques and Outcomes' Dr Emily Holmes's 30 years of research focuses on understanding the role of mental imagery and emotion, particularly in relation to anxiety, depression and bipolar disorder
2009	**The closure of the last military hospital in the UK** – The Royal Hospital Haslar in Gosport (founded in 1753)
2010	**The Arab Spring** and increased displacement of large groups of adults and children
2010	Andrew Murrison MD MP publishes the report 'Fighting Fit: A Mental Health Plan for Servicemen and Veterans'
2013	APA publishes DSM-5 that moves PTSD disorder from the anxiety disorders category to a new category entitled 'Trauma and Stressor-related Disorders'. Also, it delineates a separate diagnostic sub-classification for diagnosing PTSD in children under age 7
2014	New Art Studio set up by Tania Kaczynski and Jon Martyn
2014	Bessel Van der Kolk publishes 'The Body Keeps The Score: Brain, Mind, and Body in the Healing of Trauma'
2018	Publication of 'Art Therapy with Military Veterans' (edited by Janice Lobban)
2018	UK NICE guidelines for PTSD updated and published
2019	ICD-11 published that includes Complex PTSD (CPTSD) as a diagnostic disorder for the first time
2019	**The Global Climate Protests**
2020	**The Global Covid-19 Coronavirus Pandemic**
2020	**The Global Black Lives Matter Protests**

*Bolded text indicates historical events that have pushed forward and led to the development of concepts. It has not been possible to list all the significant conflicts that have occurred in this period and so I have only listed conflicts made reference to within the chapters.

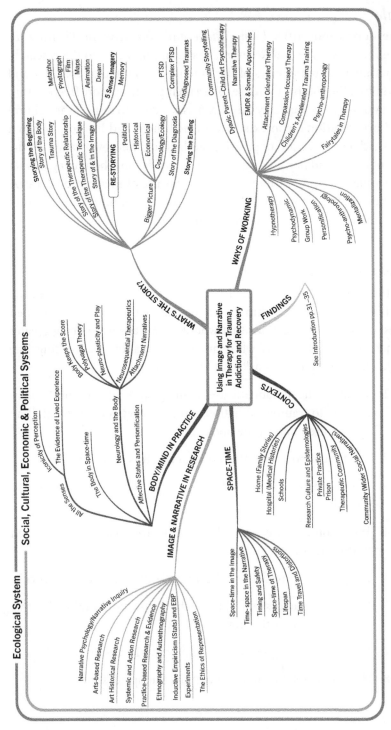

Figure 1.3: The UINTTAR mind map (see online colour plate)

Title

The book's long title, *Using Image and Narrative in Therapy for Trauma, Addiction and Recovery*, has been important to the research. It outlined the parameters of the practice we wanted to consider and permitted the authors then to explore their practices more freely within the boundaries outlined by the title. It assisted me to respect the cultural and organizational contexts that formed them and has resulted in a very rich cross-section of practices addressing their own 'takes' on the use of image and narrative in therapy. An additional boundary was set that while each author must represent the 'use of image and narrative in therapy', the authors could represent just two of these three areas of the practice: trauma, addiction and recovery.

Eight emergent questions

In the course of the book, as I reviewed the chapters, I checked the authors were keeping within the boundaries of the title and developed a list of emergent questions that would encourage us to bring greater coherence to the book as a whole and foster collaborative working. The eight emergent questions asked of the texts were:

1. What are the therapeutic uses of image and narrative outlined in relation to trauma, addiction and recovery? Is the text fulfilling the requirements of the book's title?

2. How is the body and affect outlined in this chapter?

3. Are there any 'findings' in the chapter that are important to identify and follow up?

4. What contextual epistemologies or methodologies are outlined in this practice?

5. Is a particular modality or 'approach' outlined in this practice?

6. Who are the actors and what are the transactions outlined in this practice? What is the story?

7. What are the origins of the trauma experiences described?

8. How is the relational holding of the therapy described?

Putting it all together...together

There were three authors' meetings that supported us in developing the mind map, leading to cross-fertilization and a sort of hermeneutic cycling of the whole (book) to the parts (chapters) and supporting a research culture of mutual interest within the project as a whole. My role as editor likewise has been to hold the overview, to synthesize the elements and feed back to the authors, so that when the reader journeys through the book they will find both commonalities and elements of uniqueness without redundancy and repetition. For example, the authors shared out the outlining of theories, histories and definitions of diagnostic terms and the etymologies of keywords for the book as a whole. (You will find discussions of diagnostic terms in Chapter 4 and etymological reflections on our terms in Chapter 13, recent neurological research is represented in Chapter 5, representations of attachment theory appear in Chapters 3 and 7, therapeutic community approaches in Chapters 11 and 15 and a cognitive behavioural approach in Chapter 9.) This work was shared out by respecting the particular contextual epistemologies of the authors' practices while fulfilling the broader needs of the book as a whole as comprehensively as possible.

On completion, the book appears like a collage where single images are assembled into a new and contemporary view. Multiple perspectives are combined into a new view. The process not only celebrates the original perspectives of each image where the parts can be recognized and appreciated in themselves, but as the eye moves from the parts to the whole we gain new insights of the parts and gain a novel view of the whole.

Findings – a thematic analysis

The eight emergent questions point to the areas that emerged across the chapters as common ground. While the book, the title and the proposal may have come from shared assumptions about this work, these independent representations of practice give us an opportunity to see how these assumptions are manifested through examples. This process may reveal contradictions but at the same time it provides practitioners with opportunities for deeper reflections on practice. Some of the chapters are justified by appeals made to pre-existing theory and empirical research, others attempt to show stories from therapy that reveal a practice and present their own and their clients' understandings of these collaborative explorations. Having read all the chapters, I have tried to list some of the common themes discovered with the authors as our 'findings' in this practice-based research, and this seems a fair way to conclude this Introduction. The 'findings' fall into a number of categories.

The categories relating to the use of image and narrative in therapy for trauma, addiction and recovery are:

- Self-care and containing the 'dangerous' process.

- The body, memory, affect and holding in therapy.

- Space-time, therapeutic timing and time travel.

- Re-storying and re-imagining in space and time.

- Addiction as a response to trauma and as an attachment disorder.

Self-care and containing the 'dangerous' process

Therapists should prepare for the danger and discomfort of revivification in this work and should have some experience of staying with such discomfort through personal experience and/or through rigorous experiential training.

Working with images and narratives in therapy helps contain and give spatial and temporal order, structure and meaning to what may appear to be random experience. It externalizes the images and affects of trauma and can help to loosen an understandably fearful and rigid grasp of reality through play, allowing both the story and its integration into the wider holding communities. The extent to which we integrate these realities together will determine the status of our collective cultural wisdom.

Therapy can present powerful opportunities for existential and spiritual renewal through integrating past experiences. This, in all societies, provides resources of wisdom based on individual and collective experience and learning across time in a process of dynamic collective myth making.

The body, memory, affect and holding in therapy

Recovery occurs through giving attention to the lived experience of the body and its affects and sensory-based imagery. The importance of embodied therapeutic presence within the session and the wider frameworks of relational holding in therapy, supervision, family, social groups, and then out again into organizations, culture, society, economy and ecological systems, represented in these chapters, underpins recovery and all our work. The aetiology of trauma shows these levels to be interdependent and interwoven layers that must be acknowledged in the process of supporting recovery in the community.

All these therapies rely on good-quality, thick, embodied, affect-laden, insider, sensory data from lived experience.

When we speak of imagery here it relates to all our senses, not just the visual sense.

Sequenced affective imagery provides the basis of therapeutic re-storying.

In a necessarily bottom-up process it is difficult to predetermine a treatment modality, but at the same time protocols and sequencing are a necessary part of the meeting and safe holding of the 'chaos narratives' of trauma.

The use of image and narrative in therapy helps to bring structure, agency, authority and authorship to the client and the process.

Space-time, therapeutic timing and time travel

Images relate to space and narratives relate to time, and so this combined work encourages us to explore space-time in its many dimensions through our subjective and objective explorations of time and space, together and separately.

The chapters point to the importance of reflections of space-time in therapy, therapeutic timing and 'time travel' as a phenomenon of traumatic experience.

Reflections on our lived experience of time and the phenomenon of traumatic experience, which we named 'time travel' in the authors' meeting, are central to this work. This spatio temporal journeying is a key ingredient of this work as we assemble and disassemble the workings of time and space in our lives, mapping out the past, the present and the future and dismantling the phenomena of 'flashbacks' by integrating the experience imaginatively back into our lives through pictures, stories and ongoing creative practice.

The notion of 'timing' in therapy also chimes with the protocols of EMDR (Shapiro 2018) and the 'neurosequential therapeutics' outlined by Bruce Perry (MacKinnon 2012). All these aim to reintegrate the fragmented experience of bio-psycho-social disruptions caused by trauma, which necessitate that practitioners 'regulate, relate and reason' and promote safety with a systemic and agile awareness.

Re-storying and re-imagining in space and time

Recovery occurs through processes of re-storying and re-imagining that provide greater adaptive flexibility to the 'takes' on trauma. This process encourages creative agency in the therapist and the client as artists and authors. Recovery can then occur dialogically within the therapeutic interaction, and this helps to externalize the perspectives and the tellings through image and story-making to provide important opportunities to reflect on the 'personifications' and conflicts that arise in these tellings and showings, and encourage 're-castings' and 're-views' of the characters and scenarios encountered.

Trauma causes deep divisions and conflicts within the self. The therapeutic frame can provide a forum and holding relationships to explore these tensions and settle the varied accounts of reality that may appear at odds with each other but that may reflect the conflicts that arise under stress between our many talents, capacities and instincts that recent neurological research points to (developmental and evolutionary triple brain and left and right hemispheres suggest a wealth of human capacity). Trauma often occurs in social conflicts, and these divisions can be reflected within the individual participants post trauma.

Sometimes a central image or scene holds a key that, when explored, changes and integrates the other story fragments and helps us to 'make sense'.

Clients in recovery begin to embrace incompleteness in their lives, tell stories and make images that leave space for the, as yet unknown, future, which holds the potentiality of imagination and creativity that can change the world. The ongoing adaptability of re-storying through images and stories permits reinterpretation, re-writes and new creations to occur in ongoing integrations and flexible adaptations while not denying 'the facts'.

Addiction as a response to trauma and as an attachment disorder

In the book 'recovery' from trauma and from addiction are conflated. Addiction has a close, complex but non-causal relationship with trauma in all its forms (single, chronic, complex) and also often reveals itself as an attachment disorder. Addiction is seen as an understandable response to trauma that has the positive aim of attempting to soothe emotional pain and manage traumatic experience, and seeks to provide state changes for unbearable feelings, yet it compounds traumas and inhibits recovery unless these underlying traumas and attachment issues are addressed.

With these findings in mind, please read on!

References

Bruner, J. (1986a) 'Possible Castles.' In *Actual Minds, Possible Worlds*. Cambridge, MA: Harvard University Press.

Bruner, J. (1986b) 'Two Modes of Thought.' In *Actual Minds, Possible Worlds*. Cambridge, MA: Harvard University Press.

Chron, L. (2012) *Wired for Story*. Berkeley, CA: Ten Speed Press.

Culler, J. (2000) *Literary Theory*. Oxford: Oxford University Press.

Eco, U. (1984) 'Lector in Fabula.' In *The Role of the Reader*. Bloomington, IN: Indiana University Press.

Etherington, K. (2002) *Working Together: Editing a Book as Narrative Research Methodology*. Bristol: University of Bristol.

Freud, S. (2001) 'Beyond the Pleasure Principle.' *Standard Edition of the Complete Psychological Works of Sigmund Freud: Vol. XVIII*. London: Vintage. (Original work published 1920)

Geertz, C. (1993) 'Thick Description: Towards an Interpretive Theory of Culture.' In *The Interpretation of Cultures*. London: Fontana.

Greimas, A.J. and Courtés, J. (1979) *Semiotics and Language: An Analytical Dictionary*. Bloomington, IN: Indiana University Press.

Johnstone, L. and Boyle, M. (2018) *The Power Threat Meaning Framework: Towards the Identification of Patterns in Emotional Distress, Unusual Experiences and Troubled or Troubling Behaviour, as an Alternative to Functional Psychiatric Diagnosis.* Leicester: British Psychological Society.

Kessler, R.C., Aguilar-Gaxiola, S., Alonso, J., Benjet, C. et al. (2017) 'Trauma and PTSD in the WHO World Mental Health Surveys.' *European Journal of Psychotraumatology 8,* sup5, 1353383.

Lévi-Strauss, C. (1973) 'The Science of the Concrete.' In *The Savage Mind.* London: University of Chicago Press.

MacKinnon, L. (2012) 'The neurosequential model of therapeutics: An interview with Bruce Perry.' *Australian and New Zealand Journal of Family Therapy 33,* 3, 210–218.

Mattingly, C. (2001) *Healing Dramas and Clinical Plots.* Cambridge: Cambridge University Press.

Merrick, M.T., Ford, D.C., Ports, K.A., Guinn, A.S. et al. (2019, 8 November) 'Vital signs: Estimated proportion of adult health problems attributable to adverse childhood experiences and implications for prevention: 25 States, 2015–2017.' US Department of Health and Human Services, Centers for Disease Control and Prevention. *Morbidity and Mortality Weekly Report 68,* 44, 999–1005.

Miller, A. (1990) *The Untouched Key.* London: Virago.

Moss, R. (2011) *Active Dreaming.* Novato, CA: New World Library.

Moustakas, C. (1994) *Phenomenological Research Methods.* London: Sage.

Ortega y Gasset, J. (2004) 'Meditaciones del Quijote.' *Obras Completas: Vol. I.* Madrid: Taurus/Fundación José Ortega y Gasset. (Originally work published 1914)

Rumi (1984) *Open Secret: Versions of Rumi* (J. Moyne and C. Barks, Trans.). Boulder, CO: Shambala Publications.

Shapiro, F. (2018) *Eye Movement Desensitisation and Reprocessing Therapy.* New York, NY: Guilford Press.

West, J.D. (ed.) (2018) *Art Therapy in Private Practice: Theory, Practice and Research in Changing Contexts.* London: Jessica Kingsley Publishers.

2

Getting Perspective

*Points of View, Positions and the Metaphor
of Visual Perspective in Therapy*

James D. West

*Now I a fourfold vision see
And a fourfold vision is given to me;
Tis fourfold in my supreme delight
And threefold in soft Beulahs night
And twofold Always. May God us keep
From Single vision & Newtons sleep!*

(William Blake in a Letter to Thomas Butts, 22 November 1802)

Obtaining, expanding, integrating or changing perspectives are
necessarily central concepts in therapy. In this chapter, focusing
on the image, we will look at visual perspective from an art history
and semiotic perspective before concluding with a consideration of
John Rowan's notions of 'personification' and 'I-positions' to show
how critical reflections on perspective can loosen some of the more
confining experiences of trauma and addiction.

In therapy we often talk about listening, yet listening occurs in the
auditory field. An equivalent visual word for *listening* would be *seeing*
or *noticing*. *Noticing* is probably the better word with less of an auditory
bias and suggestive of a multisensory approach to the therapeutic field.
We can ask the open question '...and what do/did you notice there?' It
is not laden with the therapist's nascent interpretations and allows for
an answer that could surprise the therapist as much as the client. The

question does not even need to be stated or answered; it can be carried by receptive glances or simple attentive presence.

Perspective as a symbolic form

Every visual image suggests a viewpoint. It is a quality of images to locate the viewer and suggest a subjective view. Images are inherently perspectival. The materiality of an image implies a local and experiential knowledge, and yet it is always possible to imagine a shift in location or a physical move to deconstruct or disrupt a single-point perspective. A perspectivist epistemology may create a more tolerant and permissive practice and rebuild a perspectivist notion of social selfhood, which both artistic and therapeutic work appears to demand.

In Panofsky's famous essay 'Perspective as Symbolic Form' (1991) he considers the Western tradition of single-point perspective formed in the Renaissance. He credits Cassirer with the notion of 'symbolic form', in which 'spiritual meaning is attached to a concrete, material sign and intrinsically given to that sign' and extends this concept to consider how meaning is attached to this particular concrete, material sign and asks us to consider more generally 'why it is essential to ask of artistic periods and regions not only whether they have perspective, but also which perspective they have' (p.41).

We can ask this same question of our own times and ask, for the purposes of this chapter, what sort of images we create in relation to traumas. Can our illusionary constructions in space-time help our therapeutic reflections as clients and therapists? My answer as a practising therapist instinctively would be to say 'Yes!' but this invites the question 'How?' Panofsky shows us how the development of single-point perspective achieved a number of notable landmarks. The most graspable idea is of the picture plane as a 'window on the world'. In Figure 2.1 you can see how the viewpoint of a single-point perspective image is swung sideways to become part of the flat picture plane enabling the geometric calculation of the perspectival illusion of a chequered floor upon the picture plane.

This single-eyed view of the world evolves from a drawing system like any of the others that preceded it in the history of spatial representation, but it has had a number of very significant cultural, symbolic and technological consequences that are historically unprecedented.

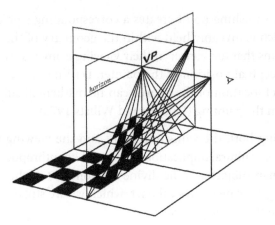

Figure 2.1: Single-point perspective

There are a number of key ideas that evolve from Panofsky's assessment:

- In pictures using single-point perspective a vanishing point (VP) is created in the geometry that comes to represent an infinite distance. The vanishing point must be located within the frame by the artist and so invites them to consider its metaphysical symbolism. An example would be in Leonardo da Vinci's 'The Last Supper'. What do you notice?

Figure 2.2: 'The Last Supper' redrawn by the author after da Vinci

The vanishing point is located at the head of Jesus. This image illustrates the solid bond alining the viewpoint, the vanishing point and its metaphorical association with the infinite and the divine. The visual and ideological terms of viewing are encoded in the picture.

- The vanishing point creates a corresponding single viewpoint which is invisibly held within the geometry of the picture and means that the viewer in their viewing is invited to stand in the perceptual position of the painter. Da Vinci wrote of how this exact location of the viewer can be mathematically calculated from the painting (Dubery and Willats 1972).

- Fixing both the vanishing point and the viewing point has a deeper cultural implication in terms of its anthropocentrism. The human subject and the divine are bonded together through an imaginary metaphysical pact, which we are still deconstructing in contemporary visual art.

- '[T]he structure of an infinite, unchanging and homogeneous space – in short, a purely mathematical space – is quite unlike the structure of psychophysical space' (Panofsky 1997, pp.29–30).

Panofsky concludes his thesis on a dual note of admiration for the cultural and technological achievements of this new perspective but with a note of foreboding regarding the narcissism of this self-enclosed conceptual loop where man (not woman) casts himself as the divine.

> Perspective, in transforming the *ousia* (reality) into the *phainomenon* (appearance), seems to reduce the divine to a mere subject matter for human consciousness; but for that very reason, conversely, it expands human consciousness into a vessel for the divine. It is thus no accident if this perspectival view of space has already succeeded twice in the course of the evolution of art: the first time as a sign of an ending, when antique theocracy crumbled; the second time as the sign of a beginning, when modern 'anthropocracy' first reared itself. (Panofsky 1997, p.72)

The semiotician Umberto Eco suggests this historical development is the first movement of a development towards and a premonition of the photographic, the televisual and other contemporary media that now possess our global society. He refers to television as the 'electronic mirror' and sees its development as the culmination of a cultural desire for the hyperreal, which we can see was offered significant impetus in the development of single-point perspective in painting.

> We have 'invented' both photography and cinema. That is, even though historically they came first, from a theoretical point of view photographic and cinematographic images are an impoverished version

of television images, clumsy inventions, so to speak, attempts to reach an *optimum* that was still technically impossible. (Eco 2000, p.375)

Eco and Panofsky both point to a line of technological advances that have evolved through Renaissance perspective in painting, to photography, into film, television and video and into the current multimodal state of the art. Baudrillard's (1983) reflections on 'simulacra' in postmodern times are also relevant as it is the same technological developments that have undoubtedly enhanced the sense of cultural and technological vertigo and invited our 'post truth' musings.

Iconicity: The play of pictures

The previous section showed the seriousness with which images must be considered as a cultural form and the profound cultural implications that painting can have. We can now reflect more positively on how a critical view of images and perspective can function in the field of therapeutic emancipation, helping us think about the nature of perception and our *being here*.

Charles Peirce, the 19th-century American scientist, pragmatist and inventor of semiotics, identified and clarified the nature of signification and the objects of the visual field we intend to explore further.

A sign, or *representamen*, is something which stands to somebody for something in some respect or capacity. It addresses somebody, that is, creates in the mind of that person an equivalent sign, or perhaps a more developed sign. The sign which it creates I call the *interpretant* of the first sign. The sign stands for something, *its object*. It stands for that object, not in all respects, but in reference to a sort of idea. (Peirce 1931–1958, §2.228)

Nothing is a sign unless it is interpreted as a sign. (§2.308)

...thinking always proceeds in the form of a dialogue – a dialogue between different phases of the ego – so that, being dialogical, it is essentially composed of signs. (§4.6)

Peirce points out that our thinking, and ultimately therefore our selfhood, is both a dialogical and semiotic social process, and that we can create a typology of signs that defines each sign by the way it relates to the *representamen*, to *the object* to which it refers and *the interpretants* it creates in the minds of its recipients.

Our concern here is primarily with Peirce's notion of the iconic sign within the visual field, but it is worth briefly noting how Peirce conceived of realistic pictures as 'hypoicons'.

> Icons are so completely substituted for their objects as hardly to be distinguished from them... So in contemplating a painting, there is a moment when we lose the consciousness that it is not the thing, the distinction of the real and the copy disappears, and it is for the moment a pure dream – not any particular existence, and yet not general. At that moment we are contemplating an icon. (Peirce 1992, p.226)

For Peirce it is only when we fall into the illusion of a picture that it becomes iconic, when it is experienced at some level 'as if' it were a direct perception of its object. He relates this experience to states of trance and dreaming and recognizes the icon as a copy or substitute for its 'real' object.

Eco states similarly of the visual imagery that it is 'something that offers itself to the perception' and provides 'surrogate stimuli' to perception. In a discussion in which he explores a number of examples of hypoicons (mirrors, waxworks, realist painting, scientific drawing, photography, film and television) he also considers the 'prosthetic' quality of iconicity (Eco 2000). I would argue that it is in this illusionary bridging space of prosthesis and mirroring that reality can be reworked therapeutically and we can relocate ourselves in relation to the symbolic, imaginary and the real and begin to reconfigure past, present and future frames; a vital step in recovery.

We can easily confuse the image for its object as we enter the experiential territory of trance states, flashbacks, dreams and storytelling, but, as Eco points out, a simple movement of the head can usually suffice for us to check our actuality because the image usually carries with it the circumstances of its creation and with it a suggested viewpoint. Lived experience, however, is characterized by mobility, flux and a multidimensional and multimodal quality. It is not homogeneous. The notion of mirroring has been thoroughly explored in the psychoanalytic literature by Lacan (1949/1977), Winnicott (1971) and Wright (2009). Is this zone of iconicity not the same territory referred to in psychoanalytic literature as the realm of mirroring, transitional objects and transitional phenomena, where all of us are seen to be dyadically and dialogically formed, gently coaxed into selfhood in our early lives and then enculturated as subjects of society from infancy to old age across the lifespan? The risks associated with the ambiguity of images at this moment become the very source of their therapeutic virtue. Iconic slipperiness and an openness to interpretation provides the *possibility* on which our good humour, adaptation, creativity and recovery depend.

Peirce defined all signs under these three headings, Icon, Index and Symbol, which evolve from his notions of firstness, secondness and thirdness in a hierarchy that becomes more conventional and less experiential the more 'symbolic' they become. Hypoicons for Peirce slide down the scale of conventionality and are subject to what he aptly calls 'semiotic degeneracy', as they begin to have more and more in common with their objects through resemblance. It is important for us to distinguish the particular qualities of icons as they approximate more closely to the moments of our perception that are so central to the work of trauma recovery. They necessarily become the tools of our trade. Here Peirce further subdivides types of hypoicons in relation to their 'semiotic degeneracy':

> Hypoicons may be roughly divided according to the mode of Firstness of which they partake. Those which partake in simple qualities, or First Firstness, are *images*; those which represent the relation, mainly dyadic, or so regarded, of the parts, are *diagrams*; those which represent the representative character of a representamen by representing a parallelism in something else are *metaphors*. (Peirce 1931–1958, §2.277)

Icons for Peirce represent the preliminaries of our encounter with the world, and in returning us to our primary perception they have a vitalizing quality (whether in joy or fear) that is closer to our perception, sense and bodily experience than the signs that have become more conventionally routine. Art therapy in this way appears to depend therapeutically on this 'semiotic degeneracy' as images, as signs, closer to perception are more likely to be affect-laden. They are the foundation of all thinking based on our actuality in the world. Peirce writes of 'possibility', 'perception without reflection' and 'feeling' in relation to hypoicons.

We will see in the course of the chapters that follow how the reintroduction of the image into therapy is vital to understanding its place in trauma recovery – whether trauma memories and the 'target images' of eye movement desensitization and reprocessing (EMDR), trance inductions and visualization (Chapter 10), imagery work in Children's Accelerated Trauma Technique (CATT) (Chapter 4), or the concrete images made in art therapy, the maps and diagrams made in groups (Chapter 13), memories of film (Chapter 7), the making of stop-frame animation (Chapter 12) or the dramatic sensory reconstructions of story in Narativ workshops (Chapter 16). Images can intrude, disrupt and demand an altered understanding. Images trouble logocentric discourse just as trauma memories disturb the conventionally held identities that we may struggle to hold together post-traumatically. The authors in the following chapters welcome images. Images are actively invited to participate in these therapies to integrate and process trauma, assist recovery and support ongoing self-actualization. In these chapters images take us on journeys to our earliest development, our dreams and nightmares, trauma memories and to imaginative trajectories and visions of the future. Images have at once a basic perceptual and power-fully transcendent imaginative force. We should welcome them!

Perspectivism

Nietzsche was probably the first philosopher to propose a perspectivist epistemology. It is inherent in the practice of artists to be open to stagings, perspective, listenings, performances and enactments. It is not just for pleasure but a stance in the world. Nietzsche was committed to the arts in philosophy, or artful philosophy, which respects local knowledge. His theory of knowledge is necessarily anti-foundational, energetic and mobile. A perspectivist epistemology privileges lived experience, the actual and local knowledge, is suspicious of universals and generalization and yet can still present a coherent art-based epistemology that is not conventionally or contextually confining.

An image that comes to mind is of a life class. As we move around the room we notice the conventions of life drawing, its traditions and the styles the various artists adopt. We see the artists responding and gathering round the body of a particular life model as each image inscribes each work with physical presences and locations within the room. Context, discourses, genres, styles of representation are all in play, but there is a historical and actual moment held there in these multiple representations. A written report, attendance register, or a photograph of the room at a particular moment of the class would merely provide other perspectives or representations. We can nonetheless assume there is a particularity and actuality of things beyond what each text reflects there but this will always remain ungraspable in its totality and forever mediated by signs. There can be no ultimate view of the ongoing event.

Nietzsche did not disavow the troubling nature of art but embraced its capriciousness as an avowal of the flux of life. In our semiotic terms he celebrates what Peirce called the 'semiotic degeneracy' of icons and presents this as a philosophical virtue providing us with a positive reframing of philosophy that honours openness, potentiality and play. He stated that Art

> continuously muddles the rubrics and the compartments of concepts, presenting new transcriptions, metaphors, and metonymies; it continuously reveals the desire to give the subsisting world of waking man a figure so multicoloured, irregular, devoid of consequences, incoherent, exciting and eternally new, which is that provided by the world of dreams. (Nietzsche quoted in Eco 2000, p.46)

Like Peirce, Nietzsche suggests that the iconic nature of Art and its chimerical products echo the flux of lived experience, which our more conventional sign systems tend to fix. Images get us to think of images, which get us to reconsider perception, which in turn gets us thinking about Being. I would like to suggest then that it is in the nature of iconicity to create an opening for further thought; infinite and indeterminable. Importantly for our consideration here Art, through its proximity to lived experience and perception, also evolves from the same flux and chaos from which traumas intrude upon us. The therapeutic use of images therefore provides a mediating space for re-befriending the world and building an integrated post-traumatic recovery.

Bion (1992) illustrated well the value of a dual perspective in psychiatry in a passage entitled 'The hatred of learning from experience'. He presents an illustration of an oblique projection of a cube to give us a real example, that you can experience now, of the shifting perspective he felt so necessary in therapeutic group work. This type of drawing system is used in engineering and has no vanishing point as in single-point perspective and therefore suggests no fixed viewpoint (Figure 2.3). Interestingly, a single-point perspective would not permit such a perceptual shift.

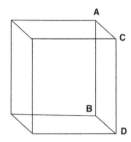

Figure 2.3: A box for shifting perspectives

Can you notice how it is possible to invert the box perceptually (by alternatively placing AB or CD at the front)? Single-point perspective in contrast denies other perspectives. It assures us of our place but this stabilization simultaneously stultifies thinking by discouraging the multiple and shifting viewpoints of a perspectivist epistemology that acknowledges a multiplicity of views.

Examples in practice

Figure 2.4: 'Las Meninas' redrawn by the author after Velázquez

In the image in Figure 2.4 Velázquez depicts a scene in which the artist paints a picture of the Spanish court. There are multiple perspectives suggested (12 positions if we include the viewer and the dog and 24 if we include each eye). This image deconstructs single-point perspective and opens up all sorts of imaginative opportunities and puzzles. Who is/are the viewers? The mirrored figures or the man in the doorway or simply ourselves? Velázquez gets us to look at looking.

The following 'made up' examples aim to provide opportunities to reflect on perspectives in therapy. I have found Grinder and DeLozier's (1987) thoughts about 'perceptual positions' in therapy useful and have presented the following examples in the first, second and third positions as examples in practice. The commentary (non-italicized) provides a fourth perceptual position.

First position (pronoun 'I') – The safety of the woodland floor
It is night and I look up at the moon that floats above me. The trees rise over me and seem to gather around me. The human animal with all its mischief and deceit is far away. It is quiet. I feel the soft earth beneath me and I am safe. As I look up, the moon is at the centre of my vision and the trees seem to point to it. They surround me and I feel comforted.

Figure 2.5: From the woodland floor

In this escape into the woodlands the human animal is cast by the artist as the most dangerous animal. Recovery from trauma requires the creation of safe spaces in order to work with states of acute vigilance apparent in unprocessed trauma memories. In recovery from trauma it is necessary to unlock these single-pointed vigilant intensities, move around, locate other safe spaces and deconstruct the images in order to integrate them into the wider stories and/or create new ones that will accommodate this known but exiled perspective.

Second position (pronoun 'You') –
Dissociation: Panning in and out

In the image you look from a hilltop and see down into the valley where a group of people stand. The colours and lines you have used in the painting make a pleasing representation of the landscape. You don't notice that the therapist is looking shocked as they have realized, in coming closer to the image, that some of the figures represented have missing limbs... you do not feel those feelings even though it is your picture. You do not speak about it.

In supporting trauma we learn to contain these unexpressed and unexplored emotions, something that the person who experiences it may hold at a distance...panning out. The process continues and the alliance may enable a gradual process of encounter and re-view. The holding and ongoing process permits this visual and affective panning in and out of the scene allowing a tentative and consenting engagement with the picture's meaning. We share the unbearable burden until it becomes bearable. The picture, the evolving story and relationship holds it until then.

Third position (pronouns 'He/She/They/It') – Locked out

A man draws a picture in coloured pencil and later shows it to the group. It is a picture of his family home. He speaks of the house and his family. There is smoke in the chimney and the curtains are open, but we view it as if from the garden gate. It is a pleasant view suggesting a happy home. The sun is bright and the sky is blue.

As the discussion progresses it becomes clear that this is a house he can never re-enter, having alienated his family over many years with extreme behaviour, which came as a consequence of deep insecurity, rages, domestic violence and addiction, similar to those that formed him as a child. The 'happy home' is a now a no-go area and has become a monument to his exclusion. In the picture, positioned by perspective, we, as viewers, join him outside the 'home' for ever. This picture illustrates how this imaginary architecture and perspective can help us understand how 'it' happened and of course other pictures can be made. We can experience the artist's world by empathically taking their place(s) before it or in it.

In these examples we may assume certain voices belong to the therapist, the client and maybe a supervisor or carers, partners, etc....though none of these roles were stated. There is value in changing places.

Personification: The dialogical self and multi-point perspective

John Rowan concludes in his book *Personification*, following a thorough examination of 'personification' in the history of psychotherapy, that we should aim towards a 'mature multi-vocalism' (Rowan 2010). Translated into a visual metaphor, that would be a 'mature perspectivism' that maybe Nietzsche would have also embraced. Rowan came across 27 different names for I-positions in the literature and proposes the general term 'I-positions', which fits well with our notion of viewpoints in visual perspective outlined here.

Rowan encourages us to take up the use of 'I-positions' within a dialogical understanding of the self in therapy and asks us to bear in mind this helpful quote from Valsiner (2002, p.252):

> The dialogical self entails two domains – intra-psychological and inter-psychological – both of which are equally important. A person operates on the basis of two dialogical processes: *heterodialogue* (with others, including imaginary others) and *autodialogue* (within oneself). In fact, these two dialogues are mutually intertwined. A person who tries to state something to a listener is simultaneously hearing (or reading) his or her own statement, which becomes part of the auto-dialogical process, irrespective of any answer from the listener.

You will also recall Peirce's suggestion that 'thinking always proceeds in the form of a dialogue – a dialogue between different phases of the ego – so that, being dialogical, it is essentially composed of signs'.

Therapies have used an abundance of terms for different aspects of our encountered selves but have often failed to see the common factors, maybe due to possessive theoretical patents. Rowan's thesis draws out the common factors and outlines a case for the therapeutic use of personification that honours the positions, selves, parts, ego states, etc. that clients (and therapists) bring to therapy. Each I-position offers a perspective that can be explored as each 'I' invites a view. The visual metaphor of perspective encourages us to take on these multiple vantage points as part of the therapeutic process. As Greenberg, Rice and Elliot (1993) make clear, trauma shatters the self that experiences them and creates conflicts, held within the individual, which must be resolved. 'I-positions' are a useful concept as we encounter these divisions and begin to reassemble the broken vessel, the nature of the wounds (traumas), the shrapnel and the history they mark as we re-story them into a newly narrated whole.

As you read on, it appears it is a finding across the chapters of this book that it is useful to consider personification in therapy and for practitioners to continue to use these 'vantage points' imaginatively with ongoing curiosity without needing to seek finality or totality in therapy. The chapters show that it is the ongoing adaptability, flexibility, openness and the return to play that show up as symptoms of vitality in post-traumatic growth. Our understanding of trauma and the way it impacts on the triune brain, its hemispheres, and the complexity and diversity of the global village that sustains and encultures us, all suggest the need for a multilevel, open and flexible approach to both internal and external diversity and conflicts.

In overtly using the visual and spatial metaphors of perspective, we can help hone the visual skills of therapists and clients in their construction of images in art therapy, but also support those working more generally with imagery within addiction and trauma services in their therapeutic application of 'positions', 'parts', 'ego states' and 'persons' in therapies such as Gestalt chair and dream work, NLP perceptual positions, clinical hypo-therapeutic trance inductions and visualizations. Considering these various 'vantage points' literally and/or metaphorically, we can help clients to work more concretely with where those figures 'stand' in space-time constructions, and consider how and what they 'see' and 'feel' from 'there', using the insights that come to us as productive feedback to 'the work' in the 'here-and-now'.

There are a number of points that follow from these reflections on perspective and personification in therapy:

- We accept a de-centred notion of the self.

- We consider the self as a process.

- We see the self as a staging of characters.

- We recognize the importance of play.

- We are open to things not being as they seem.

- We recognize the need for client-centred and flexible processing.

- We recognize the importance of the resolution of conflict within the client, in the therapy and beyond through integration of image and storytelling.

This chapter began with an evocation of Blake's unfolding vision and so we could end with Nietzsche's affirmation of perspectivism, asserting that objectivity is not

> contemplation without interest... There is *only* a perspective seeing, only a perspective 'knowing'; and the *more* affects we allow to speak about one thing, the *more* eyes, different eyes, we can use to observe one thing, the more complete will our 'concept' of this thing, our 'objectivity' be. (Nietzsche quoted in Nehamas 1985, p.50)

It has been an aim in this book to present such a multiperspectival vision of our topic for the reader. It is clear that the notion of the dialogical self in therapy radically contradicts the illusion of single-point perspective. Panofsky pointed out that what single-point perspective creates through 'the structure of an infinite, unchanging and homogeneous space – in short, a purely mathematical space – is quite unlike the structure of psychophysical space' (Panofsky 1997, pp.29–30). Through these reflections we have discovered that if we move on from the 'failings' of single-point perspective as a particular type of spatial representation, we can develop it into a wider exploration of perspectives and iconicity in therapy. In thinking about icons, we discover that iconicity approximates our perception, is fundamental to our development and therefore gives enduring value to the use of the arts and perspectival reflections on pictures and mental imagery in therapy. It is this proximity to our primitive, instinctual and sensual responses, where we find an inherent iconicity of the post-traumatic vigilance and its 'looking out for...' that suggests the notion of iconicity is fundamental to helping to deconstruct the alert system whilst retaining its necessary truths and warnings (the wisdom that comes from suffering), which may be contained in the 'tale', and then to integrate that learning into contemporary tellings. The stories told in, through and by these trauma images presented in sequence then have purpose. The therapeutic tales told in this book make this point repeatedly as we move from affecting confrontations with the startling shards of meaning towards their integration into stories that become 'takes on the world that we can take' and then fruitfully 'tell', reclaiming the ancient value of storytelling. You now have the rest of the book to test these theses. Take care and enjoy!

References

Baudrillard, J. (1983) *Simulacra and Simulation*. London: Semiotext(e).

Bion, W.R. (1992) *Experiences in Groups*. London: Routledge.

Dubery, F. and Willats, J. (1972) *Drawing Systems*. London: Studio Vista.

Eco, U. (2000) *Kant and the Platypus*. London: Vintage.

Greenberg, L.S., Rice, L.N. and Elliot, R. (1993) *Facilitating Emotional Change*. London: Guilford Press.

Grinder, J. and DeLozier, J. (1987) *Turtles All the Way Down*. Portland, OR: Grinder DeLozier Associates.

Lacan, J. (1977) 'The Mirror Stage as a Formative Function of the I.' In *Ecrits*. London: Tavistock Publications. (Original work published 1949)

Nehamas, A. (1985) *Nietzsche: Life as Literature*. London: Harvard University Press.

Panofsky, E. (1997) *Perspective as Symbolic Form*. New York, NY: Zone Books. (Original work published 1927)

Peirce, C.S. (1931–1958) *Collected Papers*. Cambridge, MA: Harvard University Press.

Peirce, C.S. (1992) 'Design and Chance.' In *The Essential Peirce*. Bloomington, IN: Indiana University Press.

Rowan, J. (2010) *Personification*. London: Routledge.

Valsiner, J. (2002) 'Forms of dialogical relations and semiotic autoregulation within the self.' *Theory and Psychology 12*, 2, 251–265.

Winnicot, D.W. (1971) 'Mirror Role of Mother and Family in Child Development.' In *Playing and Reality*. London: Tavistock Publications.

Wright, K. (2009) 'The Search for Form.' In *Mirroring and Attunement*. London: Routledge.

IN THE BEGINNING...

Complex Trauma, Embodiment and
the Supervisorial Holding of the Work

3

Attachment Narratives and Images in Dyadic Parent– Child Art Psychotherapy

Anthea Hendry

Narratives and images in therapy are explored here through an attachment lens. There are three main sections: first, from attachment research, an examination of how a parent's responses to their child's behaviour influences the narrative patterns of attachment identified in childhood and adulthood. Second, a brief description of how attachment is used in diagnosis, psychological formulation and therapeutic practice with children, young people and their parents. Third, a clinical case study guided by, amongst other theoretical influences, this attachment perspective and describing joint engagement and co-construction of narrative approaches to dyadic parent–child art psychotherapy.

Narratives and images in attachment research

Bowlby's attachment theory proposed that psychological wellbeing is contingent upon the stability and strength of caregiving during infancy and young childhood (Marrone 1998). His belief that the human need for protection at times of threat is an instinctive primary drive was controversial in the psychoanalytic circles in which he worked in the 1950s, 60s and 70s. Now it is acknowledged that this developmental theory, with its relational and narrative perspective, makes an important contribution to our understanding of emotional development.

It was the conceptualization of when and why early communications go wrong and, crucially, how this can be measured (Ainsworth et al. 1978) that led to a better understanding of the intergenerational transmission of attachment (Fonagy et al. 1993). Ainsworth's research provides detailed evidence of the evolution of the attachment system and the importance of maternal sensitivity in shaping an infant's sense of security. The Strange Situation Procedure (SSP) she devised, a 20-minute filmed laboratory experiment, is still used in research and clinical settings to measure an infant's pattern of attachment. She differentiated between three primary patterns of attachment in infants:

- securely attached

- avoidant

- ambivalent/resistant.

The infant defined as *securely attached* has received sensitive and responsive caregiving from an adult who is not preoccupied with their own needs and is interested in their baby's state of mind. Such adults have the capacity to repair things quickly and easily when there is a disruption in their capacity to meet the baby's needs. For the infant recipient of this caregiving the internal attachment narrative will be something like: *'I am worthy and lovable. I feel understood. I can trust adults to look after me. I feel safe in the world.'* The image is of a contented, relaxed baby who is usually quickly calmed by their caregiver when distressed.

For infants who consistently receive care that is not sensitive to their needs Ainsworth describes two other patterns. The *avoidant* pattern of attachment is usually observed in babies who have caregivers who reject them in times of need. The child's internal narrative might then be: *'I don't feel wanted'* (Bowlby 1973, p.204) *'but I'll pretend I don't feel needy. If I do that, I can stay near and won't feel so rejected. I'll be self-sufficient.'* The image of the avoidant infant in the SSP is one who often shows little or no distress when the caregiver leaves the room and ignores or shows only mild interest in their return. They want to approach for comfort but they expect rejection. They stay close but do not show neediness. Anger will lurk under the surface (Geddes 2006). The caregiver–careseeker relationship is defined by the caregiver feeling anxious or angry when the baby is needy.

The *ambivalent/resistant* infant is anxious in the caregiver's presence but upset when they are separated. At reunion they want contact but resist it. This pattern emerges when the caregiver is inconsistent, unpredictable and preoccupied with their own needs. Such a caregiver is not rejecting and may want physical contact with their baby but on their own terms. The ambivalent child's internal narrative when their attachment system is activated might be: *'I feel very anxious so I will demand a lot of attention. I will need to keep demanding because I don't want to be forgotten. I'm angry and frustrated because I don't get enough of what I need.'* The image is of a frequently irritated infant/child who is constantly demanding and difficult to satisfy.

These three patterns of attachment describe developmental pathways representing repeated child–parent interaction in a particular family constellation. Given that infancy experiences are predominantly sensorimotor, these patterns are imprinted in the body. They persist over time and across relationships and can be observed in the therapeutic encounter.

Following Ainsworth, Mary Main identified an additional pattern of attachment in her research using the SSP (Main and Solomon 1990). This pattern is particularly relevant to this book. Using the SSP she found that a small per cent age of one-year-olds showed very odd behaviours at the point of reunion with their caregiver. They showed apprehension, disorientation, freezing or repetitive hand or head movements. Their behaviours indicated they were afraid of their caregivers (Holmes and Slade 2018). The *disorganized* pattern of attachment was identified. These infants do not have a consistent strategy for managing stress. The internal attachment narrative of the infant with a disorganized pattern of attachment will be something like: *'I don't know what to do. It must be my fault. I'm not lovable. I can't trust adults to care for me. I'm frightened.'* The personality that develops is one dominated by shame, self-blame and fear. A flight, fight or freeze response takes over. The image is of a frozen, or disconnected or unregulated angry child. The infant has no strategy for seeking comfort, because those that should be comforting them are the people who are frightening them. This is particularly associated with caregivers who had experienced early unresolved loss or trauma.

Lyons-Ruth (2005) extended this understanding by describing the parents of these children as 'either frightened by or frightening to their infants' (quoted in Holmes and Slade 2018, p.12.) The caregivers are overwhelmed and incapable of noticing their baby's needs. The infants are likely to have been exposed to any or all of the following: domestic violence, drug and alcohol abuse, physical and sexual abuse and frequent changes of caregiver. Their lives have been dominated by threat and fear. Within these broad attachment categories observed by Ainsworth and Main other variations and reframings have been suggested such as those by Crittenden (2006), who introduced an extended range of subtypes, but the broad categories by Ainsworth and Main are most often used in the clinical setting (Holmes and Slade 2018).

Main's research also led to the development of the Adult Attachment Interview (AAI), which led to our current understanding of the importance of narrative coherence in adulthood (Holmes 2001). The AAI is a semi-structured interview, which was innovative in the 1990s because it concentrates as much on the discourse style of the narrative as the content. It has been found over many years to produce stable and reliable categorization.

Main identified systematic attachment-related patterns in adults' narrative accounts of their childhood that were comparable to Ainsworth's patterns of infant behaviour identified in the SSP. The four narrative patterns that have evolved from the AAI are described in terms of their coherence and reflective capacity. The *secure/autonomous* pattern has a coherent narrative from a person able to reflect on both the good and more problematic aspects of their childhood. The *dismissing* pattern in adulthood, corresponding to the avoidant infant, lacks the ability to back up comments about their childhood. There is no depth to their narrative and they are derogatory or dismissive of attachment-related experiences. The *preoccupied* pattern, which corresponds to the ambivalent child, does not have a coherent way of talking about their childhood because they are still so preoccupied by it. The narrative is often long, entangled and can be angry. They appear overly involved in family relationships. The past still feels very alive. Positive and negative feelings about family relationships are not integrated. The fourth and final pattern is the adult with an *unresolved or disorganized* pattern who is still deeply affected by memories of loss and trauma. They are unable to speak about traumatic experiences in any coherent way. They lack the capacity for reflective functioning in critical areas. They have difficulty mentalizing. These adults in their parenting will be challenged in their ability to make sense of their child's mind, and it is this capacity that is a protective factor in the intergenerational transmission of insecure attachment patterns (Holmes and Slade 2018).

Attachment in diagnosis, psychological formulation and therapeutic practice

Attachment theory and research is part of the story relating to the challenges mental health clinicians have in finding appropriate diagnoses for children and adolescents who have experienced complex trauma. Raby and Plant in Chapter 4 describe these challenges by tracing the history of post-traumatic stress disorder (PTSD) from the 1980s and the recent attempt to capture more child-sensitive elements in the International Classification of Diseases 2019 (ICD-11) new diagnosis of complex post-traumatic stress disorder (C-PTSD). These challenges can similarly be traced through attempts to define disorders of attachment in children and young people over the same period in the American Psychiatric Association's *Diagnostic and Statistical Manual of Mental Disorders* (DSM-IV) and in ICD-10. O'Connor and Zeanah (2003) describe the dissatisfaction with the diagnostic criteria for reactive attachment disorder (RAD) in these manuals because of the inconsistency in terminology. The manuals used the terms 'inhibited' and 'disinhibited' attachment disorders, while clinical reports and research on attachment disorders use the patterns of attachment terminology defined by Ainsworth and Main. This led to inconsistencies and confusion in diagnosis. For example, in the 1990s and early this century RAD was commonly diagnosed in children who had experienced complex trauma, most particularly those who were adopted or in foster care (Byrne 2003). Byrne emphasized the need to distinguish between the core symptoms of RAD and the many co-occurring problems displayed by these children, such as conduct problems, disturbances in attention and concentration and problems in peer and family relationships. In DSM-5 (2013) the inhibited and disinhibited reactive attachment disorders became two distinct disorders. Disinhibited attachment disturbances become disinhibited social engagement disorder and RAD refers only to the inhibited disturbance.

Assessment and treatment of these disorders still lack consistency among practitioners, and in my experience they are not frequently diagnosed. However, attachment disturbances have their place in other recent attempts to describe complex trauma in children. For example, attachment is one of the seven domains of impairment in the National Child Trauma Stress Networks (NCTSN) White Paper on Complex Trauma in Children and Adolescents (Cook et al. 2003).

This was the research that led to Bessel van der Kolk's proposal for a diagnosis of developmental trauma disorder (van der Kolk 2005; see also Brenninkmeyer 2017), which is still used by mental health clinicians descriptively, despite the fact that it is not in the diagnostic manuals. Although diagnosis is not the objective of holistic approaches to therapeutic work with children and families, it can be useful in some circumstances, for example by giving access to additional funding, resources and support. Just as importantly it influences the intervention. The effects of inappropriate or inadequate diagnoses in children who have experienced complex trauma has led to mismatched treatments, which can exacerbate feelings of worthlessness and self-blame (see Raby and Plant, Chapter 4).

Attachment research and theory is used in the credible alternative to psychiatric diagnosis – psychological formulation (Johnstone 2018). Attachment patterns can be observed in the clinical setting. Holmes and Slade (2018) and Hasler (2017) describe how an understanding of the SSP is utilized in child and family work through careful observation and familiarity with attachment pattern concepts. Listening to an individual's narrative about their lives and relationships with an understanding of the AAI can inform formulations about a child and their parents. Psychological formulation is a process of co-constructing with a service user a hypothesis about the origins of their current difficulties that has meaning to them (Johnstone 2018). From an attachment perspective Holmes suggests three prototypical pathologies of narrative capacity: 'clinging to rigid stories, being overwhelmed by unstoried experience, or being unable to find a narrative strong enough to contain traumatic pain' (Holmes 2001, p.88).

Holmes (2001) suggests that attachment theory and research makes unique contributions to psychotherapeutic practice: it has an ability to move from external observable behaviours to mental representation; it provides a coherent theory of the patient–therapist relationship; the AAI provides a theoretical underpinning for the storytelling, story listening, and story understanding in any session; the patterns of attachment provide a theoretical basis for assessment and formulation; and it provides an understanding to some of the self-defeating behaviours seen in more disturbed clients. As he says:

> Psychological life is embodied in stories, and that is where psycho-therapists start from, helping patients to begin to tell their story, to

make sense of the stories they are caught up in, and to break free from the distorted stories which may have been imposed on them or which they have learned to tell themselves. (Holmes 2001, pp.xiii–xiv)

Case study: Attachment narratives and images in the joint engagement and co-construction of coherent narrative approaches to parent–child art psychotherapy

Introduction

Attachment theory and research provides a framework for this parent–child case study. Systemic principles underlie the work as they do most child and family therapeutic practice. There are influences from the art therapy literature, most particularly here the understanding that art-making is a means of non-verbal communication, and a bridge between inner and outer, and it is also a way of expressing non-declarative memories. The possibility that the process of making and reflecting on images in a therapeutic context may add to the development of epistemic trust by offering the opportunities for the creation of an object that is congruent with the maker's internal world is explored by Taylor Buck and Havsteen-Franklin (2013). The dyadic art therapy literature (Hendry and Taylor Buck 2017; Taylor Buck, Dent-Brown and Parry 2014) provides clarity about the preparation, structure and different approaches to dyadic work. Raby and Plant in Chapter 4 describe research findings into the use of imagery in the treatment of PTSD and C-PTSD, particularly the use of image re-scripting.

The case study features an adoptive family. Relevant literature specifically relating to this client group and case study includes Brodzinsky (1987), Brodzinsky and Schechter (1990), and Trinder, Feast and Howe (2014).

Assessment phase

This case study describes art psychotherapy with Holly, a ten-year-old adopted girl, Olivia, her adoptive mother, and Philip, Olivia's partner. The work took place in a multidisciplinary CAMHS team following an adoption clinic assessment (Hendry and Vincent 2002).

We learnt during the assessment of Holly's extreme neglect and physical and sexual abuse before her removal from her birth family at the age of five months. She then lived in two different foster homes before arriving in her adoptive family at the age of two. Olivia describes her arrival: '...a whirlwind, never still, underweight and failing to thrive, no speech, very independent and didn't seem to care about anyone or anything'. Aged two and a half she was described as unmanageable by a nursery and at the age of six years she was diagnosed with reactive attachment disorder. At the time of this assessment, aged ten years, her physical appearance at least was very different. The image I have of her from this time is of a zebra: strong, athletic, speedy, striking to look at, with signs of aggression and leaving a lasting impression. She was certainly not failing to thrive. There were clear deficits still in affect regulation, the level of attachment security, behavioural regulation and cognitive development. She was diagnosed with ADHD although we all understood this was not her primary difficulty. A best fit descriptive diagnosis now would be of a child with developmental trauma. Her adoptive parents were often confused, exasperated and exhausted by her behaviour, a common response to parenting a child with developmental trauma (Smith 2017).They were desperate to do anything that would help her both in school and at home. Holly's presentation was typical of the adopted children referred to the specialist clinic in this CAMHS team.

It was agreed initially to offer a short block of dyadic parent–child art psychotherapy using a joint engagement approach (Hendry and Taylor Buck 2017). These sessions were for me to observe interactions between Holly and her parents, encourage Holly's ability to communicate her feelings through the art-making and enhance Olivia and Philip's ability to understand what she was communicating. Olivia knew this intervention was an option and felt Holly would engage well with art therapy.

Joint engagement phase

This block of sessions involved Holly, Olivia and Philip in weekly dyadic art therapy sessions. Each session started with a brief check-in. This helped me understand the immediate feelings in the room and any significant events during the week that might impact on the session. The same room and the same art materials were always available, and Holly would doodle or sketch with felt-tips during this check-in. She would speak in short bursts, often contradicting something that had been said. We would try and make sense of these communications. A theme always emerged from this check-in. Art-making developed from this theme. Over the weeks this included an image made about a birthday celebration, a difficult journey on a day trip out, a family meal, and pets in the family and how they negotiated space and safety. The family always worked on the floor and used a large sheet of cartridge paper that they all worked on together to create one jointly made image.

After a block of six joined-up parent–child sessions and two parent-only sessions I had a meeting with the parents to review the work. Olivia and

Philip felt supported by the sessions. We were all encouraged by the way in which Holly engaged in the joint art-making. She never directly talked about her feelings, but they were communicated through her behaviour and art-making. Her parents began to verbalize what they understood from these. They understood that the first two years of her life, before she was placed for adoption, was a critical developmental stage; but just how important it was became more evident to them as the work progressed. The secure base they provided did not allow the effects of early complex trauma to magically disappear. They could see that there had been a shift from the very obvious disorganized/disconnected pattern of attachment Olivia observed when Holly first arrived at the age of two. Her attachment pattern now was a mixed picture, as is often the case, but the dominant pattern was ambivalence. She desperately wanted and needed Olivia and at times could use her appropriately as a secure base but at other times she could be aggressive and highly resistant.

During this review Olivia asked if we could move to some therapeutic work focusing on Holly's pre-adoption history. Holly had been asking questions about her birth family. Olivia had always been very open with her about her adoption and was doing her best to respond appropriately but wanted support with this. We had a joined-up session with Holly to discuss this. She too was keen for this shift in focus.

Co-construction of coherent narrative approach
Initial phase
The initial stage of this work began with planning sessions with Olivia and Philip. This included one session where the parents were invited to engage with the art materials. Using an attachment perspective I invited them each to make two images. The first image was to be connected with a memory from their childhood that evoked difficult feelings, and the second an image from their parenting experiences that held some significant meaning. After completing the image-making they shared the stories behind them. In a subsequent recorded review of this preparatory work both of them said how important this session was.

Philip: *'It was powerful and difficult...'*

'It evoked feelings that had been locked away that seemed much stronger than if we had just talked rather than made images.'

'It gave us some idea of what Holly might experience in the sessions.'

Olivia: *'Without planning to we went to a café after this session for about an hour. It took us that long to have the space between doing the art work and getting back to normal life... We learnt to incorporate this after each session with Holly. We went and did something together as we realized she couldn't just go straight back to school.'*

The other part of the preparatory work with the parents looked at information they had from social services about Holly's birth, the few months she spent with her birth family and her 20 months in two different foster homes. We considered which parts of the story needed emphasis and what words to use to describe the abuse she had suffered. Olivia said that Holly's current narrative was that her birth mother was blameless and her birth father entirely responsible for her removal into care. Social services' records clearly implicated her birth mother in the abuse she had suffered. Olivia wanted help to address this with Holly. She wanted at least a shift in her understanding to include the failings of her birth mother in keeping her safe. This preparatory work confirmed:

- Olivia and Philip's feeling that they wanted to pursue the co-construction of coherent narrative parent–child work and that they felt the timing was right.

- My confidence in their ability to reflect on their own childhood and parenting in a way that in AAI terms would indicate a relatively secure/autonomous status. A contra-indicator for dyadic work is unresolved loss and trauma.

- A main goal from the parents' perspective was to clarify for Holly that her birth mother was unable to keep her safe in the first five months of her life.

Parent–child Session 1: Two days in hospital with birth mother

Holly came into the room as usual, keen to use the art materials. Olivia and Philip confirmed they had talked about the session on the journey here. Holly immediately knelt on the floor and started rummaging through some of the art materials. I confirmed this was to be the first session focusing on Holly's life before she was placed for adoption. They all agreed they were ready to start this work. Holly knew that she had been born in the local hospital. We talked about pregnancies and births. We wondered what Holly's experiences *in utero* had been and how her birth mother had experienced pregnancy. We did not know. From the medical records we knew only that it was a natural birth and that Holly spent probably two days in the hospital with her birth mother.

Holly found some tissue paper. She seemed drawn to the colours and texture. Olivia followed this lead and suggested making the outline of a hospital bed with the blue tissue paper. She made this and Holly stuck it on to a large sheet of cartridge paper. Philip and I watched but were not active in the art-making. Olivia suggested making a crib. She did this in red tissue paper. Holly glued it beside the bed. Olivia cut out the shape of the birth mother and invited Holly to mark in the face, which she did with a black felt tip. It was a smiling face. Olivia stuck the seated figure on to the bed. Holly then drew on a piece of yellow tissue paper a figure of her as the baby. This included a baby's feeding bottle. Again she drew the features of the face. It was another smiley face and Philip remarked on this. Holly cut round the figure and Olivia put glue on the back of the baby and placed her in the crib. Holly instantly snatched the baby up and stuck it firmly into the arms of her birth mother (Figure 3.1). This was the memorable moment in the session. I held my breath as this spontaneous action with the art materials seemed to speak volumes. 'You are cradled in your birth mother's arms,' I observed. I thought her action was her way of communicating that whatever happened after this she wanted us to know that she felt she was safe and cared for by her birth mother in the hospital. Olivia acknowledged how important it was that they had shared making this image and the four of us sat back in silence for a few seconds. Holly left the session happily. I sat in the room for some time after the session looking at the image. Despite the smiling image, and a feeling that the planning and timing of the start of this work was right, there was a deep sadness. A reminder of the drastic nature of adoption and its long-term consequences for all the participants.

Figure 3.1: In birth mother's arms (see online colour plate)

At a review a few months after the making of this image, and again in a recording made some time later, Olivia and Philip reflected on their feelings about the making of this image.

> Olivia: 'Making it had a profound effect on me. It made me realize how important it was for Holly to feel loved by her birth mother in those early days of her life.'

> 'Of course I'm torn about her birth mother. I don't want to be negative about her, but I want to be truthful. I want to feel Holly had a good start in life, but I know most of the time she spent with her birth mother wasn't like that.'

> Philip: 'Holly could never have spoken about her feelings for her birth mother, but making the image made me realize that in her mind her birth mother is a very significant person.'

Parent–child Session 2: Ghosts in the nursery

The following week Holly looked at the image from last week and seemed satisfied. We talked about her leaving hospital and living with her birth parents for five months and that things were difficult because neither of her parents was ready for parenting. They had both had difficult childhoods. Olivia told Holly that in social services' records the bedroom she had slept in was described as bare and smelly with no carpeting, toys or furniture apart from a cot and that she was often left there on her own for many hours. We talked about what babies need to grow up feeling happy and secure. Olivia and Philip did most of the contributing to this with Holly engaged listening. They agreed to make an image of baby Holly in her cot. Holly directed most of the making of the picture with Olivia and Philip cutting and sticking as required.

Again Holly wanted to use the tissue paper; perhaps unconsciously, this fragile material matching the fragile nature of her existence at this time. A baby shape was cut out and stuck on the sheet (Figure 3.2). It had no facial features. The white strips were stuck over and round the baby to form the cot. We reflected on this briefly. 'The baby looks lonely.' 'She doesn't have a smile.' 'It reminds me of sticky tape, or plaster.' 'The sides of the cot look like prison bars.' No attempt was made by Holly to change this negative narrative. Instead, after this period of reflecting, she squeezed some thick mauve paint into a large palette and grabbed a mould of sponge and dabbed this into the paint. She then quickly filled the bottom half of the sheet with prints from the sponge, jabbing quite violently. Holly was communicating her feelings. Olivia and Philip said how bleak the picture was and how sad it made them feel. I said how frightening it must have been for Holly to be such a helpless tiny baby with no one there to make her feel safe and comfortable. It was time for the session to end, and Holly wanted to leave the room immediately. The parents understood this and left with her.

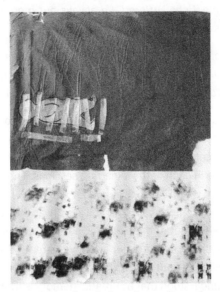

Figure 3.2: Neglected and alone (see online colour plate)

Again I sat with the image after the family had left, initially overwhelmed by the power of it. Feelings of confusion, anger and sadness followed.

When we reviewed this work together a few weeks later, Holly said she didn't like looking at it because it made her feel sad and angry. In a recording made some time later with just the parents they described some of thoughts and feelings about the image.

Olivia: *'It makes me feel very sad.'*

'She was a neglected, abused and a failure to thrive baby.'

'I find it hard to think about what she might have experienced when she was so small.'

'It's hard not knowing what really happened.'

'It became clear to me through this work that she held memories of this time in her body.'

'She would never have had words to describe this.'

'She really had no coherent narrative about her pre-adoption history, even though I have talked to her about it several times before. It reminded me how important it is to revisit the story.'

Philip: *'Watching this image being made and seeing it now makes me realize the neglect she suffered. I'd always put more emphasis on the abuse, but this reminded me of the neglect.'*

'We could collaborate in building a picture of what it must have been like for her. We could never have done it in any other way. It was making the images that allowed us to get to the real narrative and the feelings.'

This block of therapy continued for eight joined-up sessions with child and parents, and two sessions just with parents, interspersed with some phone contact with Olivia between sessions when it was needed to reflect and plan. An image was made in each of the joined-up sessions. The significant known events in the first two years of Holly's life were thought about and represented. The adoptive family's home, where they still lived, was the final image made.

These two sessions out of the block have been described because they had the most impact on Holly and her adoptive parents. They allowed Holly to express her feelings about her birth family through the art-making. The adoptive parents understood that traumatic memory is fragmented and that Holly held some of those memories in her body, and that sometimes these still dictated her behaviour in times of stress.

During the course of this co-construction of narrative work Holly asked if her birth mother had read the annual letter they had sent through the social services letter box contact agreement. The adoptive parents did not know but enquired. It was very hard for Holly to learn that the letters remained unread in a social services file. Olivia asked if a social worker could find Holly's birth mother and remind her that the letters were there. Her birth mother was visited on Holly's behalf, but she did not want to read the letters. For Holly this felt like a huge rejection, but it also allowed her to begin to accept that, for whatever reasons, her birth mother did not want any contact with her at this time. The yearning for and belief that there was a fairytale all-loving mother with open arms had to be put aside.

Postscript

Over the years since this piece of therapeutic work Holly and her adoptive parents have dipped in and out of psychotherapeutic support. Holly attended a psychotherapy group for adopted young people for two years in her teens, and her parents have had both group and therapeutic parenting support. Parents of children who have experienced developmental trauma often need long-term support.

Holly had a particularly stormy adolescence; but through all the ups and downs in their relationship her adoptive parents have remained her parenting parents. She has sometimes struggled with intimate relationships but she lives independently, works and is parenting her own child with amazing support from two sets of grandparents. Olivia and Philip get enormous pleasure from seeing their grandchild pass through early developmental stages without the traumas her mother suffered. They know there are 'ghosts in the nursery' but they have been modified by their capacity to provide that secure base for Holly and her child when they need it.

My long-term contact with this family has contributed to choosing to write about it. Holly, Olivia and Philip have all read my account here. These are their reflections on it.

Holly

> 'It was the right time and the right sort of therapy for me... I liked always having the art materials to use... The work we did about the time I had before I was placed for adoption probably stopped me from trying to make contact with my birth mother when I was a teenager...it would have been a bad time for me to do this.'

Holly has made the choice not to have face-to-face contact with any of the members of her birth family over the intervening years.

> 'I still feel very angry with them and wouldn't want to put myself in the position of being that angry. I'm better off not seeing them because I think they would be a bad influence on me. They have done nothing for me.'

> 'I wish my mum (adoptive) had given birth to me. She's my mum. I am glad I know where I stand with my mum and family. They are my real family because they are the ones that haven't given up on me and have stuck by me through thick and thin.'

Being a parent herself has helped her understand in a deeper way the serious nature of the neglect and abuse she suffered in her early months and the reasons why she was permanently removed from her birth family. She knows this has influenced her own parenting and some of her life choices.

> 'During my own daughter's first two years there were very few people I

could trust to look after her. I'm very cautious of what information I put on social media. I don't want my birth family to have contact with her.'

'I've chosen not to live in the city where I was born and grew up. I feel safer further away.'

Olivia and Philip

'The therapy we experienced was very powerful, and had a huge effect on us all. It shaped our parenting, and helped us react more calmly and rationally to Holly's sometimes challenging behaviour. It gave us deeper insight and understanding of how events in her early life continued to impact on her later years. It helped us carry on and try again.'

'It opened up a lot of areas, such as abuse, neglect, and the birth family, which we were then able to discuss more easily later on, up to and including the present [17 years on].'

'The therapy has also been a basis to talk with Holly about her parenting of her own child, and how she can be a more nurturing and protective mother than was her birth mother.'

'Doing the work together enabled Holly to move from a false belief that we had not protected her from abuse and neglect, and placed them firmly within her early experiences in her birth family. Holly could shift her own thinking about villains (birth father) and heroines (birth mother) as she became older and revisited this topic. She developed a more balanced view.'

'Art therapy was a fantastic medium as it involved us in an activity together and produced something tangible which we could then discuss. We could not have achieved the same results in a talking therapy.'

'It certainly was a big factor in enabling us to remain a family, and to continue to offer love and support and guidance, even though it was rejected at times.'

'We honestly don't believe that we would still all be together as a family without this therapeutic work.'

My grateful thanks to Holly, Olivia and Philip for agreeing to revisit this therapeutic work years after it was completed. Their voices add a vital dimension of co-construction and multiple viewpoints. I hope they feel they have retained control of their narrative in the therapy. They have given consent to the publication of the two images, and quotes from the recording and from a reflective conversation about the therapeutic work. Names have been changed to preserve anonymity. They chose the names to be used in this account.

References

Ainsworth, M.D.S., Blehar, M.C., Waters, E. and Wall, S. (1978) *Patterns of Attachment: A Psychological Study of the Strange Situation*. Hillsdale, NJ: Lawrence Erlbaum.

Bowlby, J. (1973) *Attachment and Loss: Vol. 2. Separation*. New York, NY: Basic Books.

Brenninkmeyer, F. (2017) 'Complex Trauma in Children: An Overview of Theoretical Developments.' Chapter 1 in A. Hendry and J. Hasler (eds) *Creative Therapies for Complex Trauma: Helping Children and Families in Foster Care, Kinship Care or Adoption*. London: Jessica Kingsley Publishers.

Brodzinsky, D.M. (1987) 'Adjustments to adoption: a psychosocial perspective.' *Clinical Psychology Review 7*, 25–47.

Brodzinsky, D.M. and Schechter, M.D. (eds) (1990) *The Psychology of Adoption*. New York, NY: Oxford University Press.

Byrne, J. (2003) 'Referral Bias and diagnostic dilemma.' *Attachment and Human Development 5*, 3, 249–252.

Crittenden, P.M. (2006) 'A dynamic-maturational model of attachment.' *Australia and New Zealand Journal of Family Therapy 27*, 2, 105–115.

Cook, A., Blaustein, M., Spinazzola, J. and van der Kolk, B. (eds) (2003) *Complex Trauma in Children*. White Paper. Los Angeles, CA: National Child Traumatic Stress Network.

Erikson, E. (1963) *Childhood and Society* (2nd edn). New York, NY: W.W. Norton.

Fonagy, P., Steele, M., Moran, G., Steele, H. and Higgitt, A. (1993) 'Measuring the Ghost in the Nursery: An empirical study of the relationship between parents' mental representations of childhood experiences and their infants' security of attachment.' *Journal of the American Psychoanalytic Association 41*, 4, 957–989

Geddes, H. (2006) *Attachment in the Classroom*. London: Worth.

Hasler, J. (2017) 'Healing Rhythms: Music Therapy for Attachment and Trauma.' Chapter 7 in A. Hendry and J. Hasler (eds) *Creative Therapies for Complex Trauma: Helping Children and Families in Foster Care, Kinship Care or Adoption*. London: Jessica Kingsley Publishers.

Hendry, A. and Taylor Buck, E. (2017) 'Dyadic Parent Child Art Psychotherapy with Children Who Have Been Exposed to Complex Trauma.' Chapter 6 in A. Hendry and J. Hasler (eds) *Creative Therapies for Complex Trauma: Helping Children and Families in Foster Care, Kinship Care or Adoption*. London: Jessica Kingsley Publishers.

Hendry, A. and Vincent, J. (2002) 'Supporting adoptive families: An interagency response.' *Representing Children 8*, 2, 104–118.

Holmes, J. (2001) *The Search for the Secure Base: Attachment Theory and Psychotherapy*. London: Routledge.

Holmes, J. and Slade, A. (2018) *Attachment in Therapeutic Practice*. London: Sage.

Johnstone, L. (2018) 'Psychological formulation as an alternative to psychiatric diagnosis.' *Journal of Humanistic Psychology 58*, 1, 30–46.

Main, M. and Solomon, J. (1990) 'Procedures for Identifying Infants as Disorganised/ Disorientated During the Ainsworth Strange Situation.' In M.T. Greenberg, D. Cicchetti and E.M. Cummings (eds) *Attachment in the Preschool Years: Theory, Research and Intervention* (pp.121–160). Chicago, IL: University of Chicago Press.

Marrone, M, (1998) *Attachment and Interaction*. Gateshead: Athenaeum Press.

O'Connor, T.G. and Zeanah, C.H. (2003) 'Attachment disorders: Strategies and treatment approaches.' *Attachment and Human Development 5*, 3, 223–244.

Smith, J. (2017) 'Putting Theory into Practice: Implications for Caregivers.' Chapter 3 in A. Hendry and J. Hasler (eds) *Creative Therapies for Complex Trauma: Helping Children and Families in Foster Care, Kinship Care or Adoption*. London: Jessica Kingsley Publishers.

Taylor Buck, E., Dent-Brown, K. and Parry, G. (2014) 'Dyadic art psychotherapy: Key principles, practices, and competences.' *Arts in Psychotherapy 41*, 2, 163–173.

Taylor Buck, E. and Havsteen-Franklin, D. (2013) 'Connecting with the image: How art psychotherapists can help to re-establish a sense of epistemic trust.' *Art Therapy Online 4*, 1.

Trinder, L., Feast, J. and Howe, D. (2014) *The Adoption Reunion Handbook*. Chichester: Wiley.

van der Kolk, B. (2005) 'Developmental trauma disorder. A new, rational, diagnosis for children with complex trauma histories.' *Psychiatric Annals 35*, 5, 401–408.

4

The Development of Children's Accelerated Trauma Technique (CATT)

A Human Rights and Child-centred Psychological Approach to Treating Post-traumatic Stress Disorder (PTSD) and Complex Post-traumatic Stress Disorder (C-PTSD)

Carlotta Raby and Dominic T. Plant

Figure 4.1: CATT in practice (see online colour plate)

Imagery, narrative and trauma

Ubuntu is a term from Nguni Bantu, translated to mean 'I am, because we are'. It posits that our humanity (the qualities which make us intrinsically human) is not a rigid concept, but rather that our sense of self is dynamically created through our interactions with and dependence on others (Eze 2011) and created through a delicate balance of involvement in (and distance from) relationships.

Group membership provides us with emotional and physical protection, offering a biological survival advantage. Participation in social groups also promotes emotional wellbeing, and can mitigate the impact of traumatic exposure (Haslam et al. 2016). Threat of rupture from our social group can then, understandably, lead to distress and anxiety.

Experiencing a traumatic event can threaten to isolate individuals from their social group through mechanisms such as shame, guilt or societal stigma of mental distress (to name just a few). Maya Angelou (1969, p.74) remarked that 'there is no greater agony than bearing an untold story inside you'. Judith Herman (1992) described that sharing traumatic narratives with others who could bear witness to the content was necessary for reconnecting with social groups, regaining a sense of humanity and belonging, and easing the agony of carrying their otherwise untold story.

However, trauma survivors who subsequently develop symptoms of post-traumatic stress disorder (PTSD) or complex post-traumatic stress disorder (C-PTSD) could encounter significant obstacles to being able to effectively communicate their experience(s). For example, they might not have words to convey the horror that they have endured. Or it could be that they have flashbacks when they try to, which creates distress akin to that which they experienced during the original event. Possibly they believe that their story is so psycho-toxic that they would rather protect the listener than risk inflicting psychological pain on them. Perhaps some individuals are conscious that sharing their narrative(s) could lead to the involvement of additional agencies (such as the police or social care) and are unsure what the consequences could be for themselves or others. These are just some of the many possible reasons that such stories remain untold. And yet, how can reparative therapeutic support be effective without finding a way to do so?

Trauma therapy fundamentally aims to facilitate people being able to share and update their untold narratives safely, so that they recognize that they have survived, and can express and process their personal distress, reconnect with their social group, reclaim their humanity and imagine a future for themselves.

The phrase 'a picture paints a thousand words' suggests that complex thoughts, feelings or behaviours may at times be better captured by imagery. Perhaps that explains why, for over 20,000 years, imagery has been incorporated into what could be considered as therapeutic practice (Edwards 2011, and Edwards and Arntz 2011, as cited in Arntz 2012). Rigorous evaluation of the use of imagery (particularly image re-scripting) in the treatment of PTSD and C-PTSD has been more recently explored. Research findings have indicated that:

- Adding imagery re-scripting and reprocessing into trauma work reduced the likelihood of treatment drop-out, and assisted with additional emotions (such as anger, anger control, shame or guilt) better than prolonged exposure (Arntz, Tiesema and Kindt 2007; Grunert et al. 2007).

- Imagery use in re-scripting was comparable in its effect to using real stimuli (psychologically and neurobiologically) (Holmes and Mathews 2010).

- Adding imagery into trauma therapy could be protective for trauma therapists, in that it reduced their sense of distress and helplessness (Arntz, Tiesema and Kindt 2007).

- Imagery had much stronger emotional effects, and could more effectively address automatic interpretations than verbal processing alone could (Holmes and Mathews 2010, and Holmes, Arntz and Smucker 2007, as cited in Arntz 2012).

- Imagery could be more effective than traditional CBT methods alone in addressing implicational meaning or felt beliefs in trauma work (Cooper, Todd and Turner 2007, and Edwards 2007, as cited in Arntz 2012).

Although most studies have focused on the survivor's experience of using imagery in trauma therapy, the finding relating to the experience of trauma therapists is also of importance if we keep in mind the high risk of compassion fatigue, secondary trauma exposure and burnout for this group of professionals. Finding ways to mitigate such risks is important for therapists' wellbeing, and makes it more possible for them to offer effective therapeutic interventions to those who could benefit from them.

This chapter will reveal a previously untold narrative about why and how a trauma therapy technique called Children's Accelerated Trauma Technique (CATT) (which involves the creation of characters, images and imagery re-scripting, see Figure 4.1) was first developed, and how the use of CATT has facilitated individuals to share experiences of survival that had otherwise felt unspeakable, freeing them from the unimaginable distress caused by PTSD/C-PTSD symptoms.

What has CATT been designed to treat?

In everyday dialogue, upsetting events are often referred to as 'traumatic'. Indeed, 'trauma' may be described differently throughout this book. CATT was specifically designed to treat PTSD and C-PTSD. The first half of this section will offer insight into the historic difficulties in encapsulating PTSD and C-PTSD diagnostically. Currently recognized symptoms of PTSD and C-PTSD will then be outlined so as to demarcate what this intervention was created to treat.

Historic difficulties in encapsulating PTSD and C-PTSD diagnostically

Primary contemporary diagnostic manuals used by clinicians and academics include the fifth edition of the *Diagnostic and Statistical Manual of Mental Disorders* (DSM-5) published by the American Psychiatric Association in 2013, and the eleventh revision of the *International Statistical Classification of Diseases and Related Health Problems* (ICD-11) published by the World Health Organization in 2018. Professor Allen Frances (chair of the development taskforce for DSM-IV-TR) described that 'our classification of mental disorders is no more than a collection of fallible and limited constructs that seek but never find an elusive truth. Nevertheless, this is our best current way of defining and communicating about mental disorders' (Frances and Widiger 2012, p.125).

Some mental health professionals use psychological formulation alongside diagnosis; others use it as a preferred model to diagnosis, offering a person-centred narrative of an individual's strengths and difficulties, and sharing information communicated by them and the systems around them to better understand these contextually. Formulations also interact with diagnostic theory, particularly in illustrating where well-matched evidence-based treatments could be offered as an effective intervention.

Clinicians have historically encountered challenges in formulating and/or diagnosing PTSD or C-PTSD in children and young people. This historic controversy will be outlined briefly.

PTSD was initially introduced as an adult disorder in DSM-III (APA 1980). At that time it was mainly perceived as a psychological condition experienced by adults returning from combat. Although perhaps difficult to conceptualize now, until the 1990s, it was inaccurately assumed that children and young people could not develop PTSD (Cohen and Scheeringa 2009; Rutter 1985).

Subsequent research (Yule 1992; Yule, Perrin and Smith 1999) found that children can in fact have a more unremitting and disabling course of PTSD as compared with adult populations (Alisic et al. 2011; Levendosky et al. 2006; Meiser-Stedman et al. 2008; Mongillo et al. 2009; Scheeringa 2003; Scheeringa, Zeanah, Myers and Putnam 2003; Scheeringa, Zeanah and Cohen 2011). The introduction of DSM-IV (APA 1994) acknowledged these findings, and DSM-5 (APA 2013) saw further revisions, which to some degree addressed concerns regarding developmental sensitivity and validity (specifically for infant and preschool-aged children).

Despite this, criticisms regarding the failure to include developmental trauma categories for children and young people, and to accurately assess and treat children and young people continued (for fuller discussion, see Schmid, Petermann and Fegert 2013; Scheeringa 2011). Furthermore, research indicated that the criteria included in DSM-5 offered over 600,000 symptoms that combined with other diagnoses (Brewin 2013; Sachser et al. 2018). This potentially risked children's and young people's needs being overlooked, or misdiagnosed (Alisic et al. 2011; Drury et al. 2009; Meiser-Stedman et al. 2008; Scheeringa, Zeanah, Myers and Putnam 2003).

The National Institute for Health and Care Excellence (2018) offered examples of events that could have correlated with symptoms of PTSD. Whilst some of these described single-incident traumatic events such as an accident (or several traumatic events of a similar nature within a limited time frame), others (such as childhood or domestic abuse) suggested that individuals could have been exposed to highly toxic environments (often accompanied by unsafe and/or threatening relational experiences) across a more enduring time frame. This chronic and extended exposure to traumatic events could conceivably have left a more complex imprint than could be encapsulated by the list of PTSD symptomology in DSM-5.

Despite attempts by clinicians to advocate for this complexity to be added to diagnostic manuals, in the form of C-PTSD (Ford et al. 2013; Herman 1992), the penultimate ICD publication (ICD-10: WHO 2004) and latest DSM publication (DSM-5: APA 2013) failed to contain diagnostic criteria for C-PTSD. This created significant challenges for clinicians in offering a diagnosis or formulation which could convey the holistic impact of such life experiences, and offer well-matched and evidence-based treatment interventions to this group. We may outline some putative repercussions for people who have tried to seek treatment for C-PTSD prior to this diagnosis being valid.

People who were raised in environments where they were unprotected from abuse or trauma exposure may not have had a template of safe caregivers. If safe caregivers were not available to meet their needs, support them in self-regulating and help them to emotionally and cognitively understand themselves, others and the world around them, there can be an effect on the development of their personalities and relational templates (Ford and Courtois 2013). It is more likely, in such environments, for their personalities and relational templates to have been built predominantly on their need to maintain safety, survive and protect others. Given this, seeking help from healthcare professionals could feel extremely frightening.

If people with C-PTSD had overcome this barrier to accessing support, the inability of clinicians to offer an appropriate diagnosis could have been actively counter-therapeutic, as it likely further compounded the sense of worthlessness and self-blame that survivors of chronic relational trauma can often intrinsically feel. Not being able to recognize and validate the extent of their traumatic exposure and the developmental impact of this, diagnostically, may well have created significant barriers to effective therapeutic relationships, the core foundation for treatment and recovery.

Historically, clinicians who have found themselves without appropriate diagnostic criteria may have tried to communicate people's symptoms of distress through alternative diagnoses in an attempt to access treatment for them. However, this may at times have resulted in mismatched treatment interventions, which could have left people thinking that they were 'untreatable' thus reinforcing feelings of hopelessness. Furthermore, differential diagnoses or formulations may not have offered an understanding of the developmental and relational impact of C-PTSD. Therefore, mismatched treatments would have been unlikely to offer the necessary components for tailoring specific reparative therapeutic interventions and reducing distressing symptoms. Without an accurate diagnosis, people with C-PTSD risked remaining untreated. It has further been argued that untreated C-PTSD could lead to diagnoses in adulthood to include a combination of Axis I and Axis II (personality) disorders and symptoms, Axis III physical health problems and severe Axis V psychosocial impairments (Ford and Courtois 2013).

In 2014 the WHO initiated a review of the existing diagnostic classification process with the intention of improving classification in the upcoming ICD-11 (WHO 2018). ICD-11 offers neater diagnostic criteria for PTSD, with much reduced symptom overlap (Sachser et al. 2018). ICD-11 has also recognized the diagnostic criteria of C-PTSD; suggesting that in addition to core PTSD symptoms of re-experiencing, avoidance and sense of threat, C-PTSD would also include symptoms of affect dysregulation (to include heightened emotional reactivity and emotional numbing), negative self-concept (to include persistent beliefs about oneself as diminished, defeated or worthless, accompanied by deep and pervasive feelings of shame, guilt or failure related to the traumatic event) and interpersonal difficulties (problems in building and sustaining relationships and detachment from others).

This is the start of a new era, whereby clinicians can sensitively describe the 'toxic' trauma environments that people have survived, alongside the understandable developmental impact this may have had on their ability to self-regulate and to build a positive sense of self, others and the world around them. Using this diagnostic foundation, clinicians are better able to describe how this could have led to functional holistic difficulties for the people they are treating (to include interpersonal relationships). Crucially, this type of diagnosis and formulation can allow compassionate and targeted interventions and re-establish hope for a different future.

Currently recognized symptoms of PTSD and C-PTSD

National Institute for Health and Care Excellence (NICE) guidelines have already integrated ICD-11 changes and offer rigorous assessment and treatment guidelines for both PTSD and C-PTSD in children, young people and adults. Although not all people who have survived traumatic experiences will necessarily develop PTSD or C-PTSD, NICE identifies that serious accidents, physical or sexual assaults, abuse (including childhood or domestic abuse), work-related exposure to trauma (including remote exposure), trauma related to serious health problems or childbirth experiences, and war or conflict are commonly recognized precursors to PTSD and C-PTSD (NICE 2018).

NICE (2018) guidelines suggest that PTSD and C-PTSD are considered to comprise a cluster of symptoms associated with functional impairment, to include re-experiencing, avoidance, hyperarousal, negative alterations in mood and thinking, emotional numbing, dissociation, emotional dysregulation, interpersonal difficulties or problems in relationships and negative self-perception. It is considered that such symptoms would also be associated with functional impairment.

CATT was specifically designed to reduce the symptom clusters of PTSD and C-PTSD as described in the latest NICE guidelines. In addition, CATT can be used to treat 'clinically important symptoms of PTSD', which refers to people who score over the cut-off threshold on clinically validated scales, but who do not necessarily have a full diagnosis of PTSD following a clinical interview (NICE 2018). A description of CATT will now follow.

Development of CATT

CATT is an empirical model in nature. That is to say that CATT was developed from the ground up through an evidence-based practice approach, integrating developmental and clinical psychology theory with clinical observation and practice.

CATT shares theoretical overlap in treatment components with many other trauma-focused cognitive behavioural therapies (TF-CBTs) (Raby and Edwards 2011), such as Ehlers and Clark's (2000) cognitive therapy for PTSD (CT-PTSD) which has since been adapted and applied to children and young people (Smith et al. 2009), Cohen, Mannarino and Deblinger's (2006) TF-CBT for children and adolescents, and narrative exposure therapy for traumatized children and adolescents (KidNET: Neuner et al. 2008). In this regard, CATT can be considered an individual TF-CBT intervention.

The aim here is to offer a transparent journey through the developmental origins of CATT, contextualize the era and circumstances within which the model emerged, and summarize its basic tenets.

Project X

To share the early developmental stage of the CATT model, a description of 'Project X'[1] is needed, as this was the place where it was first recognized that there was a need for such an approach. The learning that was gifted from the lived expertise of the children and families involved in this project influenced the model significantly. It would, therefore, seem disloyal not to begin here.[2]

Project X was set up in an inner-city area of the UK, between 1997 and 1998. It was founded in response to the Children Act 1989, which outlined local authority (LA) responsibilities in creating services for children who had become socially excluded. This legislation placed a new duty on LAs to identify 'Children in Need' (CIN) and support links with their families, so that:

1. further abuse and neglect did not continue unnoticed

2. the number of children removed from family care would be reduced

3. the likelihood of these children becoming involved in future criminal activity would decrease.

Section 17(1) of the 1989 Act stated that it was the 'general duty of each LA to provide a range and level of services which (were) appropriate to the CIN in their area, so as to safeguard and promote the welfare of such children; and so far as it is consistent with that aim, promote their upbringing by their families'. The Act also clarified that in addition to physical disability, CIN would be considered 'disabled' if they suffered from a 'mental disorder of any kind', and placed an additional duty on LAs to provide services for children with mental health difficulties to prevent future areas of concern, neglect or criminal proceeding against the children they described.

These new duties motivated a particularly forward thinking LA to apply for funding to design and deliver a project that aimed to develop the social and emotional skills of children and young people (aged between four and 11 years), who had been permanently excluded from

---

1   Project X will not be named, for the purposes of anonymity.

2   The description of the project is recognized as a subjective and personal account of the project through the narrow sphere of how it related to the author's development of the CATT model. Information has been taken from research produced at this time (Raby 2002).

mainstream services in the borough due to emotional and behavioural difficulties. The LA had previously advocated strongly for children with profound physical disabilities to have experiences of play, and had been highly successful in achieving these aims. They set out to provide similar opportunities for children who had become permanently excluded from mainstream services in the hope that access to safe play environments facilitated by skilled play workers could provide social modelling to assist the children in reintegrating into mainstream education, alongside the other duties laid out above.

Funding for the pilot project was awarded. The team began without any specific framework or training, but rather with a well-intentioned belief that an unstructured environment could allow for a responsive, child-centred service, built around the needs that the children expressed. It was in this context that a young team of enthusiastic play workers found themselves running:

- a term-time day-care provision for children and young people with significant emotional and behavioural difficulties

- a 'Maintaining Positive Parenting Under Stress' programme for parents of the children

- a mentoring service during the evenings and weekends

- a respite service when needed

- a holiday play scheme running full-time across holiday periods

- a transition service for children able to reintegrate into mainstream education

- a sibling programme focused on preventative behavioural support.

Initial referrals came from primary pupil referral units, when children had become permanently excluded from mainstream education. Data captured at the time showed that all of the children had experienced socio-economic disadvantage, had lived in environments where they were exposed to socio-environmental risks (e.g. violence, drugs, gang activity) and had been exposed to domestic violence (either as witnessed between their parents/carers, or as having been directly violently assaulted themselves). In addition, some of the children had further experienced neglect, emotional abuse and/or sexual abuse (Raby 2002).

Children referred were between the ages of four and 11 years and had been permanently excluded from mainstream services, due to displaying behaviour(s) that challenged those around them (such as having violently assaulted peers or staff, or having damaged property) to a degree where it was considered that they presented an ongoing risk to others (and at times also to themselves).

Although challenging behaviour in the children was overtly apparent, as a team we strove to better understand the root cause of the behaviour. As the children began to feel safer in our care, the difficulties which emerged or they disclosed fell broadly into two categories: social care and mental health.

With regard to social care, many of the children were either continuing to be exposed to risk of harm (in the home or in the community) or were (for varying reasons) unable to get their basic needs met (e.g. due to socio-economic stress they may not have eaten regular meals or not have had a bed/bedroom for privacy and to feel safe in to sleep properly). With regard to mental health, most of the children were presenting with symptoms that might now be understood as C-PTSD (sometimes alongside other presentations, predominantly anxiety disorders, depression and neurodevelopmental difficulties). However, attempts on behalf of the team to advocate for the children's needs to be met under both of these categories were more challenging than anticipated. To understand why, some historic context regarding social care and mental health services will follow.

Barriers in accessing support – social care

In some of the children's lives, historic or continued maltreatment and abuse (emotional, physical, sexual and/or neglect) was discovered and we began to formulate that these were highly traumatized children who were trying to survive (sometimes whilst under continued threat) in ways they had learnt to be relationally effective in those circumstances. As a team, we considered it unlikely that we could effect change in these children's behaviour unless we first ensured their safety and were able to work within their family systems (Raby 2002).

The Children Act 1989 stipulated that there was a general duty under Part III of the Act to prevent CIN from suffering ill treatment or neglect (see also Gore 2011). However, when we followed LA safeguarding policies and made referrals to social services, we were left confused that these referrals did not appear to result in social care taking the action we had expected.

None of the Project X team had worked within a social-care role, and our attempts to better understand why this was did not result in clarity. We were, therefore, left disputably to hypothesize that following the findings of the Cleveland Inquiry (DHSS 1988), where social workers had been critiqued for their hasty interventions in their removal of children (O'Loughlin and O'Loughlin 2016) and over-zealousness (Kitzinger 2004), there may possibly have been a downplaying of risk to mitigate such disapproval. There was a general concern during this period of time that such caution could have led to areas of ineffectual practice (Kirton 2009; Kitzinger 2004).

Furthermore, the Children Act had included a wider conceptualization of CIN, which had undoubtedly placed an increased demand on LAs to support families in maintaining parental responsibility wherever possible. Services were therefore likely to be operating under very high thresholds at this time (for a review, see O'Loughlin and O'Loughlin 2012). These combined pressures may have contributed to the wider 'public and political image of social work in the late 1990s [as] dominated by failures in relation to children and young people' (O'Loughlin and O'Loughlin 2012, p.20).

Regardless of our speculation on the reasons why we encountered a lack of expected action, the frontline reality was that despite high levels of concern amongst the team and referrals to social services having been made, most of the children remained in their family environments without the significant level of support we considered them to need. This resulted in our attempting to create partnerships with the parents of children in our care so as to assist with some of their challenges, despite their having been informed that social service referrals had been made due to our concerns about their ability to provide safe environments for their children. Particularly in the early stages of the project, and keeping in mind that a significant amount of support was offered by 1:1 staff in the family home, this was a challenging foundation upon which to build a good working partnership.

What we learnt over time was that many of the parents/carers of children on the project had experienced environments that had been unsafe or traumatic for them during their own childhoods/adolescence. Most of them considered that they had parented in a much improved way over how they had been parented. Having heard some of their childhood stories, objectively it appeared that the majority of them had.

Our compassion towards their parenting challenges increased. Their children now demanded a level of parenting that needed to be above and beyond a 'good enough' level of parenting. They now required an exceptionally therapeutic level of parenting, which could offer repair from their previous experiences, and provide safe containment for their expressions of trauma and distress (which often included aggressive and unsafe behaviours). The children also needed their familial environments to provide a strong foundation upon which to access professional support and begin their recovery journey.

Over time, members of the team began to feel the psychological impact of attempting to meet the needs of this group of children on a daily basis. Despite working in a close team, some staff experienced secondary trauma symptoms, and others began to show signs of compassion fatigue and burnout. We became more aware, then, of what a significant demand we were placing on the parents/carers, particularly given their intergenerational trauma histories and lack of wider systemic support. That stated, we were committed to assisting however we could to increase the likelihood of this being possible.

All of the parents/carers were living with a number of everyday strains (such as inappropriate housing, poverty and lack of community safety). We identified that to work in partnership with parents/carers, we would need to advocate for them to get their basic needs met, before we could expect them to have the capacity to enter into reflective dialogues with us about the emotional needs of their children.

Barriers in accessing support – mental health services

In 1998, at a time when cutting-edge research was sharing the novel evidence that children could experience PTSD, and when C-PTSD wasn't to be included in diagnostic manuals for a further 20 years, it is perhaps unsurprising that PTSD/C-PTSD diagnoses had never been considered for any of the children attending Project X, despite their histories, which included (for many) a combination of events described in the current NICE (2018) guidance.

It is now better understood that childhood maltreatment and witnessing (or being exposed to) violence or interpersonal trauma can lead to externalizing behaviours (to include violence commission) (Greenwald 2014). However, in 1998 this was not well understood.

Conversely, conduct disorder had first appeared in DSM-II as early as 1968, with robust measures of assessment existing since 1987 (Matson and Nieminen 1987). When we referred the children on Project

X for mental health assessments, their externalizing behaviours were frequently captured within a conduct-disorder diagnostic framework. However, this did not come with any advice on how to intervene to reduce symptomology.

Some of the children were offered individual psychodynamic psychotherapy, and the team were initially relieved that they would receive psychological help. However, our experience was that they found therapeutic relationships extremely difficult to establish. We were asked to support the children in attending therapy sessions, but they became strongly avoidant, and this was both threatening relationships we had worked hard to establish and also raising discussions within the team about children's rights to have their voices heard, under children's rights legislation (such as Articles 12 and 13 of the UN Convention on the Rights of the Child: UN 1990), particularly when their avoidance increased.

When we spoke to the service about this, we were informed that children often displayed worsening symptoms before symptom relief could be seen, and were advised to facilitate their ongoing attendance. This dynamic felt deeply uncomfortable, and the team struggled to get the right balance between acting in the children's best interests according to professionals, and hearing the voices and opinions of the children involved with regard to decisions that affected their lives, and advocating for them accordingly.

For the few children who engaged with the therapeutic support offered, when they became dysregulated and/or aggressive we were told that they may anyway be unsuitable for individual treatment. Many of these children reported feeling blamed, helpless or untreatable.

When we spoke openly to the children about the balance of wanting to support them in accessing something that could offer a reduction in symptoms, whilst not wanting this to damage relationships we had worked hard to establish, they voiced that it would be their choice not to continue. Consequently, we decided to provide transport, and staff to attend with them, but we agreed to let them choose whether to accept this offer when appointment times came and to respect this. For the children for whom this still remained an option, they voted with their feet and refused to attend. Having seen the distress it had created when they had attended, we decided that accepting this informed decision was fair.

Our judgement to give children with behavioural difficulties such a strong voice in decisions such as these was critiqued by some.

Our subjective observation was that giving them some control had improved relationships with our staff team, in that it demonstrated that their difficulties in establishing safety in therapeutic relationships and the upset this caused had been heard, and that it offered them an opportunity to have choice about this and discuss it, as opposed to expressing their discontent through aggressive behaviour and becoming involved in power battles with us. This increased their apparent responsibility in working alongside us to find a way forward to reduce their distressing symptoms.

Ultimately, then, we were left with a highly vulnerable group of children who appeared to present with what we would now describe as C-PTSD symptoms, in a context that didn't recognize this, and therefore with no satisfactory diagnostic framework within which to advocate for their clinical needs.

Dilemma

Acknowledging a lack of expertise at this point, the first author weighed up the options of creating an innovative approach for children and young people versus their not receiving treatment, and decided to try to develop a way forward. The first author's observation of the unmet needs of this group of children and young people, and the high level of distress it caused them, affected her deeply and remained a great motivator throughout the development of the CATT model.

Particularly as this was a novel approach, patient autonomy and informed consent became a cornerstone of the developing model. Each stage involved information sharing, transparency and choice, and we designed CATT as a holistic model that positioned people with parental responsibility centrally, and that supported them in weighing up each juncture, to ensure that engagement was in the best interests of their child.

Furthermore, we sought opinions from professionals claiming expertise in this area (nationally and internationally), and these individuals were invited to discuss the developmental stages of the model and witness training in use of the model; we also made it clear that constructive criticism was welcomed. Lastly, we designed the model to be dynamic in nature so that

- evaluation of clinical delivery
- development in the research field

- feedback (from children, families and practitioners)

- learning from staff working within different services and cultural contexts

could all be incorporated into its ongoing development. Although published consequent to the development of CATT, this process of developing ethical innovative therapeutic models of care for children is excellently captured by Eyadhy and Razack (2008).

It took many years beyond the first author's involvement in Project X for the model to come together, and it was additionally influenced by many other factors (see Raby 2010 for a full overview). The following section will offer an overview of other influencers of the model.

Influencers of CATT
Children's rights
The first author worked in a number of children's rights roles within mental health organizations and undertook further academic studies in the subject of international human rights law. Specifically hearing about a range of children's rights abuses during this time, and also listening to a diverse range of children's and young people's voices across the country regarding how they would like their mental health care to be delivered, influenced the overall model. It also further enforced the model as one of a partnership, where children were given as much autonomy and control as possible, and where the model was flexible to accommodate individual, cultural and contextual difference.

Individual clinical work with children and young people
Academic teachings from integrative arts psychotherapy, clinical psychology and psychotraumatology alongside clinical practice with children, young people and adults has added to the model in that

- it was guided by psychological research and was developed as a cognitive behavioural approach, which used a memory-based understanding of PTSD whilst integrating imagery as a key therapeutic tool

- it added a structured arts-based imaginal reliving and imaginal re-scripting technique for reducing emotional arousal of memories

- it was often led by how children chose to engage (e.g. the creation of the restorative character-based imaginal reliving came from children's natural inclination to offer a more hopeful and empowering narrative).

Application of CATT to areas affected by conflict/violence/natural disaster

The first author received an invitation to travel to Rwanda in 2007 from a local Rwandan non-governmental organization (NGO) that worked in communities affected by violence perpetrated during the genocide. The NGO aimed to achieve peace and reconciliation, and wanted a model of trauma treatment for adults, but also for children and young people affected by the mass trauma.

The experience of delivering the CATT model in this context (in conjunction with necessary research undertaken during this time) (Raby 2010) led to a formalizing of the CATT model, and demonstrated that

- CATT was applicable for cases of acute PTSD and led to symptom reduction

- CATT was culturally flexible and adaptable (Allard, Bates and Skaarbrevik 2016; Edwards 2011; Raby 2010; Raby and Edwards 2011; Rolington 2014).

This trip engendered interest in CATT being delivered to other countries affected by war, conflict or natural disaster. This ultimately led to the first author establishing a charity organization, Luna Children's Charity, in 2008. This charity has since 2018 been operating under the name of Action for Child Trauma International.[3]

The purpose of setting up Action for Child Trauma International was to enable local organizations supporting survivors of trauma and conflict (who did not possess the resources to buy in specialist therapeutic support) to access free training in CATT. It also aimed to establish culturally appropriate and locally owned sustainable methods of ongoing CATT training for children and young people in their communities.

An immense amount of feedback and learning was accorded from the application of CATT to a variety of countries for over a decade,

---

3   www.actinternational.org.uk

and from feedback from frontline staff, clinicians and children/families across diverse settings. This has led to the continued development of CATT training programmes.

TraumaPsychology (Trauma Psychology Global Limited)

The only training route for CATT used to be through Action for Child Trauma International. However, this required clinicians to then volunteer their time for the charity. This left clinicians who did not have the capacity or desire to volunteer with the charity without a training route. Only organizations without funding to otherwise buy in specialist trauma training were able to access resources and training from Action for Child Trauma International. This meant that organizations and practitioners with a budget that wanted to train in CATT had no route to access it.

TraumaPsychology was, therefore, launched in 2017 by both authors to meet these needs. TraumaPsychology recognized that there had been changes in the needs of clients, practitioners, thresholds for clinical services and developments in research since the CATT model had first been established, and therefore

- undertook a review and audit of feedback from CATT trainees

- analysed training materials

- updated the training package accordingly to incorporate the formal diagnosis of C-PTSD

- set up robust quality assurance and support systems for participants

- established a Register of CATT Practitioners.

The CATT protocol

CATT is a trademarked protocol for the psychological treatment of PTSD and C-PTSD. In-depth training in the model and its clinical application is provided by the authors through the training organization TraumaPsychology. Successful completion of a training course by licensed mental health practitioners is required to use CATT in clinical practice. Action for Child Trauma International offers a licensed version of the CATT training, for humanitarian purposes, for delivery to organizations best placed to offer such support following conflict, war or natural disaster. This section offers a very brief synopsis of the CATT model (shown in Figure 4.2).

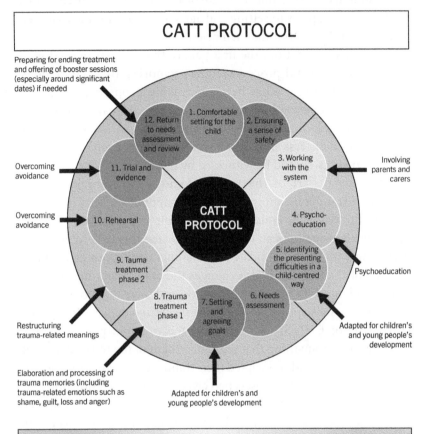

Figure 4.2: Steps of the CATT protocol

CATT is a 12-step holistic model. The model begins with ensuring that the setting is comfortable for the child, before secondly ensuring safety (both internal and external safety). The third step is in place to ensure that clinicians contextualize the treatment of the child or young person within their wider familial, societal and cultural system.

Psychoeducation on PTSD and the identification of difficulties using child-centred practice is an essential part of the model, and helps with assessments and the establishing of goals for treatment alongside person-centred formulations. Before further therapeutic work is undertaken, the CATT model has integrated a needs assessment, which places an onus on the clinician to advocate for any basic or emotional needs to be met, prior to setting and agreeing more specific treatment goals or attending to trauma memories.

Upon this foundation, the first part of the trauma-focused work aims to elaborate and process trauma memories, through demonstrating and detailing what happened using props made with art materials, and overloading working memory, to maintain internal emotional regulation. Grounding techniques can accompany this stage. Reduced distress and a reduction in what are often referred to as 'trauma hotspots' should be witnessed by the end of this step.

The second part of the trauma-focused memory work is to restructure trauma meanings, images and appraisals. This stage gives an opportunity for the child to re-script their story in a way that feels reparative. It also allows an opportunity for the therapist to engage in discussion with them to update any dysfunctional appraisals made at the time of the trauma. It also changes the emotional tone, allowing for reduced intensity of negative emotion and increased hopefulness.

The rehearsal step of CATT aims to tackle avoidance. Most people with PTSD or C-PTSD will have started to avoid places, people, conversations or anything that reminded them of the traumatic event. Having processed and re-scripted their trauma experience, they should be able to more accurately assess perceived threat in such situations and re-engage with things that they may have been avoiding without their previous level of distress. It may be that imagined trials of this can be undertaken through guided imagery prior to revisiting these *in vivo*. Otherwise reducing avoidance and practising confronting reminders of the trauma can further update accurate threat perception.

Evidence is then gathered, through triangulated information gathering, of improved functioning (such as a change in previous avoidance behaviours). Reports from the child themselves, communication from school and feedback from their family can all contribute to providing evidence that the child has improved. This can be further supported by post-treatment assessment measures, risk reviews and a clinical interview.

Finally, the clinician is asked to consider the limitations of the service and to review whether there are any pragmatic or clinical needs outstanding. Depending on the answer to this question, the clinician may need to attend to these, or make an onward referral for other needs to be met prior to discharge. Endings are carefully planned and paced, with 'check-in sessions', particularly at times where things might feel more difficult (such as anniversaries of deaths, etc.).

For readers wanting to learn more about clinical training, information can be found at TraumaPsychology's website.[4] Unfortunately, there is not capacity in this chapter to elaborate on the clinical techniques employed in each step of the protocol. For readers interested in reading a full case study, the treatment journey of a 12-year-old boy named Paul offers insight into how CATT was used to reduce symptoms of PTSD in more detail (Raby and Edwards 2011). A shortened case example of CATT treatment for a ten-year-old boy named Patrick features at the end of this chapter to give a flavour of how CATT uses the creative imaging techniques as props to demonstrate the traumatic narrative, whilst the clinician ensures that the child remains emotionally regulated, and that their trauma narrative is contained within a wider linear script to include that there was a safe beginning (before this event happened) and, crucially, an ending (where they were able to recognize that they had survived). It demonstrates that as a child's 'trauma hotspots' reduce, they can integrate their trauma narrative within the wider script in a way that they are able to neurologically process and store as a past memory, as opposed to a current potential threat. When stored in this form, it can be seen that they are better able to bring up the memory without overwhelming affect, and speak about it with others; reconnecting with their support network. The example shows that they can thereafter reduce their vigilance to current threat, and therefore do not need to avoid potential triggers, allowing for a reclaiming of their lives. Overarchingly, they are left with a sense that, although they have been through a harrowing event, they have survived it and can therefore move forwards towards a different future.

Reflections

When the first author thinks back over the development of CATT, she is reminded of a second quote by Maya Angelou: 'Do the best you can, until you know better. Then when you know better, do better' (cited

---

4   www.traumapsychology.co.uk

in Boutte, Lopez-Robertson and Powers-Costello 2011). Following 20 years of research and practice, Project X (the start of the journey of the creation of the CATT model) seems on the one hand to have been a chronically naive approach. On the other hand, this freed a young and highly enthusiastic team up from working within the somewhat restrictive narratives of the time, narratives that denied the experience of PTSD or C-PTSD in children and young people and often devalued their voices and expertise in the process of their treatment. It allowed a group of young staff to do the best they could to see and hear what the children were communicating to them, and respond to their needs and the needs of their families directly, flexibly and without preconception. These precious interactions significantly contributed to the later CATT model.

Conclusion

CATT is a 12-step trauma-focused therapy informed by developmental psychology and CBT theory, which has been woven into this grass-roots therapeutic approach to understanding children's developmental needs and rights, and observational responses to traumatic events.

CATT has been applied cross-culturally and with children of varying ages (from three years to 18 years) who have survived traumatic events of varying natures (including single-incident traumas, multiple-event traumas, and chronic and prolonged traumas) resulting in reduced PTSD symptomology. It has also been used effectively with adults. Results of pre-and post-treatment scale scores (alongside personal testimonies) demonstrate that CATT has achieved what it set out to: to offer a compassionate, person-centred and safe facilitation of traumatic narrative sharing, allowing the agony of bearing the otherwise untold story to dissipate and for rapid reconnection with others to be made.

The CATT model contemporaneously fits comfortably within UK NICE (2018) guidelines for treating children, young people and adults with PTSD and C-PTSD, as an individual TF-CBT intervention, alongside other reliable and valid child-centred TF-CBT models. This is all within a context where PTSD and C-PTSD are now thankfully recognized as valid and treatable diagnoses in children, young people and adults. It is the hope of the authors that this will lead to timely identification of need, and access to evidence-based interventions that can offer trauma survivors a more promising future.

Case study: A shortened example of CATT being used in practice[5]

This case offers a description of how the use of creative arts methods, alongside CBT and psychotherapy techniques, within the CATT technique, have effectively reduced psychological distress and symptoms of PTSD.

Patrick is a ten-year-old boy who lived with his mother, father and younger brother in Uganda. His elder sister had been tragically killed in a hit-and-run accident on her way home from her cousin's house.

Since discovering his sister had died, Patrick was described as having become withdrawn, confused and highly agitated. His mother shared that he continued to have repetitive nightmares about her being killed, and would wake up screaming, crying or having wet the bed. His mother shared that he refused to attend the burial service, and still avoided speaking about her. Since her death, he had also not attended school or seen friends, as this involved crossing the road she had been killed on, and upon approach he would become highly distressed and run home.

Steps 1 through to 12 of the CATT model were applied. The therapeutic task of each stage is briefly explained below. Steps 1 to 7 were:

1. to create a comfortable therapy setting for Patrick

2. to ensure a sense of (internal and external) safety (grounding and stabilization) for Patrick

3. to involve suitable individuals in sustainable relationships with Patrick's therapy work

4. to provide psychoeducation on PTSD

5. to identify Patrick's presenting difficulty in a child-centred way

6. to assess for additional needs that Patrick had

7. to set therapy goals with Patrick.

Steps 8 and 9 involved the trauma memory processing and re-scripting techniques. At this stage, narrative and imagery techniques were applied alongside cognitive therapy techniques.

Patrick was first supported to make a list of characters and things that were present when he heard about his sister's death, and to create these out

---

5   The primary purpose of sharing this case is to illustrate the use of CATT. Therefore, all significant identifiable information has been changed, to ensure anonymity.

of locally sourced art materials. He made himself, his sister, his mother, his father, a local police officer and his brother.

Patrick was encouraged to choose some art materials to create a representation of a point before he had been aware that anything bad had happened. He made a football pitch and named this point as 'playing football'. Patrick was supported to choose some art materials to represent a point at the end of his story, where he knew he had survived. He chose 'in my bed' and made a bed to represent this.

Patrick was invited to choose a title for his story. He chose 'The eyes of death'. Specific instructions from the clinically taught technique were utilized to overload his working memory so as to facilitate processing of his narrative without his becoming too emotionally overwhelmed. Patrick was supported by his therapist to safely retell the traumatic narrative, using the characters and imagery, in order to process the strong emotions generated at the time of the traumatic event.

In the next step, Patrick was encouraged to choose a new title for this story. He titled this story 'I carried my sister home'. He made himself, but attached lots of screwed-up tissue paper taped to his arms, sharing that these were big muscles that he would need if he were to do this effectively. Patrick then used the new character to create an imagined alternative story, which was a platform for updating his trauma narrative, with the cognitive message that the trauma was over and that he could move forward.

The therapy then continued, to complete the following therapeutic tasks:

1. behavioural techniques to practise re-engaging with previously avoided activities

2. to reassess whether therapy goals were achieved

3. to administer PTSD psychometric measures and reassess for additional needs for onward referral.

As compared with pre-treatment scores, by the end of his treatment, Patrick no longer presented with symptoms of PTSD, and Patrick's CRIES-8 score was at a 3 (see Figure 4.3), demonstrating a significant reduction in self-reported post-traumatic symptoms that no longer reached over the threshold for clinical significance (CRIES-8: 17, as indicated by the thick vertical cut-off line).

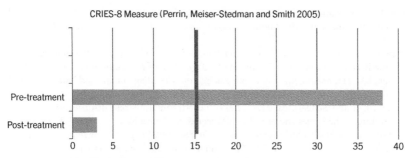

Figure 4.3: Patrick's pre-treatment CRIES-8 score, post-treatment CRIES-8 score and CRIES-8 cut-off score

Patrick co-planned an ending process (to include relapse prevention) and was offered a booster session at the anniversary of his sister's death, which also served as a review point. Patrick was able to share that he had been able to join his family in mourning his sister's memory at this event, and that his symptoms had remained sub-clinical. He and his family reported that he was continuing to function well (his teacher had reported him doing well at school, and he was described as playing with friends again and generally enjoying life). At this point he was discharged. The family were in touch a year later to inform the therapist that he continued to do well.

References

Alisic, E., Jongmans, M.J., van Wesel, F. and Kleber, R.J. (2011) 'Building child trauma theory from longitudinal studies: A meta-analysis.' *Clinical Psychology Review 31*, 5, 736–747.

Allard, S., Bates, A. and Skaarbrevik, M. (2016) *Social Impact Assessment of Luna Children's Charity CATT Training in Uganda.* Accessed on 17/3/2019 at https://static1.squarespace.com/static/5bc75ab193a6325f3c4c3ed4/t/5d66e0db35777300014c3b29/1567023325272/SIA++Uganda+2016.pdf

American Psychiatric Association (1980) *Diagnostic and Statistical Manual of Mental Disorders* (3rd edn). Washington, DC: Author.

American Psychiatric Association (1994) *Diagnostic and Statistical Manual of Mental Disorders* (4th edn). Washington, DC: Author.

American Psychiatric Association (2013) *Diagnostic and Statistical Manual of Mental Disorders* (5th edn). Washington, DC: Author.

Angelou, M. (1969) *I Know Why the Caged Bird Sings.* London: Random House.

Arntz, A. (2012) 'Imagery rescripting as a therapeutic technique: Review of clinical trials, basic studies, and research agenda.' *Journal of Experimental Psychopathology 3*, 2, 189–208.

Arntz, A., Tiesema, M. and Kindt, M. (2007) 'Treatment of PTSD: A comparison of imaginal exposure with and without imagery rescripting.' *Journal of Behavior Therapy and Experimental Psychiatry 38*, 4, 345–370.

Boutte, G.S., Lopez-Robertson, J. and Powers-Costello, E. (2011) 'Moving beyond colorblindness in early childhood classrooms.' *Early Childhood Education Journal 39*, 335.

Brewin, C.R. (2013) '"I Wouldn't start from here" – An alternative perspective on PTSD from the ICD-11: Comment on Friedman (2013).' *Journal of Traumatic Stress 26*, 5, 557–559.

Cohen, J.A., Mannarino, A.P. and Deblinger, E. (2006) *Treating Trauma and Traumatic Grief in Children and Adolescents*. New York, NY: Guilford Press.

Cohen, J.A. and Scheeringa, M.S. (2009) 'Post-traumatic stress disorder diagnosis in children: Challenges and promises.' *Dialogues in Clinical Neuroscience 11*, 1, 91.

Department for Health and Social Security (DHSS) (1988) *Report of the Inquiry into Child Abuse in Cleveland 1987*. Cd 412. London: Her Majesty's Stationery Office.

Drury, S.S., Theall, K.P., Keats, B.J. and Scheeringa, M. (2009) 'The role of the dopamine transporter (DAT) in the development of PTSD in preschool children.' *Journal of Traumatic Stress 22*, 6, 534–539.

Edwards, D.J.A. (2011) 'Invited Essay: From Ancient Shamanic Healing to 21st Century Psychotherapy: The Central Role of Imagery Methods in Effecting Psychological Change.' In A. Hackmann, J. Bennett-Levy and E. Holmes (eds) *Oxford Guide to Imagery in Cognitive Therapy*. Oxford: Oxford University Press.

Ehlers, A. and Clark, D.M. (2000) 'A cognitive model of posttraumatic stress disorder.' *Behaviour Research and Therapy 38*, 4, 319–345.

Eyadhy, A.A. and Razack, S. (2008) 'The ethics of using innovative therapies in the care of children.' *Paediatrics and Child Health 13*, 3, 181–184.

Eze, M.O. (2011) 'Humanism as history in contemporary Africa.' *Taiwan Journal of East Asian Studies 8*, 2, 59–77.

Ford, J.D. and Courtois, C.A. (eds) (2013) *Treating Complex Traumatic Stress Disorders in Children and Adolescents: Scientific Foundations and Therapeutic Models*. New York: Guilford Press.

Ford, J.D., Grasso, D., Greene, C., Levine, J., Spinazzola, J. and van der Kolk, B. (2013) 'Clinical significance of a proposed developmental trauma disorder diagnosis: Results of an international survey of clinicians.' *Journal of Clinical Psychiatry 74*, 8, 841–849.

Frances, A.J. and Widiger, T. (2012) 'Psychiatric diagnosis: Lessons from the DSM-IV past and cautions for the DSM-5 future.' *Annual Review of Clinical Psychology 8*, 109–130.

Gore, S. (2011) *Children Act 1989: Local Authority Support for Children and Families*. Bristol: Family Law.

Greenwald, R. (2014) *Trauma and Juvenile Delinquency: Theory, Research, and Interventions*. London: Routledge.

Grunert, B.K., Weis, J.M., Smucker, M.R. and Christianson, H.F. (2007) 'Imagery rescripting and reprocessing therapy after failed prolonged exposure for post-traumatic stress disorder following industrial injury.' *Journal of Behavior Therapy and Experimental Psychiatry 38*, 4, 317–328.

Haslam, C., Cruwys, T., Haslam, S.A., Dingle, G. and Chang, M.X.L. (2016) 'Groups 4 Health: Evidence that a social-identity intervention that builds and strengthens social group membership improves mental health.' *Journal of Affective Disorders 194*, 188–195.

Herman, J.L. (1992) 'Complex PTSD: A syndrome in survivors of prolonged and repeated trauma.' *Journal of Traumatic Stress 5*, 3, 377–391.

Kirton, D. (2009) *Child Social Work Policy and Practice*. London: Sage.

Kitzinger, J. (2004) *Framing Abuse: Media Influence and Public Understanding of Sexual Violence Against Children*. Ann Arbor, MI: Pluto Press.

Levendosky, A.A., Leahy, K.L., Bogat, G.A., Davidson, W.S. and von Eye, A. (2006) 'Domestic violence, maternal parenting, maternal mental health, and infant externalizing behavior.' *Journal of Family Psychology 20*, 4, 544.

Matson, J.L. and Nieminen, G.S. (1987) 'Validity of measures of conduct disorder, depression, and anxiety.' *Journal of Clinical Child Psychology 16*, 2, 151–157.

Meiser-Stedman, R., Smith, P., Glucksman, E., Yule, W. and Dalgleish, T. (2008) 'The posttraumatic stress disorder diagnosis in preschool- and elementary school-age children exposed to motor vehicle accidents.' *American Journal of Psychiatry 165*, 10, 1326–1337.

Mongillo, E.A., Briggs-Gowan, M., Ford, J.D. and Carter, A.S. (2009) 'Impact of traumatic life events in a community sample of toddlers.' *Journal of Abnormal Child Psychology 37*, 4, 455–468.

National Institute for Health and Care Excellence (2018) *Post Traumatic Stress Disorder.* NICE Guideline 116. Accessed on 17/3/2019 at www.nice.org.uk/guidance/ng116

Neuner, F., Catani, C., Ruf, M., Schauer, E., Schauer, M. and Elbert, T. (2008) 'Narrative exposure therapy for the treatment of traumatized children and adolescents (KidNET): From neurocognitive theory to field intervention.' *Child and Adolescent Psychiatric Clinics of North America 17*, 3, 641–664.

O'Loughlin, M. and O'Loughlin, S. (2016) *Social Work with Children and Families.* London: Sage.

Perrin, S., Meiser-Stedman, R. and Smith, P. (2005) 'The Children's Revised Impact of Event Scale (CRIES): Validity as a screening instrument for PTSD.' *Behavioural and Cognitive Psychotherapy 33*, 4, 487–498.

Raby, C. (2002) *Project X: A Journey Through the Development of an Inner-city Project for Children with Extreme Emotional and Behavioural Needs.* Unpublished dissertation for degree of MEd. University of Exeter.

Raby, S. (2010) *Service Evaluation of a Training Course that Teaches a New PTSD Treatment Protocol Designed for Children.* Unpublished dissertation for Mental Health Studies MSc. University College London.

Raby, C. and Edwards, D. (2011) 'Unrecognized hospital trauma as a source of complex psychiatric symptoms: A systematic case study with implications for children's rights and evidence-based practice.' *Psychotherapy Research 21*, 5, 541–553.

Rolington, L. (2014) *Children, Mental Health, and the United Nations Convention on the Rights of the Child: Investigating the Efficacy of Delivering Trauma Therapy through a Child-rights Framework.* Accessed on 30/9/2020 at https://static1.squarespace.com/static/5bc75ab193a6325f3c4c3ed4/t/5d66e09a506cd4000190fb69/1567023263231/LUCY+ROLINGTON+MA+DISSERTATION+.pdf

Rutter, M. (1985) 'Resilience in the face of adversity: Protective factors and resistance to psychiatric disorder.' *British Journal of Psychiatry 147*, 6, 598–611.

Sachser, C., Berliner, L., Holt, T., Jensen, T. et al. (2018) 'Comparing the dimensional structure and diagnostic algorithms between DSM-5 and ICD-11 PTSD in children and adolescents.' *European Child and Adolescent Psychiatry 27*, 2, 181–190.

Scheeringa, M.S. (2003) 'Research diagnostic criteria for infants and preschool children: The process and empirical support.' *Journal of the American Academy of Child & Adolescent Psychiatry 42*, 12, 1504–1512.

Scheeringa, M.S. (2011) 'PTSD in children younger than the age of 13: Toward developmentally sensitive assessment and management.' *Journal of Child & Adolescent Trauma 4*, 3, 181–197.

Scheeringa, M.S., Zeanah, C.H. and Cohen, J.A. (2011) 'PTSD in children and adolescents: Toward an empirically based algorithma.' *Depression and Anxiety 28*, 9, 770–782.

Scheeringa, M.S., Zeanah, C.H., Myers, L. and Putnam, F.W. (2003) 'New findings on alternative criteria for PTSD in preschool children.' *Journal of the American Academy of Child & Adolescent Psychiatry 42*, 5, 561–570.

Schmid, M., Petermann, F. and Fegert, J.M. (2013) 'Developmental trauma disorder: Pros and cons of including formal criteria in the psychiatric diagnostic systems.' *BMC Psychiatry 13*, 1, 3.

Smith, P., Perrin, S., Yule, W. and Clark, D.M. (2009) *Post Traumatic Stress Disorder: Cognitive Therapy with Children and Young People*. London: Routledge.

United Nations (1990) *UN Convention on the Rights of the Child*. Available at www.ohchr.org/en/professionalinterest/pages/crc.aspx

World Health Organization (WHO) (2004) *ICD-10: International Statistical Classification of Diseases and Related Health Problems (ICD-10) (2nd ed.)*. Accessed on 06/01/2021 at https://apps.who.int/iris/handle/10665/42980

World Health Organization (WHO) (2018) *International Statistical Classification of Diseases and Related Health Problems (ICD-11)*. Accessed on 17/3/2019 at www.who.int/classifications/icd/en

Yule, W. (1992) 'Post-traumatic stress disorder in child survivors of shipping disasters: The sinking of the "Jupiter".' *Psychotherapy and Psychosomatics 57*, 4, 200–205.

Yule, W., Perrin, S. and Smith, P. (1999) 'Post-traumatic Stress Disorders in Children and Adolescents.' In W. Yule (ed.) *Post-traumatic Stress Disorders: Concepts and Therapy* (pp.25–50). Chichester: Wiley.

5

The Story of the Body

Holistic Art Therapy and Neuroscience, Working with Complex
Trauma Using Interoceptive Imagery and Embodied Approaches

Nili Sigal

In this chapter I will explore the way trauma can disrupt the connection between body and mind. I will consider current research and the use of embodied processes and body awareness to support traumatized clients in their journey towards recovery, with a particular emphasis on art therapy and the role of the image.

The chapter is divided into two parts. In the first, the theoretical section, I will consider the neuroscience of trauma and PTSD and seek to demonstrate that

- the body experiences emotions as visceral sensations before we are able to identify and name them as feelings

- interoceptive ability and emotional processing are essential for psychological wellbeing and decision-making

- the above should be considered in relation to the treatment of PTSD.

In the second section, which is focused on clinical practice, I will discuss:

- somatically based, trauma-focused interventions

- the potential for improving interoceptive ability in therapy

- the importance of imagery and non-verbal processing

- some of the processes underlying therapeutic, trauma-focused work with image and narrative, and the potential for using art therapy to access implicit narratives and somatic memories.

Part 1 – Theory: The neuroscience of trauma, emotions and interoception

Most of us have felt 'butterflies in our chest', a 'knot in our stomach' or 'heartache'. These experiences are so universal that they have become part of everyday language. In *Descartes' Error*, the neurologist Antonio Damasio states that the 'fact that psychological disturbances, mild or strong, can cause diseases of the body proper is finally beginning to be accepted' (1994, p.256). Referring to the book's title, he adds:

> This is Descartes' error: the…suggestion that reasoning, and moral judgement, and the suffering that comes from physical pain or emotional upheaval might exist separately from the body. Specifically: the separation of the most refined operations of mind from the structure and operation of a biological organism. (p.250)

Fotopoulou and Tsakiris (2017) map out the shift from Freud's initial focus on bodily and sensory processes to the later abandonment of the body in psychoanalysis; not only of drive theory and sexuality, but of the idea of the self as being structured by embodied experiences. They quote Conger, who said 'the body has been invisible, for years unaddressed and ignored, left in the waiting room of the therapist's chair'. They describe this as a shift towards a 'mentalistic representation of bodily phenomena' (p.4) and consider this to be at the expense of the self's embodied nature.

Many publications in the field of PTSD and trauma treatment build on our increasing knowledge of neuroscience to understand the lingering impact of trauma. Neuroscience is the study of the nervous system, including the brain and the central and peripheral nervous systems (King 2016), and the way our body communicates with the brain. It is this very connection that often seems to be disrupted with traumatized clients, whose brains and bodies can behave as though past events are recurring in the here-and-now. They might feel distant from their bodies, or as though their bodies do not belong to them; they can experience hypervigilance, looking for danger in places of safety. They might struggle to listen to their bodies and to meet their most basic physical needs, or they might have learned to override messages from the body and have become un-attuned to themselves. The theoretical foundation upon which we understand these mechanisms will be considered below.

Survival responses and the nervous system

Located in the brainstem, the evolutionarily oldest part of our brain is often referred to as the *reptilian brain* (Rothschild 2000). It regulates the basic physiological functioning required for survival. It is 'hard-wired' and already well developed at birth. Between the brainstem and the cerebral cortex we find the limbic system, which regulates survival-related behaviours and emotions. It is part of a more evolutionarily recent part of the brain, known as the *mammalian brain*. It is shaped and formed by early life experiences, which means its development is linked with early attachment and environment (Rothschild 2000). Above the mammalian brain we find the higher-functioning, evolutionarily *new brain* – the cerebral cortex, which makes up most of the brain's weight. The cerebral cortex is associated with language, cognition, social skills, memory, decision-making and planning. Van der Kolk (2014) considers the reptilian brain and limbic system together as making up the *emotional brain*. As we will see, the processes underlying PTSD tend to happen in the emotional brain, sometimes without much access to (or input from) the new brain.

The limbic system is directly linked with the autonomic nervous system (ANS) and signals to it whether it is safe to rest or whether we must prepare for action. This mechanism can become unbalanced in PTSD as the limbic system becomes over-sensitized and overemphasizes threat when there may be little or none. This causes physiological changes as the amygdala, in the limbic system, sends output to the various brain structures, including the reptilian brainstem, which then activates instinctual survival responses. Stress hormones are released, signalling the ANS to prepare for defensive action and causing an increase in heart rate, alongside the hypervigilance we so often see with traumatized clients.

The ANS is divided into the *sympathetic nervous system* (SNS), which is activated during times of stress and effort and includes the fight or flight response to danger, and the *parasympathetic nervous system* (PNS), which is activated during times of relaxation and rest (Rothschild 2000). The arousal of one typically leads to the suppression of the other. The vagus nerve, a cranial nerve connecting the body and the brainstem, is linked with both SNS and PNS functions. Discussing its role in regulating the nervous system, Porges (2011) argues that traumatized individuals have more difficulties moving between states of mobilization for action (fight or flight, SNS activation) to feeling calm (PNS activation), which he considers to be related to issues with vagal modulation. The 'freeze' reaction in PTSD could be caused by the simultaneous activation of both SNS and PNS in the face of an overwhelming and inescapable threat, resulting in a sense of immobility. These are autonomic reactions, led by instinctive judgements about which behaviour is most likely to increase our chances of survival. They are instantaneous and overwhelmingly physical.

Expanding on the fight–flight–freeze responses, Schauer and Elbert (2010) suggest two more stages that encompass dissociative responses – flag and faint. They write that 'facing contamination and penetration/invasion may result in flaccid immobility (unresponsive immobility) or even fainting' (p.117). They consider the risk of PTSD to be increased when the victim is unable to utilize active survival responses (such as fight or flight, which are SNS activated and which could enable the victim to reconnect with a sense of agency). They argue that flag and faint are dominated by the PNS, resulting in symptoms of hypoarousal and 'shutting down'. Porges (2011) writes that 'when mobilization defensive strategies cannot be employed…a lower brainstem system, more frequently employed by reptiles, is regulating peripheral physiology. This system reduces oxygenated blood flow to the brain and leads to fainting and experiences of dissociation' (loc. 4980).

Dissociation can be described as the separation of body and mind, which is used as a psychological survival mechanism in the moment of extreme trauma. The traumatized client might be overly reactive, panicking and agitated if they are in an SNS, 'fight or flight' state, whereas the dissociated, PNS activated individual might be unresponsive and appear to be far away, out of reach; they might report feeling 'dead inside' or having no access to their emotions. Survivors of severe childhood trauma might go on to develop a dissociative disorder.

Developmental trauma and somatic memory

> PTSD seems to be a disorder of memory gone awry. Individuals
> with PTSD cannot make sense of their symptoms in the context of the
> events they have endured... Their traumatic experiences freefloat in
> time without an end or place in history. (Rothschild 2000, p.36)

The limbic system, and especially the amygdala, are important
for memory storage – with the amygdala specifically linked with
emotional memories (Craig 2015). In contrast, the hippocampus
appears to 'file' memories in a chronological way, contextual to our
life's narrative. It seems that the hippocampus can be suppressed during
traumatic threat, meaning it is unavailable to store and process the
event. As we often discover in therapy, although people with a diagnosis
of PTSD might cognitively *know* they have survived, they often don't
feel that the traumatic event is over.

Studies have shown that people with PTSD have a smaller hippocampus than the general population (Rothschild 2000). Links
have also been made between a predisposition to developing PTSD
and stressful events during childhood, including abuse and neglect.
Rothschild suggests that, potentially, 'survival mechanisms such
as dissociation or freezing have become so habituated that more
adaptive strategies either never develop or are eliminated from the
survival repertoire' (p.25). As therapy involves working with clients'
dysregulated nervous systems and related somatic experiences, it is
important to be mindful of the role of neuroplasticity (King 2016) –
both in terms of unhelpful, trauma-related learning and in terms of
healing and recovery. As therapists, it is our role to support our clients
to expand their survival repertoire and to learn to connect with feelings
of safety.

Rothschild (2000) discusses *somatic memory*, suggesting that
trauma is held in the nervous system. Van der Kolk (2014) similarly
writes about trauma's impact on the thalamus, a part of the brain that
processes sensations and integrates them into our autobiographical
memory. Referring to brain scans demonstrating that trauma can lead
to dysfunction in the thalamus, he writes that this 'explains why trauma
is primarily remembered not as a story, a narrative with a beginning,
middle and end, but as isolated sensory imprints...that are accompanied
by intense sensations, usually terror and helplessness' (p.83).

The somatic basis of emotions

Damasio (2000) argues for a biological foundation underlying emotions. He differentiates between *primary emotions* (or 'bottom-up' emotions) such as fear – which are related to survival responses and are processed by the limbic system – and *secondary emotions*, which are linked with individual and learned experiences, 'top-down' neural processes, and which link with higher-order thinking (in the new brain) to understand and evaluate the arising feelings. He further adds:

> ...emotional states are defined by myriad changes in the body's chemical profile; by changes in the state of viscera; and by changes in the degree of contraction of varied striated muscles of the face, throat, trunk, and limbs. But they are also defined by changes in the collection of neural structures which cause those changes to occur in the first place and which also cause other significant changes in the state of several neural circuits within the brain itself. (p.282)

Solms (2013) describes emotions as 'an intrinsic property of the brain' (p.7), which is automatic and evolutionarily ancient. He argues that the foundations of affective consciousness involve a separation between pleasure and unpleasure, which is expressed through approach–withdrawal behaviour and can be found in all vertebrates. This is behaviour driven by 'bottom-up' emotions at their most fundamental: approaching sources of pleasure and withdrawing from sources of unpleasure.

With increasing complexity, in the limbic system, we can find a wider range of more complex affects which are common to all mammals. Solms discusses Panksepp's idea of basic emotions (which are capitalized, to separate them from common use: SEEKING, LUST, FEAR, RAGE, CARE, GRIEF and PLAY. Solms points out that Panksepp's list does not claim to represent the full range of human emotions; however, these seven states are considered instinctual.

Interoception and homeostasis

Craig (2015) defines interoception as our capacity for body awareness: our ability to notice and to be aware of what is happening internally, inside our bodies, and in particular our affective awareness, which is related to our visceral experiences of emotions. He considers this to be key for self-awareness. Van der Kolk (2014) expands on this concept: 'Agency starts with what scientists call interoception, our awareness of our subtle sensory, body based feelings... Knowing *what* we feel is the first step in knowing *why* we feel that way' (p.113).

Critchley and Garfinkel (2017) consider the link between interoception and emotions, stating that the 'physiological expression of emotions includes changes within internal organ systems, driven by autonomic nervous responses usually independent of volitional control... People refer to internal bodily sensations when describing their emotional experience, with some consistency' (p.8). They consider studies that seek to measure interoception, including the capacity to sense one's own heartbeat or breathing rate – called respiratory and cardiac interoceptive abilities. Craig (2015) writes that individuals who perform well at perceiving their own heartbeat 'function better not only on an emotional level but also cognitively' (p.6).

Interoception allows us to have awareness and to generate predictions about information that arises inside the body. It can also help us to maintain homeostasis – a physical process comprising a set of functions that seek to 'maintain an optimal balance in the body across all conditions at all times' (Craig 2015, p.19). For example, our interoceptive awareness might inform us that we feel cold, leading us to reach for a blanket to restore homeostasis. However, reduced interoceptive ability could stop us from realizing we are cold, and therefore we might fail to meet our own basic needs and become distressed.

Additionally, PTSD seems to damage the finely calibrated systems that inform us about our ability to feel safe in the world – internally and externally – and therefore distorts our sense of homeostasis and our ability to trust information from our senses. Re-experiencing trauma from the 'there-and-then' rather than engaging with the safety of the 'here-and-now' can leave the traumatized individual confused, upset and vulnerable to mistrusting their body's messages since they cognitively *know* there is no danger. They could, consequently, develop a fractious, even hostile, relationship with their traumatized body's attempts to achieve homeostasis by replaying trauma-related experiences, which could lead to a disconnect between the mind and internal bodily processes, a disruption of interoception, an internal battle between interior narratives.

The impact on choices and decisions:
The somatic-marker theory

Damasio (1994) writes that rather than relying solely on logic and reason, emotions play a vital role in our everyday decision-making – so much so that we would not be able to operate successfully without them. Using the examples of seeking food when hungry, and of instinctively moving away from the path of a falling object, he argues that decisions often happen at a somatic and visceral level without conscious awareness. In fact, our humble 'gut feeling' can influence many of our most important decisions.

He further argues that such gut feelings, or intuitions, also inform our more complex, so-called rational choices; something just 'feels right' or 'feels wrong', and we are often able to rely on our interoceptive feedback (e.g. our gut feeling or intuition) to guide us in our choices. He postulates the *somatic-marker hypothesis*, which actively involves gut feelings and emotions in the process of decision-making. As an example, he describes the unpleasant physiological sensation we experience when we imagine a potential negative outcome to a choice we are about to make.

Conversely, positive somatic markers enable us to imagine a positive future outcome and narrow our options accordingly – it could encourage us to make sacrifices now in order to attain a future benefit as we are able to *imagine* the future advantage, which sustains us through the process of enduring the difficulties. He argues that positive somatic markers drive our willpower, especially in the face of adversity.

Like interoception, this mechanism can become skewed with extreme anxiety and PTSD, where negative somatic markers might be linked with a sensitized amygdala and a constant sense of hyper-vigilance. This can lead to catastrophizing and a narrowing of choices, resulting in the avoidant behaviour often seen with PTSD. Similarly, impulsive behaviour – also common with traumatized clients – could be linked with difficulties accessing positive somatic markers, which would make it more challenging to delay gratification. Working with somatic markers involves supporting clients to become aware of their gut feelings by learning to attune into their own internal processes – essentially, by learning to improve their interoceptive ability.

Links with substance misuse, embodied expressions of distress and somatic conditions

The overwhelming and powerful sensations in the body caused by trauma can lead to the individual seeking to self-regulate through physiological means, in order to compensate, enhance or numb what is felt to be either lacking or all-consuming. Sue Mizen (2014) has written about emotions as visceral sensations in relation to Panksepp's basic emotions model, mentioned earlier in this chapter. In her Limbus Lecture (2017)[1] she hypothesized that an overactive SEEKING system could result in the individual using stimulants to self-regulate, whereas an overactive PANIC system could lead to misuse of opiates in an attempt to self-soothe. Interoceptive processing dysfunction has been linked with drug addiction (Paulus, Stewart and Haase 2013), which led researchers to focus on approaches such as meditation and exercise to improve interoceptive abilities.

Considered from this perspective, we can think of habitual or addictive behaviours – such as compulsive sexual behaviour, self-harm, eating disorders or the use of substances – as driven by powerful and overwhelming somatically felt distress, causing clients to either take action (e.g. by cutting, restricting food, using substances) or psychologically separating from the body in order to stop these unbearable sensations (dissociation). It is therefore possible that ignoring (or being unable to attune to) messages and signals of distress originating from the body could lead to the body 'ramping up the volume' in an attempt to change a situation that can no longer be tolerated, to the point where certain physiological systems stop operating or become over-sensitized.

If extreme measures are not taken by the individual seeking to self-regulate, if the situation is not resolved and if the accompanying feelings remain unprocessed, the distress can become 'stuck' in the body, never to be acknowledged by the mind, leading to further fragmentation between the two and potentially resulting in somatic difficulties and medically unexplained symptoms (van der Kolk 2014). An example is the way many individuals with ME/CFS 'commonly report physical or emotional stress before they become ill' (US Department of Health, CDC 2018) or the link between fibromyalgia and trauma (van der Kolk

---

1   Slides available at www.limbus.org.uk/Making%20Meaning%20in%20the%20 Relational%20Brain.pptx

2014). Sapolsky (1994) writes at length about the way stress and distress can cause a range of physical illnesses.

Russell et al. (2018) explore the potential psychological causes of physiological symptoms by considering clients' experiences of attunement and attachment responses in early development. They discuss PNS and SNS activation and the somatic basis of emotions, in particular Panksepp's theory. They argue that the 'fight or flight' activation of the SNS might be associated with conditions such as fibromyalgia, backache, tension headaches and fatigue, while PNS activation is linked with gastrointestinal issues, dizziness, cognitive problems and fainting. They further explore the consequences of somatic-memory activation and somatic defence processes, which they associate with panic attacks and unexplained chest pain. It is important to note that the area of medically unexplained symptoms is controversial, and that research is in its infancy.

Trauma, imagery and emotions

Lusebrink and Hinz (2016) argue that trauma survivors of all ages often have difficulties expressing themselves verbally, especially if the trauma occurred at a very young age and interfered with the development of language. They suggest that non-verbal expressions involve various components of brain function and behaviour that differentiate them from verbal expression. Trauma memories seem to be strongly linked with visual imagery, as well as physical sensation (Gantt and Tripp 2016), and research suggests that images can induce powerful emotional states (Bernat et al. 2006). Traumatized clients might therefore find it easier to share and process their experiences through visual representation.

Damasio (2000) discusses the importance of mental imagery, which he refers to as 'the currency of the mind' (p.319). He considers mental images to be present across different levels of consciousness, echoing the psychoanalytic idea of 'the unconscious' as being accessible through imagery and art. He explains mental images as representations of *the way we interact* with the object which we are visualizing, rather than a mere objective representation of the object itself. Pearson et al. (2015) argue that mental imagery plays an important role across a variety of mental health conditions. They use as an example the insufficient or weak imagery often reported in depression, and strong, intrusive negative imagery in PTSD. They also mention studies suggesting that visual tasks performed shortly after trauma can reduce the frequency of distressing visual imagery.

Visual imagery seems to differ from other types of mental imagery, such as auditory, kinaesthetic, tactile, olfactory and gustatory imagery; Schifferstein (2009) concludes that visual imagery tends to be the most vivid of the different modalities. Professor Adam Zeman of Exeter University is currently researching aphantasia, or 'blind imagination'– the inability to generate visual mental imagery (Zeman, Dewar and Della Sala 2015). Initial feedback from people who have aphantasia suggests that they might be less susceptible to PTSD due to the absence of visual imagery. While many of these theories are at early stages of research, there is an emerging body of evidence linking emotional and visual processing that might be of particular interest to art therapists.

Part 2 – Clinical practice: Working with imagery and embodied approaches

People who have been traumatized have experienced alterations in their nervous system that over-sensitized their threat and survival mechanisms, causing them to have hypervigilant or hypovigilant responses to their environment (or both, occurring separately or simultaneously). Their bodies respond to benign situations as though they are dangerous. They have lost the ability to trust their interoceptive awareness, or 'attune' to themselves, as they have repeatedly experienced a disconnection between the instinctive messages from their bodies and their cognitive knowledge of their external reality. They might struggle with decision-making, as their somatic markers and gut feelings are not appropriate to their reality in the here-and-now. Their implicit and somatic memories can lead to a fragmented sense of autobiographical memory. They may exist in a state of nameless dread or terror, or mistrust and resent their bodies (as they sometimes experience it) for 'making them' repeatedly relive traumatic experiences.

Since these experiences are so distressing and overwhelming, traumatized clients often want these feelings (as they frequently tell me) to 'just go away!' Consequently they can become less self-compassionate, more punitive and more disconnected from their bodies; they override and silence the body's messages through overwork, substances, impulsive behaviour, medications, disordered eating, self-harm or dissociation. Sometimes this is manifested as physical symptoms, which can lead to years of testing and treatments before they are diagnosed with medically unexplained/functional symptoms, separating further the already fragile connection between body and mind. This can lead to more anger, frustration and self-loathing, with the long-suffering and ostracized body that holds the trauma now being seen, as clients have told me, as a broken vessel: 'it has let me down'.

Instead, we would like to gently invite our clients to learn to self-soothe, to find ways to ground and care for their physical selves as they would care for a terrified or distraught child (their 'inner child'). To show them ways to provide their panicked and confused nervous systems with the nurturing and calming signals associated with safety, bringing them back to the 'window of tolerance' and therefore feeling safe and integrated in order to begin to process their trauma, instead of pushing the distress away and disconnecting from it even further.

The mistrust and hostility that traumatized clients sometimes feel towards their bodies can be specifically directed towards the part of the body that has been traumatized, for example through self-harm, or it leads to clients living mostly 'in their heads'. The body is not a place that feels safe to inhabit: it holds the pain, the confusion, the hatred, the anger, the trauma. It sends them mixed signals. It presents them with distressing sensations and images. It tells them to flee, or makes them dissociate in a perfectly safe situation. Conversely, the dissociation from their own distress is also the very reason they attack their body; clients say that they feel self-harm is the only way to emerge, temporarily, from a dissociative fugue as the pain and the sight of blood makes them 'feel something' for a while. However, the feelings of guilt and shame that follow and the self-loathing when the cravings start can lead to further alienation and distancing from the body. This can also be true of impulsive behaviours, eating disorders and addictions.

The very relationship between body and mind, then, becomes distorted, corrupted. Clients have told me they consider their body to be just a vehicle that 'takes my head to where it needs to be'. They can struggle with mindfulness when asked to focus on their bodies because these practices challenge their main coping strategy of disembodiment. They might know, cognitively, the reasons for their difficulties but their body only knows pain, fear, distress and isolation.

My main therapeutic goal with these clients is to help them to re-establish and rediscover their own relationship with their bodies. To trust their body's signals and their gut feelings, while also learning to soothe and understand their physiological responses and the somatic memories leading to their distress. While the therapeutic relationship is vital, the focus is on healing internal fragmentation. This is something that can easily be overlooked in therapy, as some traumatized clients seem to struggle mostly to connect with themselves, rather than others, and especially with their own physicality. This goal can be difficult to achieve if we don't make the implicit explicit – if we don't focus on, talk about and consider these clients' relationships with their own bodies as an important and central part of the therapeutic process. As van der Kolk (2014, p.100) so famously and eloquently put it:

> The body keeps the score: If the memory of trauma is encoded in the viscera, in heartbreaking and gut-wrenching emotions, in autoimmune disorders and skeletal/muscular problems, and if mind/brain/visceral communication is the royal road to emotion regulation, this demands a radical shift in our therapeutic assumptions.

Embodied approaches to trauma treatment

Due to the sensory aspects of re-experiencing trauma (such as nightmares and flashbacks), the distressing physical symptoms accompanying these and the associated chronic hyperarousal in the ANS, Rothschild (2000) states that 'somatic disturbance is at the core of PTSD' (p.7). She mentions increasing evidence that talking alone is not necessarily helpful for PTSD. It is therefore no surprise that trauma-focused, embodied approaches are growing in popularity.

Embodied approaches might involve psychoeducation to normalize clients' experiences and symptoms, alongside grounding, resourcing and stabilization before addressing the trauma material directly. The goal is to support the client to be in the room without becoming overwhelmed and to provide them with tools to manage their own distress, in and out of the sessions. This is typically followed by trauma processing before a stage of integration, where the trauma becomes a part of the client's chronology; just another part of a bigger story, rather than being frozen and separated from the rest of their life experiences. At this point, clients can begin to form a new narrative about their lives.

Most embodied approaches seek to enable clients to reprocess or discharge the distress, which is experienced physiologically. It will not be possible to list all, or even most of them in the context of this chapter;

however, I will briefly discuss some of the more commonly practised interventions. While this includes a range and a variety of different orientations and therapeutic techniques, I refer to them as *embodied approaches* due to the shared focus on somatic processes.

Somatic experiencing was developed by Peter Levine, and is described in an article he co-authored as involving 'bottom up processing by directing the client's attention to internal sensations, both visceral (interoception) and musculo-skeletal (proprioception and kinesthesis), rather than primarily cognitive or emotional experiences' (Payne, Levine and Crane-Godreau 2015, p.1). *Eye movement desensitization and reprocessing (EMDR)* was invented by Francine Shapiro as a way to discharge negative affect associated with traumatic experiences by using bilateral stimulation, alongside resourcing, stabilization and increased awareness of body states and emotions, to help clients reprocess the traumatic material so that it is no longer overwhelming (Shapiro and Forrest 1997). Combining trauma-focused interventions with narrative and imagery, *Children's Accelerated Trauma Technique (CATT)* uses imagery to help clients to access felt beliefs and the felt sense in trauma-focused work, in order to help them re-script and reprocess their trauma. CATT is discussed in depth by Raby and Plant in Chapter 4.

Sensorimotor psychotherapy, developed by Pat Ogden, combines bodywork with psychotherapy to specifically target and heal the disconnection between mind and body (Ogden and Fisher 2015). *Focusing-oriented psychotherapy*, which places emphasis on the felt sense, was one of the approaches that inspired Peter Levine, as well as *body psychotherapy* and *embodied-relational therapy (ERT)*. The Complex Trauma Therapists' Network provides workshops on embodied approaches and the different stages of trauma-focused work, as well as working with dreams and nightmares related to PTSD. Their website[2] has free theoretical and practical resources for therapists.

Some approaches have an explicit focus on interoceptive processes: *mindful awareness in body-oriented therapy (MABT)* places a direct emphasis on developing and improving interoceptive abilities by using specific teaching strategies, including mindfulness and client self-touch. 'MABT provides an individualized protocol for scaffolding interoceptive awareness through a combination of psychoeducation and somatic approaches explicitly addressing difficulties with interoceptive

---

2   www.complextrauma.uk

processing' (Price and Hooven 2018, p.1). *Intensive short-term psychodynamic psychotherapy (ISTPP)* is not specifically a treatment for trauma, however it is an interoception-focused intervention that uses awareness of sensations, emotions and physical symptoms in the here-and-now. It is currently showing promising outcomes for people with somatic disorders or medically unexplained symptoms (Cooper, Abbass and Town 2017). *Biofeedback* and *neurofeedback* teach clients to develop conscious awareness and increased control over interoceptive process by using medical instruments, in order to improve homeostasis. *Trauma-focused CBT* requires clients to focus on their emotions and bodily sensations, while *cognitive behavioural therapy for interoceptive cue (CBT-IC)* specifically uses interoception as the main component of exposure in the therapy. Otto et al. (2014) write about attempts to use this intervention in addiction treatment. Lee et al. (2006) discuss the use of interoceptive exposure tasks, based on *interoceptive exposure-based CBT*, and report some positive results for clients with panic disorders.

Physical practices

If we consider the visceral nature of emotions, it would follow that we can attend to embodied distress at a bodily, 'bottom-up' level. Physical interventions are sometimes recommended as part of stabilization work, often alongside trauma treatment, and aim to be accessible for a variety of abilities and fitness levels. Trauma-informed therapists might encourage the cultivation of an ongoing physical practice to maintain a mind–body connection.

Yoga is mentioned by both van der Kolk (2000) and Porges (2011) as a helpful intervention for traumatized clients and is considered to be especially effective in improving interoceptive ability and helping clients to feel grounded in their bodies in a non-threatening way, as is *mindfulness* (Paulus et al. 2013). *Tai chi* and *Qigong*, *martial arts* and approaches such as the *Feldenkrais Method* are often recommended for similar reasons – the focus on movement awareness and enabling participants to foster a stronger mind–body connection. Van der Kolk also mentions *therapeutic massage*, which can be provided by trauma-informed practitioners, as a way for clients to reconnect with an ostracized body and experience safe touch. *Tension and trauma release exercises (TRE)* are a body-based practice with specific exercises to release somatic disturbances without necessarily talking about the event. *Sensory grounding* supports clients to use their senses to become connected to the here-and-now and is often used in stabilization work.

There is a great deal of evidence suggesting that exercise alone can improve mental health (Biddle 2016) and the World Health Organization recommends it as part of treatment for adults with depression.[3] For some, rigorous physical activity might be more helpful for emotion regulation than yoga or other gentle interventions. However, if exercise is used without providing traumatized individuals with tools to process and attend to distress, the core problem might stay unresolved, and mental health can deteriorate if the individual is no longer able to exercise.

A note on cross-cultural trauma-focused work

Trauma happens within society, in a multitude of cultural, communal and economic contexts. While it is beyond the scope of this chapter to go into the social aspects of trauma and trauma treatment, connection to a community has been established as a protective factor from both individual and collective traumatic experiences – and yet many trauma-focused interventions do not consider the importance of communities and cultural practices (Schultz et al. 2016).

In 'A critique of embodiment', Niwenshuti (2018) writes about his experiences of violence and genocide and the potential danger of embodied therapies taking an overly individualistic approach, which can be alienating. He mentions studies suggesting cultural differences in people's concepts of the self, with some Asian, African and South American cultures' view of people (and in some cases, nature and animals) as being an interconnected part of a collective, which differs from the Western notion of individualism. He points out that embodied approaches might therefore 'be dislocating and possibly re-traumatising if applied from a…logic that emphasises the notion of separation which locates the body to the margins, and isolates individuals and communities from themselves, each other and the world' (p.117). It is therefore important that therapists are aware of cultural and social factors when undertaking trauma-focused intervention cross-culturally.

Some clinicians view embodiment as a practice that can help to heal cultural divides by addressing and transforming collective, as well

---

3   www.who.int/mental_health/mhgap/evidence/depression/q6/en

as individual, experiences. Therapist and trauma specialist Resmaa Menakem (2017) established Cultural Somatics as 'an area of study and practice that applies our knowledge of trauma and resilience to history, intergenerational relationships, institutions, and the communal body' (p.22). He writes about racialized trauma – which he considers to be present, in different ways, in the bodies of African Americans, white Americans and American police officers. Exploring the impact of slavery, prejudice, fear and white-body supremacy, he states that 'trauma held in Black bodies shows up as a wide array of physical problems and dysfunctional behaviours – all of which are common symptoms of persistent and pervasive stress' (p.131). Looking at narratives and beliefs that are passed through the body from one generation to the next, and the embodied damage caused by racism, Menakem considers healing as a process that begins with each individual body, but that can move towards connections with other bodies: 'communal healing can help us steadily build respect, recognition, community, and, eventually, culture' (p.132). His work seeks to enable different groups to foster capacity for acceptance and a shared understanding, by using body-based exercises to build a sense of inner safety and empathy for the embodied experiences of self and others – on a personal and communal level.

Imagery and the (non-)verbal

Rothschild (2000) explores ways to connect the practice of verbal psychotherapies with body-oriented psychotherapies, as both modalities can offer resources to traumatized clients. She considers language to be vital for the purpose of understanding, processing and communicating about trauma. Somatic experiencing and EMDR similarly move from a focus on 'bottom-up' embodied experiences while processing the trauma, to 'top-down' verbal expression in order to integrate the memories. Yet arts therapies and other non-verbal and expressive approaches offer an opportunity to process and integrate traumatic material by working with the image, creativity and symbolism, rather than cognition and language. This could be especially beneficial for clients who struggle to talk about what happened to them.

It is important to mention the role of imagery in trauma-focused work: the image of the trauma itself (and related dreams or flashback material) is often explored during trauma processing and can be depicted directly by the client, especially in art therapy. Additionally, many embodied approaches use guided visualization to access the sensations clients experience in their bodies – both pleasant sensations of safety and relaxation and distressing, trauma-related sensations – effectively working with interoceptive imagery. The 'safe place exercise', which is used across a range of trauma treatments, is simply a way to enable clients to access a safe state of calm and relaxation in their bodies. As an art therapist using EMDR, I often encourage my clients to draw their safe place, in order to strengthen the client's connection with the image by creating it rather than only visualizing it.

As mentioned earlier in the chapter, images have a powerful connection with our emotions. Pearson et al. (2015) consider mental imagery as being directly relevant to mental health difficulties and suggest that imagery could become more central in future psychological interventions. Raby and Plant's chapter in this book, on the development and practice of CAAT (Chapter 4), considers the therapeutic impact of working with images, and specifically the use of imagery in trauma-focused work. They write about the powerful emotional effect of making images of a traumatic event and using the imagery to create a new narrative, helping the client to re-frame the incident and to internalize that the traumatic event is over.

Lusebrink and Hinz (2016) write that expressive therapies should be the treatment of choice for trauma-related disorders, due to the ability to access implicit memories without relying on verbal expression. As art therapy encourages a focus on image-making and working with symbolism and metaphor, they argue that art therapy can bypass some of the difficulties faced by traditional, 'talking' psychotherapies. Additionally, they argue that the creative process provides a containing space for clients to tell the implicit story of their trauma without becoming overwhelmed. They further postulate that art therapy can help to form coherent and chronological memories of the traumatic events; essentially, to construct a new narrative.

Art therapy, the client's embodied narrative and therapist self-care

So far, I have considered the ideas that emotions are non-verbal and that trauma is related to imagery and non-conscious processes; that the construction of imagery and the process of moving from unconscious to conscious imagery could be a beneficial part of trauma reprocessing;

and that many of the mechanisms of PTSD do not happen at a level accessible to cognition and language. It would therefore follow that working directly with imagery and creative processes could provide an additional dimension in trauma treatment, before the experience can be verbally expressed or cognitively analysed.

The disruption of interoception processes in PTSD indicates that imagery and art-making could have a unique role to play. As clients work on interoceptive abilities and learn to attune, notice and focus on their visceral sensations and emotions, they can visualize and locate their distressing feelings. Clients can be gently encouraged to make 'interoceptive images' by visually expressing the way the distress feels in their body, physically and viscerally. Such images have been important and at times transformative in many of my clients' journeys; depicting these nameless, disturbing sensations by creating an image or an object, while engaging the senses through the process of art-making, seems to enable a different level of processing, which is symbolic, as well as somatic and cognitive. It could also improve internal communication between body and mind, as clients become able to understand and share their sensations, and offers art therapy a unique role to play in supporting the process of healing and transformation on an embodied level.

There is a growing body of art therapy writing incorporating our current knowledge on trauma and neuroscience. *Art Therapy, Trauma and Neuroscience* (King 2016) suggests a variety of approaches and modalities for trauma-focused interventions. Cornelia Elbrecht's *Trauma Healing at the Clay Field* (2013) combines a sensorimotor approach with art therapy, considering touch, trauma, the 'felt sense' and the use of clay in a trauma-informed way. In 2014, the *International Journal of Art Therapy* dedicated a special issue to art therapy and neuroscience. In his foreword to the issue Dr Iain McGilchrist (2014, p.2) wrote:

> Now that we are able to understand more of how the brain and the body respond to activities that defy everyday language, the more we understand why art therapy should be prized and respected as among the most powerful means at our disposal to combat mental suffering.

Koch and Fuchs (2011) explore different types of embodiment and conclude that all arts therapies modalities offer valuable contributions to 'establishing the unity of body-mind' (p.278). There is currently a lively debate in the field, which it won't be possible to cover in this chapter. However, it seems that many art therapists are becoming more aware of the importance of the body and the nervous system's centrality in the process of art-making and recovery from trauma.

It is important to note that working with clients' embodied trauma, non-verbal processes and visual imagery can leave clinicians vulnerable to vicarious trauma. Developing ways to stay 'grounded' in our bodies while undertaking this type of work is essential. Therapists need to use their own interoceptive skills, in order to identify their needs and to find ways to look after their bodies and minds. Therapists might experience somatic countertransference as a response to traumatized clients' somatically held distress. Alongside commonly used strategies (such as mindfulness, supervision and creative practices), it can be helpful to have a physical practice such as yoga, exercise or movement to process difficult clinical material. In his writing on self-care for art therapists, James D. West (2018) explores the importance of 'top-down' and 'bottom-up' processes for therapists who are potentially at risk of developing secondary traumatic stress.

Feedback from a previous client

A previous client, who asked to be called 'Jenny', volunteered to share her experience in this chapter. First, she wrote about the timelines many therapists ask clients to complete at the start of the intervention and the reason she did not find this helpful:

> For every initial session I was asked to give a timeline of events in my life I was struggling with. This in itself was so destructive for me that most of the time I would pretend and gloss over a lot of it. For two reasons; firstly, no one would believe a child's timeline of so much neglect, abuse and trauma. I was told it wasn't possible at such an age. Secondly, I was so wrapped up in trying to stay mentally afloat and not drown in my own anguish and nightmare life that I couldn't bear to speak of all the horrendous events.
>
> … We did a timeline, but not in the traditional sense. In Art Therapy, I was able to express what was going on inside without fully understanding it myself, and I was helped to navigate my past gently.

She then wrote about our therapeutic work, which was art therapy with an embodied focus and EMDR:

I was able to connect pain, and a lot of my physical symptoms to memories and was able to heal from them by healing from the experience. It is vital to be told that it's ok to feel physical symptoms during therapy and to be told that it's natural. That our bodies are speaking and we can't control it.

That was the biggest step for me in my journey of recovery, and I say journey because it's not over and probably never will be. However, to have my mental illness manifest as physical symptoms and to be told that was a normal physical response was a massive breakthrough moment for me. Since working with my Art therapist and doing EMDR my physical symptoms have decreased dramatically. I am now in a loving supportive relationship and for the first time in 11 years I have managed to get a part time job and cope physically with the demands of it.

So I beg all of you to listen to people's symptoms and emotional reactions before you try to concentrate on discussing the reason they've been referred. The phrase 'gut wrenching' is so common but it seems to have been forgotten that that is a physical symptom for emotional distress; so why would it stop there? Why can't you see that it's possible to come close to death purely because your body has no way to cope with the mountains of weight caused by mental and emotional distress?

So if you want to really help your patients, treat them as a whole being, not just their mind. The body can't function without the brain and so does it not make sense that the body therefore can't function fully with a broken mind?? To heal the mind and body should be seen as one and the same thing. It is widely recognised that a panic attack can represent itself by mimicking a heart attack, so does it not naturally follow that any mental health issue will also affect the body in some way, even if the patient themselves don't recognise it themselves? I am not saying that you need to be a qualified medical doctor to help mental health, but I am saying that it is all linked. If my therapist hadn't kept checking in with what my body was trying to say with pain and other symptoms I wouldn't have benefited.

In conclusion: Making the implicit explicit and 'becoming real'

In this chapter I have explored the processes underlying traumatization and the impact on body and mind, the altered and hyper- (or hypo-)

sensitized nervous system, the disconnection between external and internal realities and the disruption of interoceptive processes. When we are unable to listen to messages from our bodies we deny the truth of what happened to us, because it is too unbearable. This raises important questions: how do we incorporate these ways of understanding trauma and trauma-related experiences? How many of us truly pay attention to our clients' physicality and physical symptoms, or their relationships with their bodies? Do we listen to their implicit, somatic narrative and would we know how to do so? Do we explore with them the somatic needs behind their choice of substance or compulsive behaviour, or what they might be seeking to regulate in their internal world? Do we ask about their physical lives, their activity levels, eating habits, sleep, sexual expression? In trauma work, we are curious about the client's internal relationship with his/her embodied experiences. We should ask ourselves: do we discuss this directly with our clients? Do we seek to encourage clients to explore this relationship in the sessions?

Many body-based therapies encourage clients to conjure images of the felt sense, initially for accessing positive sensations and then for processing difficult and distressing sensations. Being with the physicality of their distress rather than seeking to move away from it, we can encourage clients to repeatedly situate and 'ground' emotions and sensations in their body and to point out where they feel them, as a way to help connect body and mind. Art therapists can encourage clients to make 'interoceptive imagery' – to identify and situate the distress in their body and then put it to paper or clay, to express it visually.

Carolyn Spring, the founder of Positive Outcomes for Dissociative Survivors (PODS),[4] who has dissociative identity disorder as a result of childhood sexual abuse, said that the most helpful thing her therapist ever said to her was 'Where do you feel this in your body?' This enabled her to begin to become aware, to 'tune in', to understand, to connect and then to tell her story – the narrative of her body, what happened to her, and the damage it had caused. Only then was she able to begin to make sense of her experiences.

When the implicit narrative is internally understood, the explicit narrative can be shared. In art therapy, when the interoceptive image becomes externalized it can be seen, processed and acknowledged. It

---

4   www.pods-online.org.uk

'becomes real'; no longer an abstract, distressing, invisible sensation haunting the client's psyche, but something that can be 'brought down to size', viewed with the therapist, talked about and explored in a safe environment. Interoceptive imagery gives embodied distress a tangible existence that can be located outside the client's inner world and therefore considered more objectively. I believe it is only when the disturbance has been processed on a visceral level that we can help clients to put together the fragmented sense of their experiences into a new, coherent and integrated story: the story of the body, the story of the self.

References

Bernat, E., Patrick, C., Benning, S. and Tellegen, A. (2006) 'Effects of picture content and intensity on affective physiological response.' *Psychophysiology 43*, 1, 93–103.

Biddle, S. (2016) 'Physical activity and mental health: Evidence is growing.' *World Psychiatry 15*, 2, 176–177.

Cooper, A., Abbass, A. and Town, J. (2017). 'Implementing a psychotherapy service for medically unexplained symptoms in a primary care setting.' *Journal of Clinical Medicine 6*, 12, 109.

Craig, A.D. (2015) *How Do You Feel? An Interoceptive Moment with Your Neurological Self.* Princeton, NJ: Princeton University Press.

Critchley, H. and Garfinkel, S. (2017) 'Interoception and emotion.' *Current Opinion in Psychology 17*, 7–14.

Damasio, A. (1994, reprinted 2006) *Descartes' Error: Emotion, Reason and the Human Brain.* London: Vintage.

Damasio, A. (2000) *The Feeling of What Happens: Body, Emotions and the Making of Consciousness.* London: Vintage.

Elbrecht, C. (2013) *Trauma Healing at the Clay Field: A Sensorimotor Art Therapy Approach.* London: Jessica Kingsley Publishers.

Fotopoulou, A. and Tsakiris, M. (2017) 'Mentalizing homeostasis: The social origins of interoceptive inference.' *Neuropsychoanalysis 19*, 1, 3–28.

Gantt, L. and Tripp, T. (2016) 'The Image Comes First: Treating Preverbal Trauma with Art Therapy.' In J. King (ed.) *Art Therapy, Trauma and Neuroscience: Theoretical and Practical Perspectives.* New York, NY: Routledge.

King, J. (ed.) (2016) *Art Therapy, Trauma and Neuroscience: Theoretical and Practical Perspectives.* New York, NY: Routledge.

Koch, S. and Fuchs, T. (2011) 'Embodied arts therapies.' *The Arts in Psychotherapy 38*, 4, 276–280.

Lee, K., Noda, Y., Nakano, Y., Ogawa, S. et al. (2006) 'Interoceptive hypersensitivity and interoceptive exposure in patients with panic disorder: Specificity and effectiveness.' *BMC Psychiatry 6*, 3.

Lusebrink, V. and Hinz, V. (2016) 'The Expressive Therapies Continuum as a Framework in the Treatment of Trauma.' In J. King (ed.) *Art Therapy, Trauma and Neuroscience: Theoretical and Practical Perspectives.* New York, NY: Routledge.

McGilchrist, I. (2014) 'Foreword.' *International Journal of Art Therapy 19*, 1, 2.

Menakem, R. (2017) *My Grandmother's Hands: Racialized Trauma and the Pathway to Mending Our Hearts and Bodies.* Las Vegas, NV: Central Recovery Press.

Mizen, S. (2014) 'Towards a relational affective theory of personality disorder.' *Psychoanalytic Psychotherapy 28*, 4, 357–378.

Mizen, S. (2017, 11 November) 'Metaphor Making in the Relational Brain.' [Abstract.] Limbus Lecture. Accessed on 20/5/2019 at www.limbus.org.uk/Mizen.html

Niwenshuti, T. (2018) 'A critique of embodiment.' *Strategic Review for Southern Africa 40*, 1, 117–132.

Ogden, P. and Fisher, J. (2015) *Sensorimotor Psychotherapy: Interventions for Trauma and Attachment.* New York, NY: W.W. Norton.

Otto, M., Hearon, B., McHugh, K., Calkins, A. et al. (2014) 'A randomized, controlled trial of the efficacy of an interoceptive exposure-based CBT for treatment-refractory outpatients with opioid dependence.' *Journal of Psychoactive Drugs 46*, 5, 402–411.

Paulus, M., Stewart, J. and Haase, L. (2013) 'Treatment approaches for interoceptive dysfunctions in drug addiction.' *Frontiers in Psychiatry 4*, article 137.

Payne, P., Levine, P. and Crane-Godreau, M. (2015) 'Somatic experiencing: Using interoception and proprioception as core elements of trauma therapy.' *Frontiers in Psychology 6*, article 93.

Pearson, J., Naselaris, T., Holmes, E. and Kosslyn, S. (2015) 'Mental imagery: Functional mechanisms and clinical applications.' *Trends in Cognitive Neuroscience 19*, 10, 590–602.

Porges, S.W. (2011) *The Polyvagal Theory: Neurophysiological Foundations of Emotions, Attachment, Communication, and Self-regulation.* New York, NY: W.W. Norton. (Kindle edition)

Price, C. and Hooven, C. (2018) 'Interoceptive awareness skills for emotion regulation: Theory and approach of mindful awareness in body-oriented therapy (MABT).' *Frontiers in Psychology 9*, article 798.

Rothschild, B. (2000) *The Body Remembers: The Psychophysiology of Trauma and Trauma Treatment.* New York, NY: W.W. Norton.

Russell, L., Abbass, A., Allder, S. and Neborsky, R. (2018) 'Applying intensive short-term dynamic psychotherapy to the treatment of medically unexplained symptoms: Integrating theories of cause and theories of change.' *Journal of the Academy of Medical Psychology 9*, 1, 1–23.

Sapolsky, R.M. (1994) *Why Zebras Don't Get Ulcers: A Guide to Stress, Stress Related Diseases, and Coping.* New York, NY: W.H. Freeman.

Schauer, M. and Elbert, T. (2010) 'Dissociation following traumatic stress: Etiology and treatment.' *Journal of Psychology 218*, 2, 109–127.

Schifferstein, H. (2009) 'Comparing mental imagery across the sensory modalities.' *Imagination, Cognition and Personality 28*, 4, 371–388.

Schultz, K., Cattaneo, L., Sabina, C., Brunner, L. et al. (2016). 'Key roles of community connectedness in healing from trauma.' *Psychology of Violence 6*, 1, 42–48.

Shapiro, F. and Forrest, M. (1979) *EMDR: Eye Movement Desensitisation and Reprocessing.* New York, NY: Basic Books.

Solms, M. (2013) 'The conscious id.' *Neuropsychoanalysis 15*, 1, 5–85.

U.S. Department of Health & Human Services, Centres for Disease Control and Prevention (CDC) (2018) *Myalgic Encephalomyelitis/Chronic Fatigue Syndrome.* Accessed on 20/05/2019 at www.cdc.gov/me-cfs/about/possible-causes.html

van der Kolk, B. (2014) *The Body Keeps the Score: Brain, Mind, and Body in the Healing of Trauma.* New York, NY: Viking.

West, J.D. (2018) 'Self-Care in Art Therapy Private Practice.' In J.D. West (ed.) *Art Therapy in Private Practice: Theory, Practice and Research in Changing Contexts.* London: Jessica Kingsley Publishers.

Zeman, A., Dewar, M. and Della Sala, S. (2015) 'Lives without imagery: Congenital aphantasia.' *Cortex 73*, 378–380.

6

On Seeing What We Expect to See

Mentalizing Trauma and Narratives in Art Therapy Supervision

Dominik Havsteen-Franklin

This chapter describes the supervisory process within which we use narratives and discourse about the image in art therapy to aid mentalizing. Mentalizing, a form of social cognition and theory of mind (Overwalle 2009), is seen as the foundation for human relatedness and 'mind-mindedness' (Barreto et al. 2016) that precedes successful bonding and relational alliances (Zeegers et al. 2017). Explicit mentalizing is a core process in mentalization-based supervision of reworking interpersonal narratives, defined as a relational experience of validating, discovering, exploring, challenging and re-imagining fixed ideas about our relationships. Within the narrative, the supervisor develops curiosity and attuned perspective-taking. This chapter argues that the art psychotherapy supervisory encounter is a narrative dialogue between the patient, therapist, image and cultural context. This places the supervisor as a dynamic entity with specific perspectives that also enables a sensitive disruption to the dominant discourses assumed to be true to the patient experience. The supervisor's responsibility to sustain a capacity to mentalize is crucial to questioning narratives that undermine or privilege perspectives at the cost of mentalizing. A mentalization-based approach to supervision encourages challenging implicit and explicit bias and acquiring a deeper knowledge about the presenting issues (see also Mattan et al. 2018).

What is mentalization-based art therapy supervision?

Art therapy clinical supervision methods are varied and draw upon a wide range of different models (Case 2007). At one pole supervision focuses on maintaining best practice and offering guidance to ensure that a framework or standard is followed (Malchiodi and Riley 1996), at the other end of the spectrum the supervisee is offered a contained space to enable non-judgemental elaborations on experience and to help develop dynamic formulations in relation to the unique nature of the clinical encounter (Wood 2007). The former is likely to be more practice-focused with examples of 'how to' conduct therapy, and the latter is likely to be more theory-focused with an emphasis on cognitive comprehension, equipping the therapist with the understanding that will enable the therapist to be more reflective. In practice, it is likely that most supervisors draw upon good practice examples and ground the supervision in a theoretical framework that makes sense of relationships and the image-making process. The aims differ depending on how health and effectiveness are conceptualized. For example, aims for supervising clinicians working with adult populations are described as developing a space within which learning can happen (Gilroy 2007), the internalization of the supervisory experience to support self-agency (Wood 2007), understanding the countertransference or when processing the images developing a capacity of being (Laine 2007). Carpendale (2002) describes the fundaments of a phenomenological approach to supervision as 'uncovering the essence of those situations and relationships'.

Mentalization-based art therapy supervision draws together the most essential factors of art therapy supervision under an umbrella aim of enabling, encouraging and promoting mentalization in the supervisory context and the clinical situation. However, mentalizing often falters or is derailed by self-preserving mechanisms. In severe mental health conditions we expect to see profound distortions of shared relational reality in high-arousal situations, where real or imagined interpersonal events stimulate profound anxieties about attachment and separation, and in conditions of trauma this often results in disassociated states of mind (Bloom 2010). These conditions of apparent interpersonal rupture also serve to attempt to reconstruct reality to preserve some psychological integrity (Schumaker 1995).

Emotional responses to trauma are also physiological responses, that form part of a social and cultural system of communication. 'This is because, historically and globally, human cultures take the lead in reorganising and restructuring bodily sensations into symbolically and linguistically specific feelings and emotions' (Burkitt 2019, pp.6–7). Where the threat overwhelms our physiological response, in a mentalization-based model there are principally three forms of emotionally driven cognitive response that attempt to restructure events at the cost of social cognition (Fonagy and Bateman 2016).

The first non-mentalizing state (see also Havsteen-Franklin 2019) is a presentation of a rapid and urgent concrete solution for a problem that is primarily a relational one. For example, in art therapy we might find image-making being conducted unthinkingly, with immediacy, high affect and a solution focus. In severe mental health conditions, using the concreteness of the materials can help to offer a sense of safety that avoids relationships and offers a successful psychological retreat. Similarly, in trauma reactions, strategies can be employed to avoid relational contact, such as gaze aversion, social withdrawal and disassociation.

The second form of non-mentalizing is 'psychic equivalence', when internal experiences and emotions are rigidly equated with external events, often expanding on a restricted appraisal of the situation. For example, one patient told me, 'You want to be my therapist, because you want to keep me safe from the world. It's a safe haven, essentially you are my mother and I am your son.' The patient equated me with a mother that would hide him from his father. When he was a child, his father would beat him until he became numbed to the pain. The equation of me being his mother required us to use the image-making to reveal his sense of hopelessness and vulnerability and how this felt unmanageable and often resulted in his avoiding contact where there was a different perspective.

The third area of non-mentalizing is referred to as 'pretend-mode' (Target and Fonagy 1996) or 'pseudo-mentalizing' (Fonagy and Allison 2014). Pseudo-mentalizing is the capacity to develop beliefs and ideas that are detached from felt content and make sense of experience from an intellectual and egocentric perspective. This single-perspective narrative offers a meaning often under the guise of didactic thinking but is against thinking about thinking. Pseudo-mentalizing functions to find a solution in the face of helplessness or hopelessness, where there are profound levels of psychological and relational disturbance and disconnection.

Developing relational narratives requires allowing differences, thinking about thinking and developing relationships between causes and effects, correlations and meanings that require multiperspective turn-taking whilst keeping the emotional communication in mind.

Questioning narratives

A primary aim of mentalization-based art therapy is to help people to reconstruct narratives that are more salient to their environmental stimuli. Narrative is closely identified with a sense of identity, social positioning, communication and as mediation with the environment. Narrative concerns how we envelop scenarios within a time frame, holding events together meaningfully. This sense of 'being' (see Laine 2007) as contained and meaningful relates to the development of the self as conceptualized by Anzieu (1993) who describes the ego as developing functions being synonymous with the experience of the skin. Anzieu and Briggs (1990) state that our sense of identity, experiences and memories are formed by and inform narratives that like a skin contain a fundamental sense of being. The skin is a sense organ enabling contact with the world in all directions; sufficiently containing, flexible and permeable, whilst also forming the shape of the person in the world. Similar to skin, the narration of the image must be sufficiently flexible to allow for movement, so that we know that what 'factual' interpretation we arrive at is how we understand something from that point in time, from one perspective, and is subject to change.

In mentalization-based art therapy supervision, narrative coherence functions as a metaphor illuminating a relational context. For us as social animals needing sustained relationships, object constancy (Solnit 1982) and attachment security (Bowlby 2008), these assumptions are also supported, if not defined by narrative coherence (Hyvärinen 2010). Our metaphorical relational narrative representations guide our social behaviours. However, as Bohm (2013) stated, 'we automatically assume that our representations are true pictures of reality, rather than relative guides for action that are based on reflexive, unexamined memories'. In other words, as Tenzer (1985) suggests, 'we see what must be'. We arrive at conclusions based on what we expect to see. Successful supervision necessitates a fluctuating tide of coherence and non-coherence, between feeling safe with the security of well-grounded knowledge and being challenged about fixed perceptions. In a supervisory context this happens primarily through perspective-taking, allowing for embodying different viewpoints, to reduce dualistic comparison that results in a divisive biographical and cultural understanding. The mentalizing supervisor as witness introduces a third perspective, emotionally attuning to several perspectives, including the emotional embodiment of people within the relational system. For example, mentalizing requires demonstrating an explicit curiosity about family, friends and the patient and therapist to enable the development of emotional vividity and plausible hypotheses. The image assists in this process, allowing for the flexibility of imagination to develop associations, mapping new ways of seeing.

Whilst the supervisee's primary concern is conveying the clinical narrative, through the unfolding form of the image, it is the supervisor's role to playfully, gently and supportively disrupt expected and well-trodden narratives that have lost openness to possibility and emotionality. In many respects this can only happen if the space feels safe and well attended to, where the art therapist feels kept in mind. This poses a parallel to therapy, and the supervisor must mediate the risks of creating a therapeutic relationship where the inevitable personal resonances to the clinical material risk overshadowing the primary tasks of the supervision.

Developmental narratives

The earliest types of contact that enable safeness are in relation to the gaze, holding and playful physical contact, regulating and responsive sounds and familiar olfactory experiences of being with another. Our senses are the precursor to social understanding, and mentalization-based treatments are building conceptual knowledge to encompass a wider appreciation of the effects of our sensed experience. '…our usage differs in that we are assuming that the term "mentalization" specifically includes inferring the imagined causes and implications of sensation that impact on the individual' (Duquette and Ainley 2019, p.3). The quality of eye-contact, touch and bodily articulation is key to the image impressions that a patient makes in art therapy. Memories and learned associations, made up of spatial and temporal experiences cognitively woven into narratives, provide a conscious or pre-conscious cohesion enabling social cognition and adaptation.

In art therapy, memories are codified through the image expression as a method of communication within a relational dialogue (Bucci 1984). However, the images we make hold a particular language that also remains independent from dialogue. I have conducted an experiment many times in supervisory workshops asking the supervisee to describe a picture and the supervisor to imagine the picture described. This helps to differentiate the value of words, the supervisory alliance and the use of the image. It often forms an impression in the supervisor's mind and there is extra material drawn from associations that informs an understanding of the clinical work; however, the image constructed by the supervisor rarely has the same characteristics as the one being described. The image-making process involves a physical and interactional space which the supervisor is not a part of. The fundamental therapeutic aim to disconfirm beliefs based on misattuned and invalidating prior experiences begins with communicating pre-reflective bodily processes within a relational context through the image-making. This is near to impossible to convey in the supervisory context except through parallel processes (McNeill and Worthen 1989) and the bodily articulation (Duquette and Ainley 2019) in the form of the image. The physicality of the image in supervision is closer to the patient's experience and therefore provides anchorage for the affect, which can be easily lost and give way to elaborate pseudo-mentalizing. Producing conditions for successful mentalizing in art therapy requires a third object (Ogden 1994) that will enable a shared narrative developed from an affectively focused image-based representation. As Duquette and Ainley (2019, p.10) state:

> …acknowledging the influence of bodily sensation on the processes of mind, and creating a window into the influence of the body and sensory experience on emotional states and cognitions, allows therapists a much wider range of interventions based on the body than when engaging relationally with our patients in 'just' talk therapy.

In mentalization-based art therapy theory, early experiences of well-mentalized representations of mental states, inclusive of affects, is more likely to produce secure attachments (see Fonagy et al. 1991), whereas poorly mentalized representations that invalidate the infant's experience are likely to produce maladaptive fixed narratives about social norms (see also Havsteen-Franklin 2019). Art therapists require supervision because in the clinical situation the offer to be helpful is frequently in the context of the helper being perceived as unreliable, invalidating and abusive. Where there has been pervasive and compounded trauma, the ensuing stories are often about self-hatred, having no self or a worthless sense of self, where they are alone, helpless and are required to be self-sufficient. The mentalizing therapist is often validating, curious, and imaginatively explores the arts form from a range of perspectives. However, this process often leaves the therapist with similar feelings of fear, guilt, shame, despair and hopelessness (Wright 2016). Similar to parental care of the infant, this marks an important part of a therapeutic process: to be within the emotional world of the patient, where not everything is processed at a conscious level and therefore remains relationally active within the intuitive socio-emotional experience. As Schore (2003, p.52) suggests, the maternal attitude bears a similar resemblance, 'But she is also listening and interacting at another level, an experience-near subjective level, one that implicitly processes moment-to-moment socioemotional information at levels beneath awareness.'

When the narrative has become a familiar place, where there is little progress or movement, the mentalization-based supervisor can assist the therapist by re-framing and reconstructing the narrative. Within the frame of the supervision it requires a more specific challenge that reconstructs the therapeutic discourse beyond traditional notions of containing and surviving emotional turbulence (Winnicott 1969). In this sense the meta-narrative is reworking from a perspective outside of the therapeutic encounter.

Our patients have internalized and live through narratives just as therapists do, and this shapes identity, communication and interpersonal worlds – stories about what can and can't be done and what their role is. Narratives appear to automatically unfold in the same ways that we find what we expect to see. Thus, the image often holds the expected narrative, the pseudo-mentalized experience within which we must search for the emotional meaning and what vulnerability is being defended against. This requires both therapist and patient using what is immediately visible as a starting point for a deeper emotional inquiry. Shared understanding is imperative to establishing a good alliance, as is validating the supervisee's experience. Therefore, building narrative coherence to develop the therapeutic alliance is as important to the supervisory relationship as it is to the therapist–patient relationship.

Trauma, memory and narrative reconstruction

Having a shared narrative is a sequence of events, with cause and effect, where conclusions are drawn based on prior experiences and what we expect to see. It is part of the supervisor's role to become sensitive to 'false cause fallacy' where sequences of events are identified as being causally related without there being reliable evidence. The mentalizing therapist utilizes a genuine curiosity about the narrative to unpack and offer alternative hypotheses.

Apart from the troubles of assuming correlations between events, there is another key issue with assuming causal relations based on memories. Our memories are highly plastic, and, under stress, trauma causes memory impairment, impacting negatively on recalling memories and uncontrolled recollection, for example unwanted triggering of traumatic memories (McEwen 1999). In the therapeutic process, it is likely that directly or indirectly the traumatic events will be remembered and retrieved. The therapist may express compassionate interest; even demonstrate an open curiosity to elicit more detail about the event. Retrieval of those memories causes a reconstruction of the memory which potentially draws upon a range of similar experiences and is vulnerable to false correlations or cues (Alberini and LeDoux 2013). However, traumatic events are partially reconstructed from similar experiences which distort features of the original events. For example, Gabbard, Miller and Martinez (2006, p.113) state: 'Perception of reality is based on what one remembers. Reality is based on expectations on what it should be, which is based on our memories.'

In art therapy, the work often focuses on the areas of greatest emotional intensity. Intensely emotional experiences are stored more accurately (Payne, Joseph and Tudway 2007). In a therapeutic context the therapist may use emotive words such as 'shocking' or 'frightening' when asking questions, which can influence, shape or even assimilate related memories within the neural encoding process during the reconstruction (Loftus 2005). Facing this inevitability of the emotional nucleus of memory being nested in associations, the image helps us to reveal and name the emotions produced in relation to the trauma, which remain consistent and relational. Whilst the memories of traumatic events are important in a mentalization-based model, the affective focus in the present is initially of primary importance. It is the supervisor's task to ensure that the emotions are listened to and felt at an intuitive experience-near level of reconstructing the narrative (see Schore 2003).

Sparkes and Smith (2008) describe from a social constructionist perspective that biographical narratives are the points in time strung together, 'where emotions or memories are merely psychological states but are also narratively performed social enactments' (p.299). Accordingly, the narrative ultimately becomes a constructed metaphor, transposed on to a situation out of reach except in the ways we construct and reconstruct it as a composition of, as (Haraway 1997) suggests, 'diffracted' perspectives. In the supervision, the primary agent of change is not locating the memory as a 'factual' account of the narrative, but sensitively holding in mind, empathizing and building curiosity to enable the development of a sense of a social self where experiences are recognized, validated and attuned to within the present.

Case study: Sandra – 'Screwed up'

An experienced art therapist arrived at the supervision with some sense of unease. She had recently begun working with a middle-aged white woman called Sandra who had two sons, was a single mother and had been in a series of violent relationships that she had found difficult to leave. She was known to social services and had received verbal psychotherapy in the past. Her children were known to have behavioural problems, including being aggressive to others. Now in the early sessions of her art therapy, the therapist described feeling afraid that the patient was disengaging and felt that the therapeutic alliance was poorly established.

In the supervision, the therapist produced the artwork from a cardboard box and placed it on the table between us. The object was a screwed-up piece of white A4 paper which had been painted black after being screwed up. The therapist described the flat affect when the patient was describing sexual and emotional abuse. The patient did not want to take legal action and the therapist felt stuck. The therapist felt that the carefully constructed screwed-up paper represented her withdrawal from the therapy, devoid of emotionality. The therapist felt a powerful sense of absence and hopelessness and wanted to be more directive; she wanted to ensure safety and be protective against the potential abusers, and the suggested directiveness was also about providing strategies for how the patient should use the session time more constructively to be assertive.

I made notes during the supervision of my emotional narrative and associations. My first impression of the image was of a 'throw away' art object; a screwed-up piece of paper ready to be discarded. However, the paper appeared to have a form that was deliberate and intended. It was carefully held and shaped. I noted that the worthlessness of the discarded object, because of its form and lack of colour, appeared to more closely represent her depressed condition – self-enclosed and indistinct, held as a closed form. The image appeared to be something in the moment that she was close to rather than throwing away and at the end of the session she carefully stored it. My internal narrative developed as I focused my attention on the quality of painting on the surface and what it would be like if the paper unfolded. This felt empty, fragmented, hungry and absent. The lack of an empathic, enabling curiosity felt to me to be intrusive and demanding. I understood the feeling of urgency in the face of perpetual threat, and perhaps action was needed to be taken to be more effectively assisting her in her domestic life. However, when the therapist explained as she did, I felt the concern about her physical safety was overshadowing her communication and vulnerability and offering a quick solution that protected and sustained her role as victim whilst appearing to be supporting a change to her behaviour.

When the inquiry about intentional states of mind is reduced to a change in behaviour, this also marks a change in mentalizing. We were moving toward a teleological concrete response to a relational problem in the therapy. The solution that was being offered by the art therapist responded to the sense that the patient felt helpless and emotionally disconnected, and this became the motivating factor. In this patient's interpersonal world, there was often a radical attempt by the other to reconnect when she appeared to be in a condition of perceived withdrawal. Just like the screwed-up piece of paper that she had made, the potentiality of contact was reduced as she turned in on herself, with self-criticism, loathing and eventually hopelessness. In the narrative that she described, she said that she could not express her felt experience but had felt hopeless. The therapist and others that had been close to her attempted to make a firmer contact, but failed in a similar way to the invalidating environment where the emotionality was not held in mind. This pattern of invalidation and directive contact from another, in its most severe state, left her vulnerable to violent intrusions. This does not suggest that she is responsible for the violence towards her, simply that she appeared to have a pervasive epistemic distrust of others based on anticipated relational ruptures.

The final part of my internal narrative within the supervision as the form became more apparent was of the patient's attempt to reach out to connect with another when she offered the object for the therapist to view. After attuning to the therapist's experience, I attempted to embody the position of the patient making this form, the tactile construction, making careful contact with the paper and the offering as not simply a communication of her condition of withdrawal, but the way in which this form was offered by the patient appeared to be a veiled attempt to make contact with the therapist. The struggle to convey the vulnerability and pain regarding her experiences left the art therapist feeling excluded and helpless. However, the patient's reach for another helped the therapist to identify the maladaptive attempt to use the therapy and to reconsider the use of rules to offer her safety and to engage instead in an emotionally explorative process of what it is like making emotional contact with another. Whilst empowering her to take action and be stronger might still be a good idea, the therapist was responding differently to previous attempts to support her and stepping outside of the anticipated narrative. In this sense, the supervisor is attempting to enable a disruption of the relational narrative that may evolve into an implicitly invalidating experience.

After this new narrative, the patient began to form a more secure working relationship and was able to share that an experience worse than an invalidating relationship was rejection and abandonment, which was avoided at all costs. Developing an affect-focused narrative based on the interpersonal experience of the image and a formulation of the co-constructed relationship within a contextual narrative provided the basis for relational change. Through being more curious about what making contact with another was like for her and reflecting on the artwork, the patient felt that her struggle to connect and the associated anxieties and pain could be heard by another.

On mentalization-focused supervision

Being a supervisor is dependent on and is guided by the clinician's experience of the patient. There are distinct ethical parameters for the supervisor and supervisee based on similar contractual arrangements to the clinical work, such as time, place, frequency, shared aims and agreement about how the material from the supervision will be used. Berger, Quiros and Benavidez-Hatzis (2018, p.128) state:

> Effective strategies in addressing challenges that stem from the interplay of trauma work and intersectionality are those that empower supervisees, attend to relational components in supervisory interactions, create a feeling of emotional and physical safety and support, address parallel process, emphasize knowledge, and advocate self-care.

It is arguable that supervision is another form of therapeutic interaction that emulates and models therapy from an emotional standpoint rather than being competency-based (Fish 2008). However, within the healthcare context the focus is primarily on enabling sustainable clinical change and resourceful management of the quantity and quality of contact required to enable the clinical change warranted by the health organization. Stefano, Piacentino and Ruvolo (2017) suggest that supervision is an important part of enabling sustainable mentalizing within organizational spaces. They state that a mentalizing process should initiate

> an attitude of caring and compassion, enhance the curiosity which members of the group have about each other's thoughts and feelings, be careful to identify when mentalization has turned into pseudo-mentalization (pretending to know), and focuses on misunderstanding. (p.221)

In the clinical context the verbal/non-verbal narrative interpretation works across several domains that require attention in the supervisory context: the patient experience, the therapist experience, the organization and the socio-cultural contextual narratives. The case study below provides an example.

Case study: Therapist feeling 'cut off'

One of my supervisees shared concerns about using the supervision effectively. To my mind there did not appear to be a way of understanding this in the clinical work, which he appeared to explore and reflect on in an articulate and insightful way. I extended our exploration beyond the immediate clinical work to the wider context. He worked on a triage ward in a large psychiatric hospital where patients were discharged quickly and whilst planned could leave with a few days' notice. The therapist was in a cycle of often beginning and forming relationships that enabled comprehensive psychiatric assessments, providing access to art materials and facilitating relational and emotional development. The therapist then experienced this attachment as being repeatedly 'cut off'.

It emerged that the losses and lack of support from staff resulted in the art therapist feeling left in the art therapy room with the emotive images and the absence of the patients. This ultimately reflected how the therapist felt, and he conveyed that even in supervision he felt that he was without support, cut off from meaningful relationships. The supervisee did not know why he felt the way he did, and a lot of questions arose regarding the experience of not being held and how this might impact on the work. The supervision focused on the ward function, staff defences against loss and retreat as a way of managing feelings about loss (Bowlby 1973). In this sense, by focusing on the emotional quality and associations, a credible evidence-informed hypothesis was developed that could be successfully explored with the supervisee.

This brief example illustrates a relational mentalization-based model of supervision, exploring dynamic clinical issues, where the roots of the issue are considered within an attachment-based framework. As his supervisor, I explored the clinical encounter and the expected narratives, embodying narrative perspectives at different levels of experience, from the pre-reflective expression in art therapy to the organizational need to manage discharge targets (Figure 6.1).

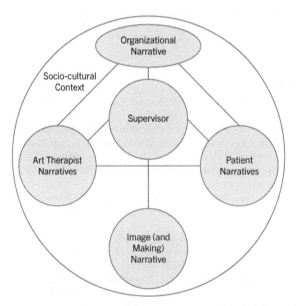

*Figure 6.1: Position of the supervisor at the interface
of narratives about the patient experience*

Conclusion

As illustrated, the mentalization-based supervisor explores multi-layered narratives with an aim to engage in a mentalizing process. In a mentalization-based art therapy model, the supervisor is part of a collaborative journey with the art therapist and the patient. The supervisor assumes the role of traveller attempting to navigate different perspectives, to enable groundedness when a narrative is dramatically shifting, and exploration when the narrative becomes static or rigid. It is part of the human drive for security that 'we find what we expect to see', and the supervisor will slip into premature knowing. Sometimes this is a restricted view and at other times this is to hold on to knowing rather than experience feelings. However, this is part of the supervisory journey as parallel process; a modelling of practice; a collaborative space for the unfolding narratives bringing the affect into sharp relief. In this model, the authority of the supervisor is embodied as reflective guide and benign investigator and as an ally in the exploration of the clinical work. As a process of investigation, akin to narrative constructionism in art therapy (Riley 1997), the formation of narrative is in collaboration and therefore requires trust and confidence that the supervisory relationship can allow for multiple perspectives in the co-creation of social meaning.

References

Alberini, C.M. and LeDoux, J.E. (2013) 'Memory reconsolidation.' *Current Biology 23*, 17, R746–R750.

Anzieu, D. (1993) 'Autistic phenomena and the skin ego.' *Psychoanalytic Inquiry 13*, 42–48.

Anzieu, D. and Briggs, D. (1990) *Psychic Envelopes*. London: Karnac Books.

Barreto, A.L., Fearon, R.M.P., Osório, A., Meins, E. and Martins, C. (2016) 'Are adult mentalizing abilities associated with mind-mindedness?' *International Journal of Behavioral Development 40*, 4, 296–301.

Berger, R., Quiros, L. and Benavidez-Hatzis, J.R. (2018) 'The intersection of identities in supervision for trauma-informed practice: Challenges and strategies.' *The Clinical Supervisor 37*, 1, 122–141.

Bloom, S.L. (2010) 'Bridging the black hole of trauma: The evolutionary significance of the arts.' *Psychotherapy and Politics International 8*, 3, 198–212.

Bohm, D. (2013) *On Dialogue*. London: Routledge.

Bowlby, J. (1973) *Attachment and Loss: Vol. 2. Separation*. New York, NY: Basic Books.

Bowlby, J. (2008) *A Secure Base: Parent–Child Attachment and Healthy Human Development*. New York, NY: Basic Books.

Bucci, W. (1984) 'Linking words and things: Basic processes and individual variation.' *Cognition 17*, 2, 137–153.

Burkitt, I. (2019) 'Emotions, social activity and neuroscience: The cultural-historical formation of emotion.' *New Ideas in Psychology 54*, 1–7.

Carpendale, M. (2002) 'Getting to the underbelly: Phenomenology and art therapy supervision.' *Canadian Art Therapy Association Journal 15*, 2, 2–6.

Case, C. (2007) 'Review of the Literature on Art Therapy Supervision.' In J. Schaverien and C. Case (eds) *Supervision of Art Psychotherapy* (pp.1–27). Hove: Routledge.

Duquette, P. and Ainley, V. (2019) 'Working with the predictable life of patients: The importance of "mentalizing interoception" to meaningful change in psychotherapy.' *Frontiers in Psychology 10*, 2173.

Fish, B.J. (2008) 'Formative evaluation research of art-based supervision in art therapy training.' *Art Therapy 25*, 2, 70–77.

Fonagy, P. and Allison, E. (2014) 'The role of mentalizing and epistemic trust in the therapeutic relationship.' *Psychotherapy 51*, 3, 372–380.

Fonagy, P. and Bateman, A.W. (2016) 'Adversity, attachment, and mentalizing.' *Comprehensive Psychiatry 64*, 59–66.

Fonagy, P., Steele, M., Steele, H., Moran, G.S. and Higgitt, A.C. (1991) 'The capacity for understanding mental states: The reflective self in parent and child and its significance for security of attachment.' *Infant Mental Health Journal 12*, 3, 201–218.

Gabbard, G.O., Miller, L.A. and Martinez, M. (2006) 'A Neurobiological Perspective on Mentalizing and Internal Object Relations in Traumatized Patients with Borderline Personality Disorder.' In J.G. Allen and P. Fonagy (eds) *Handbook of Mentalization-based Treatment* (pp.123–140). Chichester: Wiley.

Gilroy, A. (2007) 'In Pursuit of an Object.' In J. Schaverien and C. Case (eds) *Supervision of Art Psychotherapy: A Theoretical and Practical Handbook* (pp.213–231). Hove: Routledge.

Haraway, D.J. (1997) 'The virtual speculum in the new world order.' *Feminist Review 55*, 22–72.

Havsteen-Franklin, D. (2019) 'Creative Arts Therapies.' In A.W. Bateman and P. Fonagy (eds) *Handbook of Mentalizing in Mental Health Practice* (2nd edn, pp.181–197). Washington, DC: American Psychiatric Association.

Hyvärinen, M. (2010) *Beyond Narrative Coherence*. Amsterdam: John Benjamins.

Laine, R. (2007) 'Image Consultation: Supporting the Work of Art Therapists.' In J. Schaverien and C. Case (eds) *Supervision of Art Psychotherapy* (pp.135–154). Hove: Routledge.

Loftus, E.F. (2005) 'Planting misinformation in the human mind: A 30-year investigation of the malleability of memory.' *Learning and Memory 12*, 4, 361–366.

Malchiodi, C.A. and Riley, S. (1996. *Supervision and Related Issues: A Handbook for Professionals*. Chicago, IL: Magnolia Street Publishers.

Mattan, B.D., Wei, K.Y., Cloutier, J. and Kubota, J.T. (2018) 'The social neuroscience of race-based and status-based prejudice.' *Current Opinion in Psychology 24*, 27–34.

McEwen, B.S. (1999) 'Stress and hippocampal plasticity.' *Annual Review of Neuroscience 22*, 1, 105–122.

McNeill, B.W. and Worthen, V. (1989) 'The parallel process in psychotherapy supervision.' *Professional Psychology: Research and Practice 20*, 5, 329–333.

Ogden, T.H. (1994) 'The analytical third: Working with intersubjective clinical facts.' *International Journal of Psychoanalysis 75*, 1, 3–20.

Overwalle, F.V. (2009) 'Social cognition and the brain: A meta-analysis.' *Human Brain Mapping 30*, 3, 829–858.

Payne, A.J., Joseph, S. and Tudway, J. (2007) 'Assimilation and accommodation processes following traumatic experiences.' *Journal of Loss and Trauma 12*, 1, 75–91.

Riley, S. (1997) 'Social constructionism: The narrative approach and clinical art therapy.' *Art Therapy 14*, 4, 282–284.

Schore, A.N. (2003) *Affect Regulation and the Repair of the Self* (Vol. 2). Norton Series on Interpersonal Neurobiology. New York, NY: W.W. Norton.

Schumaker, J.F. (1995) *The Corruption of Reality: A Unified Theory of Religion, Hypnosis, and Psychopathology*. Amherst, NY: Prometheus Books.

Solnit, A.J. (1982) 'Developmental perspectives on self and object constancy.' *The Psychoanalytic Study of the Child 37*, 1, 201–218.

Sparkes, A.C. and Smith, B. (2008) 'Narrative Constructionist Inquiry.' In J.A. Holstein and J.F. Gubrium (eds) *Handbook of Constructionist Research* (pp.295–314). London: Guilford Press.

Stefano, G.D., Piacentino, B. and Ruvolo, G. (2017) 'Mentalizing in organizations: A psychodynamic model for an understanding of well-being and suffering in the work contexts.' *World Futures 73*, 4–5, 216–223.

Target, M. and Fonagy, P. (1996) 'Playing with reality: II. The development of psychic reality from a theoretical perspective.' *International Journal of Psychoanalysis 77*, 459–479.

Tenzer, A. (1985) 'Constructing new truths.' *Contemporary Psychoanalysis 21*, 228–236.

Winnicott, D.W. (1969) 'The use of an object.' *International Journal of Psychoanalysis 50*, 4, 711–716.

Wood, C. (2007) 'Agency and Attention.' In J. Schaverien and C. Case (eds) *Supervision of Art Psychotherapy: A Theoretical and Practical Handbook* (pp.185–199). Hove: Routledge.

Wright, S. (2016) *Dancing Between Hope and Despair: Trauma, Attachment and the Therapeutic Relationship*. London: Palgrave.

Zeegers, M.A.J., Colonnesi, C., Stams, G.-J.J.M. and Meins, E. (2017) 'Mind matters: A meta-analysis on parental mentalization and sensitivity as predictors of infant–parent attachment.' *Psychological Bulletin 143*, 12, 1245–1272.

MEETING TRAUMA AND ADDICTION IN PRACTICE

7

Media and Culture

*An Attachment-informed Search for Healing, Transformation
and Repair Through the Treatment of Addiction*

Charles Brown

The view that addiction (an emotional, physiological or psychological desire for a substance, activity or behaviour) is in essence an attachment disorder underpins this chapter. I define addiction as a process whereby people become dependent on a substance, behaviour or activity despite negative effects and within that process become detached from reality. I set out to explore the relationship between traumatic experience and these processes. Psychoanalysis views symptoms as manifestations of the unconscious. That which cannot be expressed through language is expressed in the form of physical, behavioural, emotional or psychosomatic symptoms. Psychoanalysis recognizes that the symptom is a defence or survival tactic created by the unconscious as a solution to a problem. In this chapter I attempt to illustrate, through a clinical case study, the relevance of attachment theory when working with such disorders.

Attachment theory was formulated to explain patterns of behaviour and the propensity to make intimate emotional bonds that were formerly conceptualized in terms of dependency, resulting in the reformulation of psychoanalytic metapsychology. I argue that the performatory activity of post-traumatic experience may be understood not only as a search for meaning but also as a means for repair.

Trauma is recognized as a sudden brief and unexpected event or an enduring persistent and repetitive situation (Herman 1992). Trauma disrupts functionality, is the source of fragmentary processes and produces a distorted sense of self, of the environment and shared reality. A traumatic response can come from the stuff of everyday life in varying forms that threaten an individual's integrity. This chapter raises some implications for the treatment of this client group, the development of 'earned security' for those individuals whose experiences might have created an insecure attachment status and who have demonstrated a resilience that would not have been anticipated. These individuals as adults are then able to describe their experiences in a coherent and contained way.

Attachment theory (Bowlby 1958) hypothesized that children build mental models of self and others based on their primary attachment relationships. Importantly, Bowlby theorized that the role of attachment relationships in human development is crucial to survival. Bowlby's colleague Mary Ainsworth (1990) further added that attachment systems evolved to enable proximity and provide soothing at times of distress as well as a safe haven. The relationships between trauma, attachment and dependency are multilayered and complex. I will focus on some of the parallels encountered in treating those clients who struggle to cope with trauma and dependency, whether substances, activities or behaviours.

I present one client's trajectory towards earned security despite deprivation and lack of a safe facilitating environment. The client that I shall present is a composite representative whom I shall call 'Juliet'. I describe Juliet's early experiences that were indicators of her emotional and psychological experiences that led to a maladaptive internal working model. I discuss her sense of existence and how this was expressed. The maladaptation aims to ensure the survival and the integrity of the individual through hope that the lost equilibrium between the individual and her environment will be restored.

When the child's needs are left unmet and the caregiver instead becomes the source of a misattuned and disorientating attachment system, therapy must recognize the developmental disruptions that underlie the symptoms. Clients who suffer from dependency problems present with complicated and entrenched difficulties encompassing mental, emotional and physical aspects stemming from attachment problems. Neglecting this during treatment contributes to the high treatment dropout rates and relapse in this client group. Whilst not all substance dependants share the same historical experiences, underlying trauma is invariably present in their lived experiences. The need for responsive trauma-informed dependency treatment is an important part of treatment and essential for the healing and recovery process.

Psychoanalytic theory had its origins in hysterical trauma and carried 'three ideas over on to the psychical level, the idea of a psychical excitation, the idea of a wound and the idea of consequences affecting the whole organism' (Laplanche and Pontalis 1973, p.466).

Attachment behaviour as described by Bowlby and his collaborators (Ainsworth 1964, 1967; Bowlby 1958, 1969, 1973; Main and Hesse 1990) is conceived of as any form of behaviour that results in a person attaining or retaining proximity to some other differentiated and preferred individual, usually the caregiver. Attachment behaviour is a class of behaviours distinct from feeding and sexual behaviour but of equal significance (Bowlby 1977). Attachment theory proposes that human development be understood within an evolutionary context and attachment as an enduring emotional bond, the main purpose of which is affect regulation. Bowlby thought that whilst suffering and loss are inevitable, relationships are healing. Working relationally with addiction, complex trauma, grief and loss are key to bringing about change.

Unconscious fantasy can be thought of as a defensive narrative that protects the psyche from reality. In attachment theory the purpose of defence is to regulate affect. Affect regulation is linked to the experience of relationship to the caregiver and to the internal working models built from that experience. An attachment-informed approach to dependency might be useful in helping these clients self-regulate and in restoring the human relational system. Neuroscience has given us new and deeper insights into the nature of trauma. We can now see what happens in the traumatized brain and in the nervous system both during and after a traumatic event. Psychotherapy can make use of these important contributions that show the ways in which trauma can shape experience and provide understanding of how trauma is always about a present event.

Addiction and its concomitant behaviours can be understood as responses to trauma in the here-and-now suggesting that these conditions can and should be treated synonymously.

Trauma sits at the heart of many mental and emotional presentations met with in the consulting room, in our streets and in treatment centres, and readily observed in the schools and homes of the people living in our communities. What constitutes traumatic experience therefore has to be broad enough to include the stuff of ordinary life, such as divorce, illness and accidents, as well as extreme experiences such as war, torture, rape and murder. Further, definitive trauma must be the subjective experience of the objectively perceived events that determine whether an event is experienced as traumatic or not. Trauma is an experience of an event in which the individual's ability to integrate his/her emotional experience is overwhelmed, or the individual experiences (subjectively) a threat to life, bodily integrity or sanity (Pearlman and Saakvitne 1995).

Freud (1914) linked trauma to the repressed memory of a painful and intense experience that was then evoked by a later event that had some similarity or association to the first. However, he later realized that memories are not fixed but subject to rearrangement and transcription (Massom 1985). The psychoanalytic concept of trauma does not have a precise definition, and psychoanalysts have referred to 'catastrophic trauma' (Anderson and Gold 2003), 'cumulative trauma' (Auerhahn and Peskin 2003), 'strain trauma' (Hurvich 2003), 'pure trauma' (Baranger, Baranger and Mom 1988) and 'developmental trauma' (van der Kolk 2005). Often these references make no distinction between whether trauma is thought of as the event itself or the experience of it, subjectively or objectively. Trauma has been regarded as a process, a state, and at other times attributed to changes in the affected subject.

Neuroscientific insights made during the 1980s corroborate and augment psychoanalytic theory. Damasio (2000) found that stress reactions can also be physical because our sense of ourselves is anchored in our bodies. Herman (1992) in her seminal book further stated that the child makes use of compulsive, obsessive behaviours to regulate their internal states.

As a result of traumatic experience, because of what happened, the body produces more stress hormones than it normally would and continues doing so after the event. These abnormally high stress levels can impact long-term physical health and cause difficulties in recalling and regulating affective experiences (Schacter 2008). The stream of hormones also disrupts the hippocampal (episodic memory) functioning and injures neurones, and traumatized individuals experience their traumatic memories as timeless, intrusive, sensory fragments that cannot be expressed as language (Ogden, Minton and Pain 2006). The need to defend against remembering and to render events and feelings unconscious creates a hysterical symptom formation that manifests as a repetitive performance of the traumatic event or events. Those children who experience complex stress situations in relation to their primary attachment figure are likely to encounter difficulties in later life, such as repetitive self-defeating behaviours (Panksepp, Siviy and Normansell 1985). Freud (1920) proposed that trauma arose from intrapsychic or environmental determinants. He proposed that intolerable danger, anxiety or instinctual arousal led to 'repetition compulsion', a fixation that remains immortal so long as it is not understood. Holmes (2014) says implicit memories that are laid down before the cerebral cortex has fully developed, and 'before the development of language', are a 'unique response to experience'.

Children of drug-using caregivers are likely to encounter complex multiple traumas, such as domestic violence, parental incarceration and sexual, physical or psychological abuse (Hussong et al. 2012; Larkin, Shields and Anda 2014; Taplin et al. 2014). The link between parental addiction and their children going on to use substances is complex. The research indicates that, in fact, most children do not become problem drug users themselves (Cleaver, Unell and Aldgate 2011; Tonmyr et al. 2010; Velleman 1993).

Case study: Juliet

Juliet, a 30-year-old mother of an 18-month-old son attended once-weekly therapy for just over two years in an NHS outpatients setting. Her mother was 15 when she had her and resident in a local authority care home. Juliet had been taken into foster care when she was around six weeks old. After three years her mother regained custody of her. Life was very chaotic with her mother who was involved with violent partners. After her mother moved without leaving a forwarding address, Juliet stayed with her maternal grandmother. When Juliet was five years old her mother remarried. However, the marriage was not a good one, with Juliet witnessing considerable violence between her mother and stepfather, who drank heavily. Her stepfather would be violent towards Juliet too. Moreover, she was terrified that she would be raped. When she was in the bath her stepfather would come in to use the toilet and when his friends came over they would try to get her to sit on their laps. There was no image of a parental couple that could co-operate.

Juliet initially came into contact with the child mental health services when she was ten after some trouble at school. When she was 11 years old she took an overdose of her mother's medication and at 12 years old, after witnessing her mother and stepfather arguing, she again used her mother's medication to attempt suicide. The couple eventually separated and contact was re-established with her biological father, who suffered from mental health problems and alcoholism and was in poor physical health.

At 14 Juliet and her mother were attacked and her mother was killed. Juliet was severely injured but survived by playing dead. After some time in hospital she moved in with her grandmother. Juliet was offered counselling support; however, she was unable to engage with her therapist and didn't stay in therapy. A further suicide attempt occurred when she was 16. When she was 21 she was sentenced to a term of imprisonment for drug dealing.

At the start of the therapy with me Juliet had been in a relationship for almost three years.

Juliet sought therapy because she kept finding herself in violent and abusive relationships where she felt she had little control over her life. Juliet had given some thought as to why she got into these relationships but felt this was always by accident rather than anything to do with herself. Juliet had not used any class-A drugs, but she continued to use marijuana as she did not consider it a drug. Juliet made use of the therapy to tell her story. Gradually she moved from a mimetic historically performed narrative to a storied autobiography. Juliet arrived 20 minutes late for her first appointment and announced that she 'couldn't stay as her son was outside in the car'. I later learned that there had been difficulties with the childcare arrangements with her partner. Initially the therapy focused on the relationship with her partner, who was unreliable and dishonest and also a gambler. Her partner would often disappear for days, and she felt their relationship and their son were not a priority. She had fought to keep her family together and to get him involved in being a father and being part of a family, but he never did.

When her partner moved out of their flat and began seeing someone else, Juliet started using drugs again and began a relationship with someone who was using drugs. Her boyfriend often wore shell suits, and Juliet linked his clothing to the image of her tracksuit-wearing stepfather. She had found some athletic awards from school that had her stepfather's surname on them (her mother and Juliet had taken the stepfather's name). She had thrown them in the bin. She was able to follow my links between her drug use and her need to feel accepted. Links were made to her own childhood experience.

She had recently come across some pictures of herself when she was a baby with her mother. This led to associations of a mother who would hug her so tightly sometimes she would feel smothered and memories of not 'getting a look in' with her mother, who was 'all about my stepfather'. In a similar way, Juliet felt that her son did not get a look in with his father. When Juliet left her grandmother's home she did not maintain contact but met again during Juliet's labour. Juliet refused to see her grandmother and would not let her grandmother see her son. I wondered whether this might have been an expression of anger and resentment at having had an abortion when she was 16. Juliet became emotional and started to feel the therapy was making her 'soft...too emotional'.

'I hate feeling like this...like a four-year-old... I feel strange and stupid. I can't make sense of things.' I came to understand this as a communication for a therapist/mother who could be accepting and containing and bear witness to her story without rejecting or judging her. She could not trust what emerged in the work and sought validation of her own mind from the 'expert doctor'. Juliet was shifting from a basic form of regulating herself to a more reflective functioning.

Juliet brought a fragment of a dream. In the dream she was being chased by snarling werewolves. Associations to the dream were that she was trying to protect everyone. Her dreams, she told me, 'were often about trauma, imminent or happening' and usually of her 'saving a friend...being a super woman or something like that'. She told me that her dreams were 'always about killers and escaping from aliens or monsters'. This led to the disclosure of an earlier preoccupation with horror films that she used in order to process and manage her traumatic experiences.

As a teenager, she would watch endless horror movies and obsessively read 'True Crime' magazines. She would also take 'acid' (a hallucinogenic drug) to see whether she could 'survive the trip'. For Juliet, it felt like there was no escape from her horror and no possibility for any conversation through which a solution might be found. Frames of reference that offered a perspective on her experience were not available to her; instead, Juliet performed a bizarre, and seemingly unconnected, enactment of her experience. Narratives from Juliet's lived experience from witnessing domestic abuse and alcohol misuse in an environment where there was little safety or security meant that she had to adapt psychically. Feelings were not spoken about and any communications that might have illuminated her experience were not available. Language and meaning for Juliet was constituted in enactment.

Bowlby's (1969) environmental and organismic model situates psychical problems as the result of interference with the innate potential for interrelatedness, and the recognition patterns of relating and meaning of behaviour in terms of its interpersonal function are crucial for treatment. At the first break, which coincided with her mother's birthday, Juliet became anxious that she was not talking about her relationship with her mother, and she wondered whether she should go and visit her mother's grave. She had not been to the cemetery since the funeral. Juliet had driven to the cemetery before but had crashed her car after getting lost. She remembered her visit to the chapel of rest where her mother was lying and as she gazed at the body she saw her mother's eyes open. She decided that there was no point her going to the cemetery: 'There isn't anything up there – a skeleton! Do I go and talk to it?' she wailed. 'The funeral was horrible... I cried my eyes out... I haven't cried for ages, I used to cry all the time.' She got through the wake by chain-smoking in the garden. After a few minutes' silence Juliet said that she was 'itching'. She thought a bug in the room had bitten her. 'See what happens when I come to this stupid place!' she cried. Reflecting on this, Juliet came to see that her response was linked with the time of the year – the anniversary of her mother's funeral. She was able to think then about her arrival in therapy the same age her mother was when she died. This session ended with her saying that she was doing 'all right and didn't need to come here... Goodbye, Doctor!'

During a break Juliet had spoken about her therapy with her friends and grandmother and found that she was 'moaning about not going to therapy'. Juliet had not previously felt able to tell her story 'except in little bits and short sentences' to others. She couldn't talk to whomever and had never told anyone the details. She felt strange talking about it to me and remarked that she noticed that I wore ear studs and asked whether it would be ok to call me Charles. In the retelling of her narrative, through which her experiences were being reconstructed, Juliet recalled living in a house as a child that was enclosed by 'a white picket fence, she had been adopted by a loving family and a rabbit fur jacket'. It emerged that Juliet had been placed with several foster carers. It seemed that her grandmother had stayed in contact with her throughout this period. Reflecting, Juliet noted the contradictions and asked, 'Does it matter? Funny the way your memory works... I think that I just went to anyone... I was that kind of kid... I shouldn't have come here today.'

The violent conflicts between Juliet's mother and her husband included fights between Juliet and her mother, and at other times, fights with her stepfather. 'There must have been good times,' she said. 'There are things that I don't remember and you might be putting things in my head.' I came to understand that Juliet had developed an 'outer person' that could 'deal with things'. A picture emerged of a child struggling to survive. Juliet wondered, 'If Mummy was here, would we be friends? Probably not.' Whenever Juliet thought about her mother she felt angry with her. Juliet spoke of being physically and verbally abused. Juliet would make light of this and say she 'found it hard to think about those things'. As the treatment approached an end, Juliet became anxious. She wondered whether I maintained a private practice where she could come in case things weren't ok. She felt that she 'needed more time' for herself. She had not used any mood-altering drugs for several months and had achieved some internal sense of security that supported her in being able to self-regulate.

This chapter has focused on the links between early trauma and addiction in discussing trauma as symptom and as a means for healing. Several factors have been considered, including environmental dispositions, the primary attachment relationship, the nature of the trauma and the availability of support. In the case study Juliet could not begin to heal until she acknowledged that her caregiver did not, in reality, exist. Therapy supported her to relinquish that which never really was. Understanding the psychobiological response to loss, and integrating the memories, images and thoughts that are processed and become deeper over time, make for successful emotion regulation and learning.

Childhood trauma has been associated with insecure attachment (Piehler, Véronneau and Dishion 2012). Attachment-orientated psychotherapy has been shown to restore deficits in self- and affect regulation (Flores 2006; Khantzian 2015). It is well known that trauma damages the neuronal pathways and hormonal systems in a similar way that illicit drugs do. Insecure attachment experiences and adversity typically disrupt the capacity to relate to how people make sense of their social world and, linked to this, the development of a coherent self-structure.

Reinstating the capacity to form coherent narratives about self and others enables the ability to regulate emotional experiences, which leads to earned security. A trauma-informed attachment approach to substance or process dependencies allows the client to find meaning and purpose after trauma and fosters the creation of a positive identity that might lead to successful lasting recovery. Earned security plays a crucial role after trauma when clients simply lack secure, healthy relationships that could help them heal. Bowlby (1973 p.442) wrote, 'Intimate attachments to other human beings are the hub around which a person's life revolves.'

Anna Freud (1967) viewed trauma as an unbearable experience

and posited a theory of affects originating from intrapsychic or environmental factors that disrupted the ego's organizing function and interrupted the self-regulating process. Neglect and physical, emotional or sexual abuse focused attention on the attachment relationship. Main and Soloman (1986) found that the disorganized/disorientated category (D) classification reliably predicted adjustment problems from childhood through to adolescence. When the attachment figure becomes a source of danger, the child in order to survive must adapt to a hostile environment, inevitably leading to aggressive, externalizing symptoms (Shaw et al. 1996). For example, when access to the attachment figure is jeopardized, fear takes precedence over other activities and leads to behaviours that normally serve to re-establish access to the caregiver.

Children learn to regulate their emotional states by anticipating their caregivers' responses. This allows them to construct what Bowlby (1973) called 'Internal working models' (p.203). Internal working models reflect interactions between an attached individual and the attachment figure. The availability of an attachment figure determines whether the attachment relationship is a safe and secure space. Main and Hesse (1990) found that infants who have been unpredictably frightened by their attachment figure displayed momentary lapses in 'metacognitive monitoring' that included disorientation in time and space, loss of monitoring of discourse and extreme behavioural reactions. They concluded that these lapses could be seen as indicators of unresolved trauma or loss that remained unprocessed at the conscious level, with reference to the range of possible adaptations to acute distress, pain and loss, particularly during early life and the links to addictions.

Attachment views the therapist's emotional availability as central to healing. Dozier, Cue and Barnett (1994) offered support for the idea that a therapist's capacity to remain open to his or her experience as well as to the client is likely to be most predictive of a healthy and successful therapy outcome. In the case study the work with Juliet gave rise to anxieties within the line-management supervision. The supervisor felt uncertain whether the service could cope with Juliet's trauma. A further risk assessment was carried out and the transference relationship was closely examined. The supervisor thought that containing the trauma would be a beneficial treatment strategy. Juliet had come to therapy at a time when her fear of the loss of an attachment relationship was at its height. First, she was approaching the age her mother was when she was killed and secondly, she was afraid her partner would take her son from her. Therapy was somewhere that could provide a safe and reliable space for Juliet to search for meaning.

Ways of being that lack the security of the attachment bond also give rise to failures in emotional regulation, the construction of representational models linked to adaptation, and difficulties forming coherent internal working models of the world and relationships between self and other (Bentovim 2002). Bowlby's ethological theory of attachment and loss has made an important contribution to the phenomenology of grief and its concomitant behavioural and emotional reactions. According to Bowlby, the absence or loss of an attachment figure activates an innate motivational system that searches for the lost object. When this fails the individual reorganizes their representational world in such a way that allows a return to normal functioning and the seeking out or renewal of social relationships. Bowlby (1980) wrote that the defensive reaction to loss was an aspect of a more general personality organization he termed 'compulsive self-reliance', where individuals place a priority on self-sufficiency with a propensity for 'switching off'. Closeness is avoided to prevent awareness of underlying attachment needs and the experience of vulnerability. All expression of feeling is frowned upon and the child grows up independent of affectional ties.

Earned security involves the client's capacity to reflect on their 'storied life' with the therapist, then to take that shared story into everyday life in a meaningful and transformative way. In the case study Juliet could not trust that what came up in the therapy was real and sought verification. Whenever Juliet felt that her memories or behaviour was unintelligible her responses could be difficult for her to contain. Treating underlying trauma as an essential part of recovery is crucial for the dependent. Van der Kolk (2014) criticizes dealing with symptoms rather than causes and argues that 'integrating' trauma by turning it into a bad memory rather than reliving it may be key to recovering from trauma. The challenge of finding a safe space to talk about trauma such as Alcoholics Anonymous or Adult Children of Alcoholics or Narcotics Anonymous is why these groups are essential.

From an attachment perspective the overall aim of therapy is to help clients become more secure. Development of internal and external resources can transform the individual's relationship to trauma and to others. When the therapist is present emotionally in a sensitive way the innate regulatory systems necessary for personal growth, relational health and wellbeing can be promoted. Therapeutic neutrality can be experienced as neglect, rejection or abandonment. The therapist may be experienced as intrusive or frightening and trigger fears of engulfment, dependency or retraumatizing. Clients who are designated unresolved/disorganized pose particular issues because most affect is dissociated and distorted. Therapy concerns itself again and again with loss, separation and reunion in consideration of the client's experience and in the separations and reunions that form part of the therapeutic process.

References

Ainsworth, M.D.S. (1964) 'Patterns of attachment behavior shown by the infant in interaction with his mother.' *Merrill-Palmer Quarterly 10*, 51–58.

Ainsworth, M.D.S. (1967) *Infancy in Uganda: Infant Care and the Growth of Attachment.* Baltimore, MD: Johns Hopkins University Press.

Ainsworth, M.D.S. (1990) 'Some Considerations Regarding Theory and Assessment Relevant to Attachment Beyond Infancy.' In M.T. Greenberg, D. Cicchetti and E.M. Cummings (eds) *Attachment in the Preschool Years: Theory, Research, and Intervention* (pp.463–488). Chicago, IL: University of Chicago Press.

Anderson, F.S. and Gold, J. (2003) 'Trauma, dissociation, and conflict.' *Psychoanalytic Psychology 20*, 3, 536–541

Auerhahn, N.C. and Peskin, H. (2003) 'Action knowledge, acknowledgment, and interpretive action in work with Holocaust survivors.' *The Psychoanalytic Quarterly 72*, 3, 615–658.

Baranger, M., Baranger, W. and Mom, J. (1988) 'The infantile trauma from us to Freud: Pure trauma, retroactivity and reconstruction.' *International Journal of Psychoanalysis 69*, 113–128.

Bentovim, A. (2002) 'Undoing the Effects of Complex Trauma: Creating a Lifespan Trauma Narrative with Children and Young People.' In V. Sinason (ed.) *Attachment, Trauma and Multiplicity: Working with Dissociative Identity Disorder* (2nd edn, pp.47–62). Hove: Brunner-Routledge.

Bowlby, J. (1958) 'The nature of the child's tie to his mother.' *International Journal of Psychoanalysis 39*, 350–373.

Bowlby, J. (1969) *Attachment and Loss: Vol. 1. Attachment.* New York, NY: Basic Books.

Bowlby, J. (1973) *Attachment and Loss: Vol. 2. Separation.* New York, NY: Basic Books.

Bowlby, J. (1977) 'The making and breaking of affectional bonds 1. Aetiology and psychopathology in the light of attachment theory.' An expanded version of the Fiftieth Maudsley Lecture, delivered before the Royal College of Psychiatrists, 19 November 1976. *British Journal of Psychiatry 130*, 201–210.

Bowlby, J. (1980) *Attachment and Loss: Vol. 3. Sadness and Depression.* New York, NY: Basic Books.

Cleaver, H., Unell, I. and Aldgate, J. (2011) *Children's Needs, Parenting Capacity: The Impact of Mental Illness, Learning Disability, Problem Alcohol and Drug Use and Domestic Violence on Children's Safety and Development* (2nd edn). London: Department for Education.

Damasio, A. (2000) *The Feeling of What Happens: Body, Emotions and the Making of Consciousness.* London: Vintage.

Dozier, M., Cue, K. and Barnett, L. (1994) 'Clinicians as caregivers: Role of attachment organisation in treatment.' *Journal of Consulting and Clinical Psychology 62*, 793–800.

Flores, P. (2006) *Addiction as an Attachment Disorder.* New York, NY: Jason Aronson.

Freud, A. (1967) 'Comments on Trauma.' In S.S. Furst (ed.) *Psychic Trauma.* New York, NY: Basic Books.

Freud, S. (1914) 'Remembering, Repeating and Working Through (Further Recommendations in the Technique of Psychoanalysis II).' *Standard Edition of the Complete Psychological Works of Sigmund Freud: Vol. XII.* London: Hogarth Press and the Institute of Psycho-Analysis.

Freud, S. (1920) 'Beyond the Pleasure Principle.' *Standard Edition of the Complete Psychological Works of Sigmund Freud: Vol. XVIII.* London: Hogarth Press and the Institute of Psycho-Analysis.

Herman, J.L. (1992) *Trauma and Recovery: The Aftermath of Violence – from Domestic Abuse to Political Terror.* New York, NY: Basic Books.

Holmes, L. (2014) 'Reaching the repetition compulsion mode.' *Modern Psychoanalysis 39,* 1, 26–37.

Hurvich, M. (2003) 'The places of annihilation anxieties in psychoanalytic theory.' *Journal of the American Psychoanalytic Association 51,* 2, 579–616.

Hussong, A.M., Huang, W., Serrano, D., Curran, P.J. and Chassin, L. (2012) 'Testing whether and when parent alcoholism uniquely affects various forms of adolescent substance use.' *Journal of Abnormal Child Psychology 40,* 8, 1265–1276.

Khantzian, E. (2015) 'Psychodynamic Psychotherapy for the Treatment of Substance Use Disorders.' In N. el-Guebaly, G. Carrà and M. Galanter (eds) *Textbook of Addiction Treatment: International Perspectives.* Milan: Springer.

Laplanche, J. and Pontalis, J.B. (1973) *The Language of Psychoanalysis.* London: Hogarth Press.

Larkin. H., Shields, J.J. and Anda, R.F. (2012) 'The health and social consequences of adverse childhood experiences (ACE) across the lifespan: An introduction to prevention and intervention in the community.' *Journal of Prevention and Intervention in the Community 40,* 263–270.

Main, M. and Hesse, E. (1990) 'The Insecure Disorganised/Disorientated Attachment Pattern in Infancy: Precursors and Sequelae.' In M. Greenberg, D. Cicchetti and E.M. Cummings (eds) *Attachment During the Preschool Years: Theory, Research and Intervention* (pp.161–182). Chicago, IL: University of Chicago Press.

Main, M. and Soloman, J. (1986) 'Discovery of a New, Insecure Disorganized/Disorientated Attachment Pattern.' In T.B. Brazelton and M. Yogman (eds) *Affective Development in Infancy* (pp.95–124). Norwood, NJ: Ablex.

Massom, J.M. (ed.) (1985) *The Complete Letters of Sigmund Freud to Wilhelm Fliess.* Cambridge, MA: Harvard University Press.

Ogden. P., Minton, K. and Pain, C. (2006) *Trauma and the Body: A Sensorimotor Approach to Psychotherapy.* New York, NY: W.W. Norton.

Panksepp, J., Siviy, S.M. and Normansell, A. (1985) 'Brain Opioids and Social Emotions.' In N. Reite and T. Fields (eds) *The Psychobiology of Attachment and Separation* (pp.3–44). London: Academic Press.

Pearlman, L.A. and Saakvitne, K.W. (1995) *Trauma and the Therapist: Countertransference and Vicarious Traumatization in Psychotherapy with Incest Survivors.* New York, NY: W.W. Norton.

Piehler, T.F., Véronneau, M.H. and Dishion, T.J. (2012) 'Substance use progression from adolescence to early adulthood: Effortful control in the context of friendship influence and early-onset use.' *Journal of Abnormal Child Psychology 40,* 7, 1045–1058.

Schacter, D.L (2008) *Searching for Memory: The Brain, the Mind, and the Past.* New York, NY: Basic Books.

Shaw, D.S., Owens, E.B., Vondra. J.I., Keenan, K. and Winslow, E.B. (1996) 'Early risk factors and pathways in the development of early disruptive behavior problems.' *Development and Psychopathology 8,* 679–699.

Taplin, C., Saddichha, S., Li, K. and Krausz, M.R. (2014) 'Family history of alcohol and drug abuse, childhood trauma, and age of first drug injection.' *Substance Use and Misuse 49*, 1311–1316.

Tonmyr, L., Thornton, T., Draca, J. and Wekerle, C. (2010) 'A review of childhood maltreatment and adolescent substance use relationship.' *Current Psychiatry Research and Reviews 6*, 223–234.

van der Kolk, B. (2005) 'Developmental trauma disorder: Toward a rational diagnosis for children with complex trauma histories.' *Psychiatric Annals 35*, 5, 401–408.

van der Kolk, B. (2014) *The Body Keeps the Score: Brain, Mind, and Body in the Healing of Trauma.* New York, NY: Viking.

Velleman, R. (1993) *Alcohol and the Family.* Occasional Paper. London: Institute of Alcohol Studies.

8

Tea at the Round Table

Trauma, Dissociation and Reintegration

Richard Kidgell and Janice Lobban

This study, co-written by a client and an art therapist, documents art therapy in practice over time and the part it played in reclaiming life after trauma. Little did we know, when our paths crossed at the veterans' mental health charity Combat Stress, that our therapeutic alliance would continue for 14 years. In 2004, treatment there typically consisted of two fortnight-long, annual inpatient admissions. However, our work sometimes involved gaps of over a year. The constraints of short-stay admissions, shaped by the funding available at the time, meant that the work had to be undertaken in titrated doses. With only two weeks available, the first few days involved catching-up and determining a therapy focus; followed by a short period of intensive work; with a final few days of consolidation before returning home. This brief therapy format meant that progress was slow but safely delivered. The intervening months between admissions gave the opportunity to put new learning into practice, then the work could be refreshed and extended the next time.

Alongside this ongoing therapy, developments in the treatment of post-traumatic stress disorder (PTSD) and other mental health problems were advancing. For example, Paul Gilbert and others introduced compassion-focused therapy (Gilbert 2009), which has now become widely used for the treatment of shame-based PTSD and self-criticism (Lee and James 2012). It is mandatory as well as crucial for clinicians to undertake continuing professional development, so over the years I (Janice) engaged in further training modules. The knowledge and tools gained were then incorporated into art therapy practice, with associated effects on treatment. We examine key stages in our therapeutic journey and how the evolving form of therapy was shaped and conceptualized. Art therapy is recognized as providing a means of communication between conflicting psychological processes, thereby facilitating self-understanding and promoting positive change.

Richard's story

I am a Royal Air Force (RAF) veteran and I suffer from chronic, combat-related PTSD. Although I was not involved in actual combat, I experienced trauma in combat-like circumstances, mostly during a three-and-a-half year posting to an air weapons range in the early1980s (Kidgell 2017). My primary role was electronics technician in charge of all electronic equipment, including, most significantly with regard to my later PTSD, a prototype electronic gun target. Because the range had a very small number of staff, my secondary duties covered many other tasks, including acting as assistant crash-rescue fireman; searching for and marking unexploded weapons; and any job that was considered too dangerous for civilian workers.

There were several incidents that threatened my life or those of my immediate companions, but the long-term problem was the constant need to be aware of hazards and dangers. The biggest source of pressure was the prototype gun target, which typically failed several times daily (unsurprisingly, as they were being fired at by aircraft cannon). I would have to work at the aiming point while loaded aircraft made practice runs – hopefully with their weapons switches set to 'safe'. Unfortunately for my state of mind, I did see several instances when the cannon fired in error.

In our society, there can be pressure to aspire to 'masculine values', where courage is one of the greatest virtues and cowardice is one of the most humiliating vices ('boys don't cry'). In training, and throughout military service, natural urges to fight, flee or hide are countered by trained reflexes, discipline, a strong sense of duty, tradition and camaraderie. Military culture places many strains on a person that are unusual in civilian life, not the least being that you might have to be prepared to kill or risk death in the line of duty. A person's mental processes will inevitably be affected by, for example, a sudden realization that their life might end in a few seconds, and this happened to me several times a day while repairing the gun targets and carrying out other duties on the air weapons range. I coped by refusing to hear the emotional side of my mind, unaware of any inner conflict. But the emotional memories built up out of sight, and their long-term effect was mentally corrosive.

I left the range to enter officer training without realizing that I was suffering the effects of trauma. Officer training is a tough regime, and although it is not bullying, it can seem like it. It exacerbated my emotional suppression. Within a few months, I suffered flashbacks; intrusive memories; 'lost time'; lost memories; and the feeling that there was a malicious 'person' who could read my thoughts if I put them into words, who would block my plans. Logically, I knew that this was a phenomenon within my mind, probably caused by high stress. However, I could not shake off the feeling that there was a cruel, disciplinarian monster who really could read my thoughts if they were put into words. I even gave him a name – 'The General'. Years later, through art therapy, I realized that this was how my dissociated, emotional subconscious had come to see my logical, disciplined, conscious mind. At the time, however, I could not tell anybody about this, or about the traumatic events that caused it. I did try at first but found that I was disbelieved, even about the nature of my work on the range. My RAF doctors accused me of malingering. So, I stopped trying to get help and, instead, quarantined my worries, bad memories and fears in a locked part of my mind that I tried to ignore.

I left the RAF in 1985 and went to work as a systems design engineer for a major electronics manufacturer, where I had a successful career for over 20 years. Actually, I guessed quite early on from watching television documentaries about 'shell-shock' that I was suffering from PTSD, but this felt a shameful condition for someone who had not been in combat, and I refused to admit the possibility. It was not until 2004, nearly 20 years after I left the RAF, that I finally accepted that I might have PTSD and contacted Combat Stress for help.

Our therapeutic journey
Foundational work
During early admissions, Richard attended the weekly art therapy group and some individual sessions. The experience of art therapy enabled him to discover a way of articulating his thoughts and feelings through images and poetry. On an individual basis, attention was given to

establishing a timeline of events over his lifespan that eventually led him to seek help. In this way, it was possible to construct a formulation to help to conceptualize how and why events from the past were affecting the present, and to explore personal meaning.

PTSD symptoms are clustered into four distinct groups to establish the diagnosis (American Psychiatric Association 2013):

- re-experiencing symptoms (e.g. through nightmares or dissociative flashbacks)

- avoidance symptoms (e.g. of thoughts, feelings or places that might prompt memories of the trauma)

- negative alterations in cognitions and mood (e.g. a distorted sense of self-blame associated with the trauma)

- increased arousal (e.g. hypervigilance or irritability).

Individuals will have a differing proportion of symptoms across the clusters. For instance, some people might be troubled more by arousal symptoms with overt hypervigilance tendencies that might lead to social avoidance; whereas others might be able to socialize but report emotional numbing and detachment, although it is never so clear cut. Through discussion with Richard it became apparent that dissociation was a significant factor in his case.

Dissociation can be viewed as the disconnection 'between things usually associated with each other' such as the 'usually integrated functions of consciousness, memory, identity, or perception' (ISSTD 2018). Herman (1992) observes how trauma causes a fragmentation of the self-preservation system. When the survival mechanisms of flight, fight, freeze or flop are in vain and escape is impossible, dissociation can act as a survival mechanism. In this case, the mind detaches from the traumatic experience in order to reduce its power. However, this causes a break in conscious awareness with disruption to the sense of self (ISSTD 2018). Consequently, the memory of the experience remains detached and un-integrated although it might be triggered into conscious awareness some time later. In such circumstances dissociation can be considered an adaptive process that not only provides analgesia to endure the traumatic experience, but also allows the person to keep functioning (Putnam 1989). When dissociation has been used for survival, it can affect subsequent emotional functioning. For example, an individual might feel nothing at the loss of a loved one (Lobban 2017).

Richard reported that he was not sure whether some of the traumas he recalled really did happen to him or if they had happened to someone else and he had just heard about them. He was able to speak about extraordinary experiences of extreme pressure and repeated exposure to life-threatening situations during his military career without appearing distressed. He would even joke about the bizarre nature of his work and the near misses he experienced, and having flashbacks involving a dual reality of past and present. There was a sense of Richard getting on with the job in hand despite the inherent dangers involved. However, he also mentioned the later emergence of high anxiety, depression and other symptoms that eventually led him to seek help.

The influence of military culture

Busuttil (2017) proposes that 'military culture is unique' (p.73). He emphasizes that when working with veterans it is crucial to be aware of intrinsic cultural features that have been shaped by military training, operations, and the severing of attachments on leaving the forces. These cultural aspects affect approaches to help-seeking and engagement in treatment. Military training places the mission over individual needs. An internal locus of control is expected whereby individuals problem-solve in order to fulfil the task, and 'asking for help is a last resort' (Busuttil 2017, p.78; see also Hoge, Auchterlonie and Milliken 2006; Mikulincer and Solomon 1988).

From clinical experience I had learned that veterans with PTSD can be highly self-critical, and how undermining this could be to progress if left unchallenged. In art therapy sessions, the presence of a veteran's 'inner critic' might promote self-sabotage, or at the very least cause a distressing conflict within. I suspected that Richard might be in such turmoil, so in 2010, I introduced the concept of 'compassionate imagery' into the sessions as a potential mechanism for moderating the effects of harsh self-criticism. This seemed to key in with symbols already latent in Richard's work.

There can be many barriers to self-compassion in veterans who have been used to putting others or the mission first. Self-compassion might be viewed as self-pity or letting oneself 'off the hook' and therefore something to be resisted. Early conversations therefore might explore preconceptions as well as defining what self-compassion might entail, and the hoped for benefits.

Theories that informed practice

There are many conceptualizations from different schools of thought that can help to decipher meaning in material as it emerges in therapy. In our work, it was Richard's experience of dissociation during trauma, his consequential sense of a divided self, and his search for reintegration that shaped understanding. Richard recognized the presence of two conflicting aspects of himself – his 'emotional subconscious' and 'logical, disciplined, conscious mind' – that had separated in order to fulfil his tasks on the range, which were later reinforced by his experiences in officer training. He developed symbolic representations of these parts through art therapy, which enabled communication between them to take place. The influence of compassion-focused therapy (CFT) played a catalytic role in this process.

CFT takes a bio-psycho-social approach and provides a model for understanding the effects of self-attacking thoughts that stimulate a threat response (Gilbert 2007). CFT theory is based on interactions between the three affect regulation systems: the *incentive system* (i.e. doing and achieving); the *affiliative system* (i.e. feeling safe and contented); and the *self-protection system* (i.e. threat-based). Developing self-soothing techniques that stimulate a sense of safety helps to moderate the threat system and consequently reduces stress (Gilbert 2009). Building a compassionate image of an inner helper/mediator can help to access the calming system. Through this image one is able to gain a third-party perspective on situations that can provide alternative viewpoints that might challenge rigidly held perceptions. The choice of compassionate imagery is up to the individual. For instance, it could be an actual person, an imaginary figure, an animal or a landscape, but associated qualities are to include wisdom, strength, warmth and non-judgement (Compassionate Mind Foundation n.d.).

Another concept that helped to inform meaning-making during therapy was that of structural dissociation of the personality, which has its origins in the work of Pierre Janet in the early 20th century. The theory suggests that trauma causes psychological division. One or more 'apparently normal parts' (ANPs) of the personality, which are motivational-driven, avoid reminders of the trauma and continue to participate in everyday life. The ANP enables continued functioning, such as holding down a job. At the same time, one or more 'emotional parts' (EPs) of the personality, which are threat-orientated, become stuck in the horror of trauma time (Steele, van der Hart and Nijenhuis

2005). First World War psychologist Charles Myers first used the terms 'apparently normal part' and 'emotional part' of the personality in the context of traumatized soldiers with shell-shock. He observed how the ANPs' avoidance of the trauma might manifest in numbing or even amnesia (Myers 1940; Steele et al. 2005). The ANP and EP are separate and dissociated. The aim of treatment is integration, and a systems approach is taken to enable the parts to work together (Lobban 2017; van der Hart, Nijenhuis and Soloman 2010).

A related notion is the formation of trauma-related ego states. For instance, ego state therapy (EST) proposes that personality is made up of numerous separate parts or conditions of awareness, and that each of these ego states has its own trait (Ego State Therapy International n.d.; Watkins and Watkins 1997). Each ego state is unique to the individual, and these states of mind can be in conflict. Hence EST sets out to resolve conflict between the separate states of mind by enabling co-operation between the parts (Forgash and Knipe 2012).

Richard's compassionate imagery and symbolic representations

Some important symbolic figures have emerged and evolved in art therapy, apparently spontaneously, without any conscious intention. Over several years, they have developed a 'fictional-reality'. I know they are mental constructs that have no existence in the actual world, but I can conjure them up in imagination as personalities with whom I can discuss problems, study my mental condition, and muster support in times of anxiety. Some represent the component parts of my dissociated mind, which I need to study and manipulate to enable healing. My current symbolic figures are: 'Taffy the Friendly Dragon', my compassionate image, who represents the best and strongest features of my personality; 'Squadron Leader Dead-Eye', who represents my logical, disciplined and courageous conscious mind; and 'The Prof', who represents my emotional, creative subconscious mind. I also have a symbol representing my present-day self who acts as an avatar, permitting me to enter and participate in the imagined scenario, rather than being just a passive outside observer.

Without doubt the most important of my symbolic figures is Taffy. I imagine him as a person inside or beside me, voicing messages of calm, resolve and confidence in times of anxiety and stress. He acts as my companion as I explore the hidden areas of my mind and past. He plays the part of my therapist when I am privately reviewing my situation or planning my next action. Taffy is an imaginary tool, but he represents a significant part of my inner self, and I could not have progressed so far without him.

In 2004 a curious symbol appeared in one of my first art therapy drawings – a small dragon curled up asleep. I sensed he was important but had no idea what he represented. In 2010 Janice asked me to list the features I would want in a guardian angel/compassionate image. As I wrote the list, I had a sudden realization and finished with the words '...or *me*, as I think I could be'. In 2011 I made an art therapy drawing in which I was digging the muck out of a cesspit representing my mind, and complaining bitterly. Then, without intending to, I added a little picture of a dragon smiling down at me and saying, 'Come on – hurry up and get digging, it's nice up here!' I had no idea what this image represented and wrote on the drawing, 'Who the heck is this?' (Figure 8.1). Being Welsh, I tried to colour the dragon red, but I couldn't. It just had to be a friendly shade of pink!

Figure 8.1: 'Who the heck is this?' (see online colour plate)

Figure 8.2: Taffy the Dragon – my friend (see online colour plate)

The dragon evolved rapidly during my next admission and it became clear that he was a symbolic representation of the guardian angel I had described in 2010. His colour darkened to a stronger shade of 'friendly pink' and, in three successive drawings, he quickly grew in size and demonstrated his essential roles. In the first, he played the referee standing over my arguing conscious and subconscious minds, holding the key that could open the mental barrier between them. In the second, I was shown assailed by various people and agencies in the real world, and the dragon was a friendly guide and protector, leading me from these miseries into a better world. In the third, my conscious and subconscious minds had the 'slings and arrows of outrageous fortune' raining down on them and, while the subconscious cowered in fear from the onslaught, the conscious mind raged at him to stand up and do his duty. Meanwhile, the smiling dragon stands between them calming and holding back the conscious mind while offering a sheltering umbrella to the subconscious (Figure 8.2). Then the most amazing transformation happened: I felt the need to write a poem, and it just flowed from my hand onto paper without planning or editing. In it, the dragon introduced himself as 'Taffy' and said that he was there, inside my mind, to help me whenever needed. In this way, the dragon became a 'person' with whom I could discuss and analyse my problems, and journey with on imaginary adventures of mental discovery. Taffy is a mental construction, a useful tool, but he remains a genuinely compassionate image and, as the poem title says, 'My Friend'.

The two other symbolic figures are more utilitarian, tools to communicate with my conscious and subconscious minds more flexibly and intuitively. 'Dead-Eye' was born in 2014, just an hour after an art therapy session in which I finally admitted the existence of my internal nemesis 'The General', and drew him. I had already realized that 'The General' was an image of how my subconscious saw my conscious mind, but it was shocking to see on paper how frightening one part of my own mind found the other. I felt exhausted and slept for an hour afterwards, but when I woke I 'heard' a strange conversation inside my head:

'Is that *really* how you see me?'

'No, not really…not any more.'

'Well, how do you see me now?'

And, with that, an image blasted into my mind of a Second World War fighter pilot, complete with leather flying helmet and 'Mae West' inflatable life jacket, giving a 'thumbs-up' sign and smiling confidently. I even heard the spoken description: 'Squadron Leader Richard (Dead-Eye Dick) Kidgell, known to his friends as "Dead-Eye", scourge of the black dragons.' He was ridiculously like a hero from a *Boy's Own* magazine, but The General was gone, and has never returned, and my conscious mind has been 'Dead-Eye' ever since (Kidgell 2017). It also gave me a new name for my problems – 'black dragons', and they could be hunted down individually, rather than being tackled as one enormous monster.

'The Prof.', the symbol for my subconscious mind, emerged just as dramatically, about two years later. I had been referred to my local NHS mental health team for cognitive behavioural therapy (CBT), and in my first session the therapist started teaching me how to use mindfulness techniques to block troublesome images from my subconscious. As I left the building, I was hit by a wave of anger so intense that I stumbled backwards against a wall, and a vivid image dominated my vision. It was a picture of a man who looked just like me, wearing a white laboratory coat, seated in a chair with the wall behind filled with shelves of books. He was pointing a finger directly at me, looking furious, saying coldly, 'Don't you DARE start ignoring me again! I am "The Prof." I am half of you and I WILL NOT be locked away again!' From then on, he was a 'person' whom I could visualize and work with. I did not attempt that mindfulness technique again; instead the therapist and I worked out a way to apply CBT techniques to art therapy-type drawings, which proved very effective for me, adding a powerful new weapon to my armoury.

Also in 2014, I drew a simple picture in chalk on black paper showing the present-day 'me' having turned around to see how far I had come (Kidgell 2017). But part-way along the road that stretched to the dark horizon was another figure with his back to me, wreathed in black depression, with his gaze fixed on the past. This image made me realize that part of my mind was trapped in the past events, needing to be rescued and brought into the present. The trouble was that I had no idea how to do this in 2014, but by late 2016 I had the necessary toolkit. I started cautiously, tackling some of the smaller black dragons by facing them on paper, while imagining that I was sending Taffy back to destroy the dragon, and lead my 'missing part' forward through time to rejoin me. I successfully 'defused' several smaller, but still troublesome, bad memories. I felt ready to tackle something more significant, but this would be using a different mode of art therapy.

Working remotely

In 2016 I had to leave a two-week art therapy programme at Combat Stress half-way through because of an emergency at home. Not wishing to lose this treatment opportunity, I kept in touch with the group by simulating the sessions at home, and submitting my artworks to Janice via e-mail, along with comments on the images. This technique worked fairly well for the remaining week of the course, but its effectiveness was severely hampered by the loss of live feedback and face-to-face conversation, especially with the therapist.

The following year I volunteered to be the test subject in a remote art-therapy pilot with Janice. It involved six one-hour, individual sessions, at roughly one-month intervals, using Skype. I was pleasantly surprised to find that the therapy sessions with Janice were very natural and felt almost identical to face-to-face contact. Having a month between Skype therapy sessions could, perhaps, have made it difficult to maintain commitment and impetus, but actually I found that the freedom increased my interest, and encouraged me to be bolder in my work. I could take longer making an image, and I could tell complex stories in poetry, prose, or through a series of linked drawings, similar to a comic book, rather than being restricted to 'snapshots' depicting a single event, or my emotions at one point in time.

When I wrote in prose, I deliberately did not plan ahead or edit the work. As with art-therapy images, it was essential to let my subconscious express itself without censorship by my conscious mind. Pictures would form in my mind, which I would record in writing. The written images were more of a movie, with different events, ideas and emotions rising and falling, and new ones emerging as the story progressed. It could be a frightening and shocking process at times, but also exhilarating as suppressed emotions and memories were released by my subconscious.

For the first two months I concentrated on a target that I had started to address during my last admission at Combat Stress. This was a particularly fearsome black dragon – the memory of working on the gun target at the air weapons range when I was in the RAF over 30 years earlier. In my mind, I sent off Taffy loaded with weapons to kill the black dragon and rescue my younger self – and then never used him! Incorporating tools I had gained from CBT, I persuaded my subconscious mind to relive, on paper, its experience of going out to repair the targets. I was astonished by the result. I honestly had no idea that part of me had felt so afraid, helpless and lonely whilst out there. My conscious memories were very different to my subconscious ones. No wonder I had re-experienced those events in flashbacks! I drew a picture showing the present me having killed the black dragon, with the part of me that had been trapped in the past running towards my present self (Figure 8.3). And then I felt, almost physically, the memory suddenly drop back to its proper place in the past – it was suddenly far away, less distinct and much less threatening. And it has stayed there ever since.

Figure 8.3: Successfully killing the black dragon

Figure 8.4: Outside the 'Conference Hotel'

In succeeding months, Janice gave me themes to explore, for example 'Refresh' and 'Round Table'. I also employed two symbols that had appeared in art therapy several months before, which now became important tools. These were places inside my mind where I could meet and discuss my problems with my symbolic figures. One is the vast 'Conference Hotel'. It represents my mind, and includes special rooms where I can encounter all my hopes, dreams, memories and forgotten experiences. The other is a comfortable living room with Edwardian decor and a comforting fire burning in the hearth. This room is reserved for Taffy and me to discuss my life and mental situation – in effect, self-therapy.

My next task was to find out how it was that I had left the range showing mild, possibly recoverable, effects of trauma, and then went to officer training, leaving there with pronounced psychological symptoms. I had kept myself functioning by imposing severe self-discipline, which had just made the problem worse. I started by making a drawing of Taffy and myself standing outside the Conference Hotel preparing to enter and start our adventure (Figure 8.4), but after that I used mainly written images. The story was too complex and extended in time for drawings to be sufficient. Surprisingly The Prof., the symbol of my subconscious mind, behaved arrogantly as though he was morally superior because he was a victim and not a cause in this issue.

When I needed to bring all my faculties to bear (for example, to analyse my situation and make a plan of action), I would assemble my personal avatar and all three symbolic figures together in a meeting room of the Conference Hotel. By this means I brought my full mind, including the symbolic subconscious, to a co-operative alertness simultaneously, all focused on the same objective. It made a very powerful combination. In the meeting room, we would all sit around a big, round wooden table and have tea and biscuits to keep us all calm and co-operative. Interestingly, the mental act of imagining a tea-break actually left me feeling calmer and more refreshed in the real world, too. I didn't hesitate to let some humour creep into the story, either, because it stopped me becoming over-anxious and blocking the process. The analogy with King Arthur's Round Table of legend was obvious, and the Taffy character was used to both exploit and soften this with humour. The resolution came when, via my avatar, I was led to re-experience a particular memory that I had almost forgotten. It showed that the key decision, from which everything else derived, namely to stay in officer training no matter what, even though I had doubts, was not a logical one – it was an emotional and powerful imperative from the subconscious mind, based on notions of honour and courage. And it might have succeeded, if I had not sustained a physical injury.

Since the Round Table, my subconscious mind has stopped trying to make me feel irrationally guilty and, while I still dissociate, it is easier and less unpleasant to bring the parts of my mind back together again.

Summary

With the help of his compassionate image, Richard has been able to revisit past trauma and retrieve and tolerate previously dissociated emotions. Essential to this process was the emergence and recognition of the conflicting ego states that he was experiencing: the highly critical General, who was later replaced by Dead-Eye as the embodiment of the logical, disciplined, conscious part of himself; and the emotional subconscious self, later manifest as The Prof. Taffy enabled communication between the conflicting factions, with Richard as the whole entity, taking an assertive role in the discussions. In this way Richard worked towards the reintegration of dissociated emotions and experiences that had been split off during trauma.

During the remote art therapy sessions, Richard experimented with the different format and timescale, and produced perhaps his most enriched and insightful pieces of work. This period also marked the end of our therapeutic work together, which provided the impetus for taking the process to a suitable point of closure. His story may offer hope to those who experienced trauma decades ago – progress can be made no matter how far along the journey. Through imagination and creativity, Richard developed effective tools for coping with the psychological aftermath of trauma.

Conclusion

Art therapy has had a profoundly beneficial effect on my condition of PTSD and, consequently, on my condition of life. I am much more at ease with myself than I have been for many years. Through art therapy I have restored a number of important suppressed memories to my life story, and my history now makes more sense. My mind still tends to dissociate under stress, but now I understand better what is happening, and I can use my symbolic images to bring my mind back together faster. When I am distressed or confused, I can resolve issues much quicker by visualizing my personal avatar, my compassionate image and representations meeting together to discuss the problem; and if I am in a stressful situation that I cannot escape (for example, if I have no option but to travel on public transport or walk through a crowd), I can conjure up an image of Taffy standing beside me, offering support and encouragement.

Soon after I started treatment at Combat Stress, their consultant psychiatrist told me that I would probably never be cured – my PTSD was far too well established for that – but they could help me control the symptoms. It took me a while to accept that, but then I thought that if I had received a physical wound, perhaps by stepping on a landmine, I would not have expected to grow a new leg, I would have been given a prosthetic leg that I would have had to master. Why should a psychological wound be different? I will always have disabilities, but art therapy, in effect, has given me the tools to build a mental prosthesis so that I can function better in society, and it prevents me from mentally falling flat on my face too often! I call that a very good result.

References

American Psychiatric Association (2013) *Diagnostic and Statistical Manual of Mental Disorders* (5th edn). Washington, DC: Author.

Busuttil, W. (2017) 'Military Culture Effects on Mental Health and Help-seeking.' In J. Lobban (ed.) *Art Therapy with Military Veterans: Trauma and the Image* (pp.73–88). London: Routledge.

Compassionate Mind Foundation (n.d.) *Building a Compassionate Image.* Accessed at https://compassionatemind.co.uk/uploads/files/building-a-compassionate-image.pdf

Ego State Therapy International (n.d.) *Ego State Therapy.* Accessed on 25/9/2020 at www.egostateinternational.com/ego-state-therapy.php

Forgash, C. and Knipe, J. (2012) 'Integrating EMDR and ego state treatment for clients with trauma disorders.' *Journal of EMDR Practice and Research 6,* 3, 120–128.

Gilbert, P. (2007) *Compassionate Mind Foundation: Introduction, Aims and Objectives.* Accessed on 25/8/2020 at https://compassionatemind.co.uk/uploads/files/background.pdf

Gilbert, P. (2009) 'Introducing compassion-focused therapy.' *Advances in Psychiatric Treatment 15,* 3, 199–208.

Herman, J.L. (1992) *Trauma and Recovery: The Aftermath of Violence – from Domestic Abuse to Political Terror.* New York, NY: Basic Books.

Hoge, C.W., Auchterlonie, J.L. and Milliken, C.S. (2006) 'Mental health problems, use of mental health services, and attrition from military service after returning from deployment to Iraq or Afghanistan.' *Journal of the American Medical Association 295,* 1023–1032.

ISSTD (2018) *Dissociation FAQs.* Accessed at www.isst-d.org/resources/dissociation-faqs

Kidgell, R. (2017) 'Trauma and Dissociation: An Insider's View'. In J. Lobban (ed.) *Art Therapy with Military Veterans: Trauma and the Image* (pp.140–151). London: Routledge.

Lee, D. and James, S. (2012) *The Compassionate Mind Approach to Recovering from Trauma.* London: Constable & Robinson.

Lobban, J. (2017) 'Two minds.' In J. Lobban (ed.) *Art Therapy with Military Veterans: Trauma and the Image* (pp.126–139). London: Routledge.

Mikulincer, M. and Solomon, Z. (1988) 'Attributional style and combat-related posttraumatic stress disorder.' *Journal of Abnormal Psychology 3,* 308–313.

Myers, C.S. (1940) *Shell Shock in France.* Cambridge: Cambridge University Press.

Putnam, F.W. (1989) *Diagnosis and Treatment of Multiple Personality Disorder.* New York, NY: Guilford Press.

Steele, K., van der Hart, O. and Nijenhuis, E.R.S. (2005) 'Phase-orientated treatment for structural dissociation in complex traumatisation: Overcoming trauma-related phobias.' *Journal of Trauma & Dissociation 6,* 3, 11–53.

van der Hart, O., Nijenhuis, E.R.S. and Soloman, R. (2010) 'Dissociation of the personality in complex trauma-related disorders and EMDR: Theoretical considerations.' *Journal of EMDR Practice & Research 4,* 2, 76–92.

Watkins, J.G. and Watkins, H.H. (1997) *Ego States: Theory and Therapy.* New York, NY: W.W. Norton.

9

Culturally Responsive Micro-formulation of Imagery in Trans-diagnostic Treatment of PTSD and Addiction

Gillian Solomon

This chapter introduces a mixed approach to treatment, using cognitive assessment and outcome measures, that emphasizes establishing a strong therapeutic and culturally responsive relationship. Trans-diagnostic use of unconscious imagery of all five senses – sight, sound, feeling, taste and smell – was micro-formulated to map perceptual processing as the dominant processing style in trauma, which integrated image and word, to facilitate cognitive restructuring and evidence change.

The tradition of examining the feasibility of new treatments through the use of a case study is one of the most natural ways clinicians in practice can engage in research. This chapter introduces a South African adolescent, and applies treatment based on Ehlers and Clark's (2000) methodology which has been shown to be effective in treating PTSD (Ehlers et al. 2005). Use is made of cognitive behavioural assessment, with a minimum data set (MDS) at the start of each treatment session. Imagery micro-formulation used a mapping template that with MDS showed positive outcomes of demonstrable psychological change and a reduction in PTSD symptoms of anxiety and depression.

Therapeutic approaches
Ethical practice

Ethical practice places an emphasis on individual responsibility (Kingdon et al. 2017). This emphasizes both the strengths and limitations of the diagnosis systems, urging their use by all healthcare professions to achieve the 'greater good', as assessment and outcome measures are crucial to feedback on progress and collaborative decision-making. The changes in the DSM from version I (1952) through DSM-5 (2013) show how assessment of anxiety has been modified, with the earlier and latest versions now more in alignment:

- DSM-I (1952): three disorders (anxiety reaction, phobic reaction, obsessive-compulsive reaction).

- DSM-II (1968): three disorders (anxiety neurosis, phobic neurosis, obsessive-compulsive neurosis).

- DSM-III (1980) and DSM-III-R (1987): nine disorders.

- DSM-IV (1994) and DSM-IV-TR (2000): 12 disorders, with various subtypes and specifier.

- DSM-5 (2013): disorders have become divided into three categories: Anxiety Disorders (11 disorders), Obsessive-Compulsive and Related Disorders (nine disorders), Trauma- and Stressor-Related Disorders (seven disorders). A total of 27 disorders (and numerous subtypes) across these three broad categories.

Clear, democratic, cost-effective treatment

Cognitive therapy is preferred by health providers as it is time-limited and structured. Management must be cost-effective and must be inclusive of the client. Permission must be obtained before treatment is commenced, and may or may not be given. Accountability is demonstrated by showing clear evidence of progress. Assessment and diagnosis of each disorder provides clarity about what is being treated over how many sessions and how. An accompanying diagram shared with and explained to the client illustrates the case formulation for each disorder, and a flexible number of sessions is planned. Clients often may make adequate progress over five sessions or may need as many as ten. This planned commitment ensures accountability to the client and ensures that the cost implications are monitored on behalf of the tax payer and health provider.

The minimum data set

The minimum data set (MDS) scores show levels of anxiety or depression, and therapists gather evidence through keeping records, case notes, video or audio recordings, rating scales (CTRS) and details of client satisfaction and feedback. These provide continuous monitoring of the effectiveness of treatment and demonstrate the ways clients improve.

Prior to the development of the cognitive model by Aaron Beck (Beck et al. 1979), treatment was loosely defined and didn't seek to demonstrate measurable progress. Therapists working in this way avoided treating many serious mental health disorders because they had no way of assessing how they function, or of analysing what they consisted of or how they commenced and generally did not produce recorded evidence of change. This meant that treatment could not be well budgeted and had no time limit. On this basis it was often deemed unaffordable. Whilst these DSM updates are in general use in many mental health settings, this system of treatment or access to psychological therapy has not been made available in South Africa, and assessment remains based upon methodologies that have been superseded.

Such lack of structure can cause insecurity, for both client and therapist. This latest update in the use of assessment and outcome measures is important as the development of multicultural care that is inclusive has a strong working alliance. The client's needs are crucial to feedback on progress and collaborative decision-making.

Simple data collection

The therapist takes a disorder-specific measurement at the start of treatment to get a fuller and more objective picture of a client's well-being and status. Therapists unaccustomed to measurement data might imagine these are cumbersome and complicated. In practice the process is simple. Weekly simple measures such as minimum dataset questionnaires PHQ9 and GAD 7 at the beginning of each session help monitor progress and coordinate and guide session content. Clients are reassured that MDS are not merely numbers but represent week-by-week information on personal progress.

Therapists often use the data gathered to inform the session, asking, 'I noticed that your scores have improved this week. Does this make sense, and are there reasons why they fit with what you've experienced? Is there something we should include and discuss this week?' Although treatment is a structured process, it is always both a scientific and creative endeavour, which is enhanced by feedback and spontaneous responses to the client's awareness of week-to-week change and progress towards negotiated goals. In this way clients become confident and curious about why and how change happens. They move quickly to being able to answer and understand the subjective meaning of questionnaires with confidence. This encourages guided discovery, progress, inquiry and reflection about the outcomes. Clients are encouraged to offer feedback at the start of the session to understand themselves, the world and relationships to others better. This provides vital support and confidence to both therapist and client, showing tangible evidence of progress and change, so that clients become their own therapist.

Formulating PTSD for DSM-5

As we will show in the case study, we moved from perceptual processing in the 'here-and-now' to 'reliving' of traumatic events in order to identify and conceptually process and evaluate thoughts and beliefs about them. This places an emphasis on the actual symptoms reported in the present rather than accounts of past events (Brewin 2005). In the case of 'Ayah', this refocused PTSD assessment around her core experience of intrusive multisensory images of the rape, using techniques to help her associate these beliefs with their impacts, and to restructure unhelpful cognitions and imagery by mapping, and micro-formulation of PTSD imagery (Holmes et al. 2019). Risk-assessment anticipated common co-morbid conditions, including substance use, depression and suicidal tendencies.

Case study: Ayah
Presenting conditions

Ayah is a 15-year-old Swazi girl, living in Johannesburg. She was brought to the clinic by her mother, who reported that she was behaving badly, failing at school and putting herself at risk. A sense of self-efficacy on the part of the parents is a critical factor in the success of treatment. In order to enhance her self-efficacy Ayah's mother was asked a number of questions:

- What would you like (or expect) to happen as a result of being here today?

- What are your goals for treatment?

- Do you think this treatment will work?

- What do you think you will need to do for your child to improve?

On this occasion Ayah's mother felt her parenting methods had failed, as her strategies of ignoring Ayah, threats of punishment, and beating had not changed Ayah's behaviour. She experienced a level of hopelessness about this situation, which seems commonplace in stressed single-parent families living in difficult circumstances, leading her to seek therapeutic advice. In the context of South Africa, where mistrust is widespread, this is unusual and to be welcomed and encouraged. The resources available are limited and it's not easy for parents to trust therapists to have the knowledge, skills or multicultural understanding necessary to assist in family difficulties. This approach by the mother provided an opportunity to develop trust and to learn to build a new alliance with cultural competency and specific agreed goals.

Individual consultation with Ayah provided additional details: Ayah's parents were separated. She lived with her mother in cramped conditions in a one-roomed flat in the inner city. Her mother stated that she found shared sleeping quarters were inappropriate for two adult women. Ayah disclosed that ten months previously she had been raped and had not reported this to her parents or the police, as she believed her family would blame her for the rape. She appeared to be suffering from PTSD and depression. Her studies suffered and she began to withdraw from social contact, avoiding friends. She now frequently left home, turned off her mobile and did not say where she was going. She had begun to drink. On returning home from such outings she was frequently punished by her mother, who beat her, saying she was behaving badly and putting herself at risk. She expressed concerns that her daughter was behaving irresponsibly by leaving home and refusing to say when she would be back, where she was going or who she was going with. Her mother complained that Ayah refused to go with her to visit family in Swaziland (Eswatini)[1] at weekends, as was the family custom. In interviews,

---

[1] Swaziland, now called Eswatini, is approximately a two-hour drive from Johannesburg and has one of the worst rates of HIV infection in the world. One in three children is orphaned. The country has a median age of 20.5 years with a life expectancy of just 31.88 years, the lowest documented life expectancy in the world and less than half the world average.

Ayah spoke about her fear of being sent 'home' to care for others and of losing her opportunity to be able to study, and to have an independent life and career in town.

Risk

The use of cognitive assessment procedures and outcome measures in the early sessions with Ayah uncovered a number of co-morbid conditions, including substance use, depression and suicidal tendencies. Assessment of risk revealed that Ayah had experienced suicidal imagery immediately after being raped. These 'flash forward' images were of her own funeral, being buried with her family standing around the graveside crying, regretful that they had let her down. In ongoing weekly treatment sessions, the PHQ9 assessment showed no current suicidal ideation, and agreed that her suicidal tendencies had subsided a few weeks after the attack. However, her negative memories continued to act to trigger, and were maintaining, her current avoidant risky behaviours.

Person-specific functional assessment with culturally sensitive modifications

The Impact of Events Scale (Weiss and Marmar 1997) and The Post-traumatic Diagnostic Scale (PDS: Foa et al. 1997) were used to establish the specific disorder within DSM-5 and ICD-11 guidelines, after which it was important to monitor mood, filling in self-report data that, when administered at each session by use of simple PHQ9 and GAD 7 and phobia scales, tracked weekly progress.

The person-specific functional assessment of Ayah's presenting problem helped to identify the disorder as post-traumatic stress disorder (PTSD). The clinician considered the importance of cognitive therapy guidelines before any adaption was made to existing treatment techniques. No assumptions where made about how a specific cultural belief had informed her subjective experience of distress. Consideration was made of cognitive processing therapy, in response to planning treatment, and engaging in the therapeutic relationship, as collaboration allowed us to include resilience factors, which included Ayah's family and personal African identity through her belief in the authority of ancestors who communicate to her in dreams. This linked to elaborated intrusion (EI) theory (May et al. 2004), which showed how a sensory trigger can maintain anxiety, and avoidance, and its relationship to the craving for alcohol and trauma (PTSD). In Ayah's case this trigger was the smell of sweat (body odour) that reminded her of her rapist. Her behavioural response was to attempt to dispel this smell, and the accompanying negative images, by consuming alcohol. Adaption of modified treatment was not motivated by awareness of Ayah's particular cultural group (Swazi). All clients are regarded as unique individuals. Further research needs to be carried out to identify any dominant themes (Sue et al. 2008).

Unconscious imagery

Multimodal images seen 'in the mind's eye', such as those experienced by Ayah, are almost always unconscious; they invoke memories of situations that caused the original feelings of anxiety. Recent cognitive psychology education shows in what way the combination of substances and negative experiences create thoughts that exert a strong influence on negative behaviour and the sense of wellbeing. Beck and Lazarus have analysed the content and nature of mental imagery-based thoughts (A.T. Beck 1970; Lazarus 1968). Judith Beck's formulations of cognitive therapy imagery and use of mental imagery techniques include: (a) imaginal exposure; (b) the direct modification of the content of aversive imagery-based thoughts; (c) the promotion of adaptive metacognitive reappraisal of imagery; and (d) imagery-based cognitive modification of maladaptive thinking habits (J.S. Beck 1995).

Approaches and methods
Conceptualization diagrams

In this case study we show three conceptualization diagrams. These are individually tailored formulations providing a framework for understanding the patient's difficulties and planning treatment. The first is Beck's longitudinal conceptualization, the second Kolb's learning cycle (Figure 9.1) and the third Ayah's own micro-formulation (Figure 9.2).

PTSD results from experiencing a traumatic event involving death, serious injury or threat to self or others (American Psychiatric Association 2013). Flashbacks (intrusive images) are the hallmark symptom of this disorder (Ehlers and Steil 1995; Ehlers et al. 2005; Speckens et al. 2007) and consist of vivid and emotional memories of the trauma, accompanied by a strong sense of current threat or 'here-and-now-ness' (Holmes and Mathews 2010). Current cognitive information processing theories of PTSD (Brewin et al. 1996; Ehlers and Clark 2000) are based upon the idea that intrusive images develop due to impaired information processing during the traumatic event (Holmes and Bourne 2008). Many studies have therefore explored the intrusive nature of this mental imagery in PTSD.

Mixed methodology

Measures of anxiety and depression monitored were taken in each session (PHQ9 and GAD7) and additional narrative techniques were used (White and Epston 1990) (the author trained at the Adelaide Narrative Therapy Centre, Australia, in 2000 with Michael White and continues to use narrative methods) as they did not assume Western cultural norms, and helped Ayah feel less marginalized and isolated. Information was gathered about:

- the nature of the trauma memory and the extent to which it is fragmented or coherent

- emotional hot spots

- problematic cognitive-behavioural coping strategies that were contributing to the maintenance of symptoms.

Ehlers and Clark's (2000) cognitive therapy (CT) for PTSD was integrated with the Coping with Stress Curriculum: CBT for PTSD in Adolescents Program, tailored specifically for inner-city adolescents (Rosenberg et al. 2005).

Participation

The therapy was properly supervised. Written consent was obtained to participate in terms of prescribed ethical procedures. Ayah met DSM-5 criteria for PTSD, and inclusion criteria for age, was fluent in English, siSwati and Zulu. There were no co-morbid acute conditions, she had a realistic appraisal of her stresses and triggers and was able to travel to the clinic from school. She requested treatment alone, which was agreed by her mother. The limitations of her specific family and environmental circumstances were taken into consideration.

Challenges

Few existing evidence-based conventions and techniques have been developed to provide guidelines for this work in South Africa. Exceptions are Padmanabhanunni and Edwards (2013). Trauma-focused CBT is the most widely replicated treatment for children and adolescents, as it emphasizes exposure through creation of a trauma narrative (Deblinger et al. 2006). The Ehlers and Clark (2000) protocol illustrates how evidence can be collected despite challenges and difficult circumstances. This flexible, formulation-driven treatment model became modified by the CBT for PTSD in Adolescents Program, tailored specifically for adolescents (Jankowski et al. 2012). The decision to include cognitive restructuring as a primary therapeutic component was made to emphasize coping skills, and every effort was made to ensure the client was exercising wise choices about her ongoing exposure to community and other environmental stressors in South Africa.

Recent studies (Hofmann et al. 2012) show we can improve the efficiency and effectiveness of CBT before modifying existing treatment to be more culturally sensitive and assess how much of the individual's presenting problems are linked to cultural identity. The person-specific functional assessment of the presenting problem was identified using routine outcome questionnaires, which were subject to Ayah's individualized case formulation. Ongoing feedback allowed us to align our work with her personal and cultural goals, enabling us to uncover possible obstacles. In this way, therapists can identify and resolve problems as treatment progresses, making adjustments to protocol-driven treatments when necessary.

Ayah's initial stated goals for therapy were:

- to be 'normal' again

- to be more in control

- to resume her relationships with friends

- to improve her schoolwork.

Treatment and application

Ayah attended nine sessions, consisting of two 90-minute sessions with her mother over a two-week period. The remaining sessions (60–90 minutes each) were treatment sessions. After initial assessment, it was decided to use treatment techniques based on mental imagery.

Mapping

To guide the therapist in the use of imagery Holmes et al. (2019) offer a detailed, four-session assessment (known as 'mapping') to explore the client's presenting difficulties. This assessment takes a cognitive-behavioural approach, consistent with Beck's longitudinal case conceptualization. Beck's longitudinal cognitive case conceptualization is the basic process where therapist and client work collaboratively to map a diagram to describe the clients' predisposing, precipitating, protective and perpetuating factors in a coherent, and meaningful way.

In order to give the client the opportunity to lead the way, Ayah was asked which issue she would like to begin with in the here-and-now. She identified her rape as the dominant issue which triggered her current problem. The micro-formulation map revealed, contextualized and made sense of her autobiographical memories, and that clarified, ordered and facilitated her prioritizing our work and direction. Other important images that contributed to anxiety, fear of being alone at 'home', exposure to poverty and illness in Swaziland, and being punished were discussed in her order of priority.

Conceptualizing PTSD

We know that intrusive, affect-laden imagery is key to post-traumatic stress disorder (Ehlers and Clark 2000) and social phobia (Hirsch et al. 2003). Imagery can feel very real, compelling and distressing to patients. Also, depressed patients can experience negative intrusive imagery of past trauma (Kuyken and Brewin 1995). Ayah was avoiding her memories of being attacked because her anxiety about the event cued and triggered, in a situational and interoceptive way, her thoughts of 'I'm not safe', 'The world is dangerous', 'I may be attacked again'. This in turn triggered her fear and avoidance of situations she was previously able to manage: her studies, walking to school, trusting friends. These anxious thought processes led to an intolerance of uncertainty and emotional biases, which caused heightened arousal, and the development of safety behaviours, including the compulsion to search for an alcoholic drink to escape. This was causing her to see herself as a victim, unsafe and vulnerable, which was undermining her current goal to be 'normal'.

Multisensory imagery

Not all images are visual, and it is important that we make this clear as part of the therapeutic process. The experience of flashbacks can be a picture in the mind's eye, or may be experienced as a single sense (sight, sound, taste, smell or somatic sensation) or in more than one sense (e.g. in this case study, the visual image of the attacker, plus the sound of his voice, the smell of his body odour, and sensation of being hurt). Because images are individual and subjective, they can be unclear, momentary or lasting, both negative or positive, and can involve any of the five senses, alone or in combination; individuals may need to be prompted to describe their experience. Imagery-based cognitions can vary in vividness, emotional arousal, and in the subjective impact that imagery has on their feelings and behaviour (Deeprose and Holmes 2010; Holmes and Mathews 2010).

Evidence-based practice

Art therapy asks the responsible therapist to embrace both art and science in order to advance the field:

> The research-informed and diagnostically driven basis of evidence based practice EBP, coupled with diminishing resources and diagnostically determined treatment frameworks in mental health care, now requires art therapists to integrate a more diagnostic approach to assessment without losing their empathic response to the individual. (Koci et al. 2012)

The premise of this chapter is that all techniques, whether they are formulation or change techniques, must be simple and easy to learn for both therapist and patient. The repeated practising of new skills and supportive reflective techniques must bring about change in a systematic way, as illustrated in Kolb's learning cycle (Figure 9.1). This must allow the behavioural and emotional change to take place, as is essential to the learning of new skills and to ethical practices.

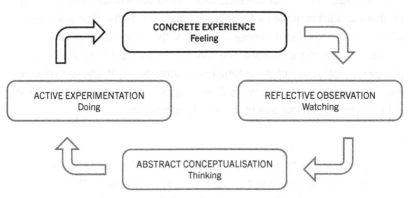

Figure 9.1: Kolb's learning cycle (Kolb 2014)

Holmes et al. (2019) suggest the following assessment steps:

1. Provide a clear definition that explains its multisensory nature.

2. Provide an idea of the different sensory types of image the patient experiences and how often they occur.

3. Identify one troublesome key image.

4. Ask the patient to describe this image in their own words.

5. Ask why it's so important, and can't be easily ignored.

6. Ask what the patient does in response to the image.

7. Ask about any other important images and their significance.

8. The micro-formulation(s) can then be integrated into the wider case formulation.

Images as an emotional amplifier

Recent neurocognitive research shows that mental imagery has a greater impact on emotion than verbal thoughts, as it acts as an 'emotional amplifier' across disorders (Holmes and Bourne 2008). Because imagery heightens our emotions, we need to consider how the use of multimodal imagery may impact on and maintain anxiety or other emotional disorders. Trauma-related, intrusive, clinically significant images are found to occur across different mental disorders (Smith, Ratcliff and Norton 2015). Making a series of images that show what happened alerts the therapist to how emotional images contributed to the diagnosis, particularly specific emotion associated with an image, linked affective states and behavioural responses. The choice of where to start is made by techniques employed by the therapist, and the client's choice to make an image or say what they see in their mind's eye will equally depend on the ability of the client, their age, ability to use language, to make logical sense of the feeling being depicted. Ayah chose to describe images seen in her mind's eye, to draw images in a diary, that showed many of her experiences, that she then described in words.

Deciding which image to formulate

Our choice of which image to use will depend upon whatever seems important to the client and is linked to the issue directly connected with the problem being dealt with. The therapist should ask for a description that makes meaning of the client's day-to-day experience. This will be identified by the client and presented in session in order to help the client describe the last time they experienced the image. The therapist should ask about details of perspective, size, placement, line and colour. Information should be elicited on how the image changes over time, the texture, sound, smell and how they communicate feelings and sensations. The therapist should allow the story to emerge in full, in the client's own subjective language. This kind of meaning is idiosyncratic and must not be interpreted in any way by the therapist.

The micro-formulation templates

A micro-formulation template is filled out jointly with the therapist(s) during the assessment phase of the intervention and is used to help identify which intervention strategies to use.

In this case study we used the imagery template provided by Holmes et al. 2019 (Figure 9.2).

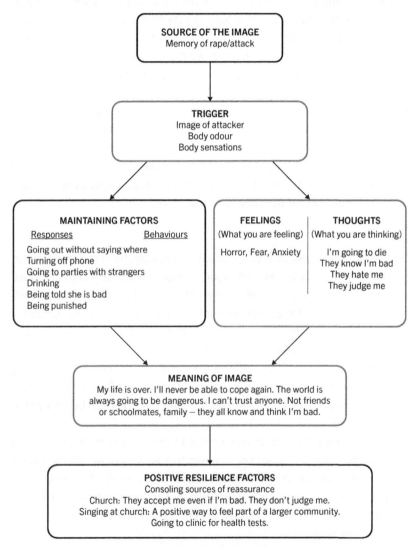

Figure 9.2: Ayah's micro-formulation

The original source of imagery was through Aya's olfactory (smell) intrusions that were a feature of her PTSD. These were triggered by her memory of being assaulted. She could describe the smell and sensations they caused her to feel; she knew they were a memory of the attack and that we could describe the accompanying images.

We asked about accompanying images to understand and make meaning of her emotions of fear and anxiety. They enabled us to understand that her negative thoughts were: 'I'm bad, like my family say', 'What happened to me is my fault', 'I have HIV AIDs. I'm going to die. My life is over.' Her belief was that 'It could happen again. No one can be trusted, I'm not safe.' These images were powerful. In addition, she had been socialized to believe she was bad and needed to be punished, beaten to keep her good. She had not described these images to anyone; they had been avoided. She had been unable to admit to having them. She 'ran away' by engaging in her avoidant behaviour, going out, seeking distractions, indulging in alcohol to soften her anxiety and make her feel 'more mellow'. Once we understood these thoughts and feelings they could be changed by various therapeutic exercises, transformed from negative to positive.

Resilience

'Resilience' and 'strength' are psychological processes that enable a person to think and act in a positive way, an important aspect of case conceptualization. It is unlikely that patients report their strengths spontaneously, so they must be asked about them in case conceptualization. The client commonly assumes that 'the negative problem' is the only experience relevant to the therapist in treatment, and therapists must ask clients directly about what they view as strengths and resilience factors. Described by narrative approaches as 'taking-it-back practices' (White and Epston 1990), this avoids a (totalizing) all or nothing description of the client as being a victim and powerless.

Ayah identified her act of going alone to the clinic to be tested for HIV AIDS as a positive action. Her test was negative. As a narrative 'taking-it-back practice', we asked what this meant about her, as an excellent example of her strength and not behaving as a victim. She replied it meant that she was able to start to regain control of her life and contradicted the negative imagery of a person who is helpless.

The therapist utilized Ayah's positive actions to conduct image-based behavioural experiments (BE) and cognitive restructuring (CR), assisting her to make similar significant changes to other negative images, reformulating them as positive events. This consolidated her resilience and belief that she was a person capable of achieving her initial stated goals for therapy of to be 'normal' again, more in control, to resume her relationships with friends and improve her schoolwork.

Conclusion

This case study has illustrated the use of imagery-based techniques and of evidence-based monitoring of treatment effectiveness. Although traditional therapeutic techniques are often less structured, it is necessary to be able to assess and offer short-term, affordable, ethical treatment and demonstrate its effectiveness. The treatment illustrated was relatively short-term and discrete. This allows the client to return to treatment at a future date, laying the groundwork for lifetime progress.

This mixed approach to treatment delivers three major benefits:

1. Because the assessment was conducted through collection and understanding of data, as relevant and important to all psychotherapists required to conform to competencies guidelines, we were able to communicate findings in a meaningful way to normalize and socialize clients, colleagues and non-researchers.

2. The therapeutic relationship is respectful, and culturally responsive, in line with the client's personal religion and spiritual orientation. This includes both images seen in the mind's eye and those made through transformation of materials. The therapist and client shared a professional and ethical relationship within which each could learn new skills and dispel cultural and racial discrimination linked to negative psychological outcomes (Asnaani et al. 2009).

3. This 'collaborative empiricism' resulted in a treatment plan based upon a structured model that showed why and how change happened through data collection and agreed goals.

References

American Psychiatric Association (2013) *Diagnostic and Statistical Manual of Mental Disorders* (5th edn). Washington, DC: Author.
Asnaani, A., Gutner, C.A., Hinton, D.E. and Hofmann, S.G. (2009) 'Panic disorder, panic attacks and panic attack symptoms across race-ethnic groups: Results of the collaborative psychiatric epidemiology studies.' *CNS Neuroscience and Therapeutics 15*, 3, 249–254.

Beck, A.T. (1970) 'Cognitive therapy: Nature and relation to behavior therapy.' *Behavior Therapy 1*, 2, 184–200.

Beck, A.T., Shaw, B., Rush, A. and Emery, G. (1979) *Cognitive Theory of Depression*. New York, NY: Guilford Press.

Beck, J.S. (1995) *Cognitive Behaviour Therapy: Basics and Beyond*. New York, NY: Guilford Press.

Brewin, C.R. (2005) 'Systematic review of screening instruments for adults at risk of PTSD.' *Journal of Traumatic Stress 18*, 1, 53–62.

Brewin, C.R., Hunter, E., Carroll, F. and Tata, P. (1996) 'Intrusive memories in depression: An index of schema activation?' *Psychological Medicine 26*, 6, 1271–1276.

Deblinger, E., Mannarino, A.P., Cohen, J.A. and Steer, R. (2006) 'A follow-up study of a multisite, randomized, controlled trial for children with sexual abuse-related PTSD symptoms.' *Journal of the American Academy of Child and Adolescent Psychiatry 45*, 12, 1474–1484.

Deeprose, C. and Holmes, E. (2010) 'An exploration of prospective imagery: The Impact of Future Events Scale.' *Behavioural and Cognitive Psychotherapy 38*, 2, 201–209.

Ehlers, A. and Clark, D.M. (2000) 'A cognitive model of posttraumatic stress disorder.' *Behaviour Research and Therapy 38*, 4, 319–345.

Ehlers, A., Clark, D.M., Hackmann, A., McManus, F. and Fennell, M. (2005) 'Cognitive therapy for post-traumatic stress disorder: Development and evaluation.' *Behaviour Research and Therapy 43*, 4, 413–431.

Ehlers, A. and Steil, R. (1995) 'Maintenance of intrusive memories in posttraumatic stress disorder: A cognitive approach.' *Behavioural and Cognitive Psychotherapy 23*, 3, 217–249.

Foa, E.B., Cashman, L., Jaycox, L. and Perry, K. (1997) 'The validation of a self-report measure of a post-traumatic stress disorder: The post traumatic diagnostic scale.' *Psychological Assessment 9*, 4, 445–451.

Hirsch, C.R., Clark, D.M., Mathews, A. and Williams, R. (2003) 'Self-images play a causal role in social phobia.' *Behaviour Research and Therapy 41*, 8, 909–921.

Hofmann, S.G., Asnaani, A., Vonk, I.J.J., Sawyer, A.T. and Fang, A. (2012) 'The efficacy of cognitive behavioral therapy: A review of meta-analyses.' *Cognitive Therapy and Research 36*, 427–440.

Holmes, E.A. and Bourne, C. (2008) 'Inducing and modulating intrusive emotional memories: A review of the trauma film paradigm.' *Acta Psychologica 127*, 3, 553–566.

Holmes, E.A., Hales, S.A., Young, K. and Di Simplicio, M. (2019) *Imagery-based Cognitive Therapy for Bipolar Disorder and Mood Instability*. New York, NY: Guilford Press.

Holmes, E.A. and Mathews, A. (2010) 'Mental imagery in emotion and emotional disorders.' *Clinical Psychology Review 30*, 3, 349–362.

Jankowski, M.K., Rosenberg, H.J., Rosenberg, S.D. and Mueser, K. (2012) *Coping with Stress: A CBT Program for Teens with Trauma*. Center City, MN: Hazelden.

Kingdon, D., McGuire, N., Stalmeisters, D. and Townend, M. (2017) *CBT Values and Ethics*. Los Angeles, CA: Sage.

Koci, A.F., McFarlane, J., Nava, A., Gilroy, H. and Maddoux, J. (2012) 'Informing practice regarding marginalization: The application of the Koci Marginality Index.' *Issues in Mental Health Nursing 33*, 12, 858–863.

Kolb, D. (2014) *Experiential Learning: Experience as the Source of Learning and Development*. Englewood Cliffs, NJ: Prentice Hall.

Kuyken, W. and Brewin, C.R. (1995) 'Autobiographical memory functioning in depression and reports of early abuse.' *Journal of Abnormal Psychology 104*, 4, 585–591.

Lazarus, A.A. (1968) 'Aversion therapy and sensory modalities: Clinical impressions.' *Perceptual and Motor Skills 27*, 1, 178.

May, J., Andrade, J., Panabokke, N. and Kavanagh, D. (2004) 'Images of desire: Cognitive models for craving.' *Memory 12*, 4, 447–461.

Padmanabhanunni, A. and Edwards, D.J.A. (2013) 'Treating the psychological sequelae of proactive drug-facilitated sexual assault: Knowledge building through systematic case-based research.' *Behavioural and Cognitive Psychotherapy 41*, 371–375.

Rosenberg, J.I., Arcinue, F., Getzelman, M.A. and Oren, C.Z. (2005) 'An exploratory look at students' experiences of problematic peers in academic professional psychology programs.' *Professional Psychology: Research and Practice 36*, 6, 665–673.

Smith, A.H., Ratcliff, C.G. and Norton, P.J. (2015) 'Transdiagnostic Cognitive Assessment and Case Formulation for Anxiety: A New Approach.' In G.P. Brown and D.A. Clark (eds) *Assessment in Cognitive Therapy* (pp.197–220). New York, NY: Guilford Press.

Speckens, A.E.M., Hackmann, A., Ehlers, A. and Cuthbert, B. (2007) 'Imagery special issue: Intrusive images and memories of earlier adverse events in patients with obsessive compulsive disorder.' *Journal of Behavior Therapy and Experimental Psychiatry 38*, 4, 411–422.

Sue, S., Zane, N., Gordon, C., Nagayama Hall, G.C. and Berger, L.K. (2008) 'The case for cultural competency in psychotherapeutic interventions.' *Annual Review of Psychology 60*, 1, 525–548.

Tarrier, N. (2006) 'An Introduction to Case Formulation and Its Challenges.' In N. Tarrier (ed.) *Case Formulation in Cognitive-behaviour Therapy: The Treatment of Challenging and Complex Cases* (pp.1–11). London: Routledge.

Weiss, D.S. and Marmar, C.R. (1997) 'The Impact of Event Scale–Revised.' In J.P. Wilson, and T.M. Keane (ed.) *Assessing Psychological Trauma and PTSD* (pp.399–411). New York, NY: Guilford Press.

White, M. and Epston, D. (1990) *Narrative Means to Therapeutic Ends*. New York, NY: W.W. Norton.

10

Accessing the Existential Narrative of Trauma Through Non-ordinary States of Consciousness

Tom Barber and Sandra Westland

Introduction: The shattering of trauma

When prolonged or sudden suffering arrives at our door, be it in our early years through neglect, abuse or sudden catastrophic events; or later on in life from war, abuse, assaults, losses or any experience that leaves us feeling overwhelmed and unable to cope, we are shattered. Symptoms and diagnosis of trauma such as post-traumatic stress disorder (PTSD) are identified as intrusive thoughts and images and increased arousal, accompanied by attempts at avoidance and emotional numbing (Joseph 2010). In essence, biologically, psychologically and emotionally, we are shattered.

> Heart racing, sweaty hands, thoughts racing, irritability and edginess. It's taking over my life. My relationship has ended because of how I am, I hate my job and I don't know what to do with myself. I either drink, go to the gym or keep myself busy with work. I don't want to keep being like this but I feel all over the place and quite broken.

These words from an ex-military man after having completed two tours in Afghanistan are an often heard account of people who have spiralled into shatteredness and who cling to addictions or other forms of self-management, as they struggle to gain control of themselves and to make sense of past traumas and where their life has ended up (LaFond Padykula and Conklin 2010; Norman et al. 2007).

Healing can be attempted through many forms: symptom reduction, behavioural change, emotion regulation and speaking about what has happened. However, we have come to notice that without going beneath the biological, psychological and emotional struggles, an authentic reconnection to one's self for long-term healing and growth will remain forever out of reach. There is a paralysis that hinders a return to what is deemed 'normal', because underneath lies existential shatteredness, which touches the very heart and soul of us, and delves deep into the complexities of the mind–body–world connection.

Greening (1997, p.125) describes this well:

> In addition to the physical, neurological and emotional trauma, we experience a fundamental assault on our right to live, on our personal sense of worth, and further, on our sense that the world (including people) basically supports human life. Our relationship with existence itself is shattered. Existence in this sense includes all the meaning structures that tell us we are a valued and viable part of the fabric of life.

Krippner, Pitchford and Davies (2012) illuminate that trauma is an existential demolition of our identity, worldview, beliefs and sense of coherence, and could not be cured by medication or simply by changing negative thoughts into positive ones. They valued the importance of confronting mortality and the necessity of finding meaning in the healing work. Krippner was also involved in a task force exploring a whole-person approach to trauma, addressing the psychological, physical and spiritual aspects of loss and healing (Serlin and Hanson 2015). The main points highlighted are that

> Trauma is a crisis of mortality, meaning, identity and what it means to be human; therefore, existential perspectives are needed; Trauma is about stuckness and numbness…therefore creative, imaginal and movement approaches are needed; Trauma is about fragmentation therefore relational approaches that connect and integrate are needed. (Serlin and Hanson 2015, p.161)

Jacobsen (2006) also conceptualized trauma, using the term 'crises' (du Plock 2010) from the whole-person approach, namely that trauma holds three dimensions: loss, adversity and the opening of existence.

Loss involves direct and physical losses of a specific object or person, psychological losses of a connection with the mind or soul, or existential losses of a relationship with self or other, resulting in grief. Nothing is the same as it was before. There is a loss of felt existence and the exposure of an unfamiliar environment to inhabit with greater awareness of one's own mortality.

In 'crisis as adversity' there is the facing up to the awareness that the world is unpredictable and offers no guarantee of security or consistency (Stolorow 2007). Individuals must learn to accept the existential 'givens' or face living inauthentically.

In the opening up of existence through trauma, there is a crack that, as Jacobson (2006) writes, 'allows the individual to look deep into something very significant. In this way, the crisis becomes existential and can become a personal turning point, a new life possibility' (p.46).

Both these views agree, as do we, that recovering from trauma is akin to an existential disentanglement and an uncovering process that expands one's consciousness, through an embodied awareness. It is only in the revealing of the deeper existential material that we can reconnect to the essential process of the emerging self (May and Yalom 2005) and to meaning. This mobilizes the forming of a new, more in-depth story or narrative, through philosophical and existential language bringing alive a new understanding of reality, the way we think and process situations, and our social connections and relationships (Richert 2010). Otherwise the ordinary 'struggles' of everyday living will be perceived out of context, with the trauma(s) becoming the reference for *all* experiences, thus creating perpetual suffering, despair and hopelessness.

As Dezelic and Ghanoum (2016) describe, pain multiplied by resistance equals suffering but 'Pain multiplied by "Meaning" equals Resilience, Healing, Hope and Transcendence' (p.32).

A narrative is the framework that organizes events. People live their stories and their stories live them, shaping the person and the world in which they live. Distress happens when 'a person's narrative is fragmented or disorganised (Neimeyer and Raskin 2000). When one's story is fragmented or partial, reality becomes disorganised and difficult to cope with…' (Richert 2010, p.38); so true for the trauma sufferer. Narrative work aims to create 'greater opportunities to find satisfaction in living and to cope creatively with challenges' (Richert 2010, p.38), thus a deep personal narrative at the existential level is essential in trauma with a new meaning-laden way to share that which has happened in and after trauma. Ratcliffe (2016, p.177) explains the importance of this:

First-person narratives not only serve to exemplify existential feeling; they also constitute evidence for my account. Most existential feelings do not have established names. So lengthy descriptions, rather than simple statements along the lines of 'I feel x', are often used to express and communicate them.

The existential domain

Unsurprisingly, there are countless philosophies of living that have been debated over hundreds of years. Life is a complex, multi-faceted endeavour. In relation to the daily struggles we face in life, Danish philosopher Søren Kierkegaard (1813–1855), widely considered one of the first 'existentialist philosophers', proposed that each individual is solely responsible for giving meaning to life and living it passionately and sincerely, or 'authentically' – a task that often feels impossible for the trauma sufferer. As Vachon, Bessette and Goyette (2016, p.184) point out: 'Surviving trauma is like waking up in a world that does not make sense anymore.'

German philosopher Martin Heidegger (1889–1976), considered to be one of the most original philosophers of the 20th century, explored in significant depth probably the most fundamental philosophical question: the question of what it means to *be*, or more so what it means to be a human being, for which he coined the term *Dasein* ('being-there'). He proposed that human beings are fundamentally 'beings-in-the-world', in a co-constituted relationship with the world and also situated in relation to time; the movement of human finitude. Trauma often arrests time – one can become frozen within trauma – taking people into an embodied awareness of their own and others' finiteness, be it physical and/or psychological, something that becomes terrifying. Heidegger also highlights the importance of the notion of authenticity in human existence and rising above the herd, or crowd – the norms of society – and in turn the notion of truth, or as Heidegger preferred, 'unconcealment'. Trauma sufferers, in feeling wretched, often try and be 'normal' and do what is expected of them in their daily lives, carrying their distress silently. There is a need for them to unveil the truth of their existence, of their trauma, of their life, admitting these truths most importantly to themselves.

The French philosopher Jean-Paul Sartre (1905–1980) also emphasized living and being authentic, this being dominant in his early work *Being and Nothingness* (1943). Along with fellow existentialist philosopher Simone de Beauvoir (1908–1986), Sartre explored the conflict between living in inauthentic 'conformity', termed *mauvaise foi*, literally meaning 'bad faith', and living an 'authentic' way of being. The idea of living in 'bad faith' is apparent when someone pretends (to themselves and others) that they are 'fine' or 'ok' or downplays the impact of their traumatic experiences on their lives and themselves.

Within this, we also frequently hear after a trauma experience, 'I just don't know who I am any more... Nothing makes any sense to me.' This is a terrifying awareness, but one that Sartre views as being human, because we actually exist within an overall condition of nothingness (no-thing-ness), trying to be some-thing, searching to define who we are. It is within this dance (between authentic and inauthentic living) that a reality is formed, and it is one where coping with living feels, at the very least, possible.

In our work, we so often, through imagery, hear clients who experienced considerable trauma as a child talk about their different selves (perhaps a bird of prey ready to attack or a puppy eager to please and be loved), which they project into the world, because if not there would be nothingness...just dark, black, and an overwhelming void. In the face of this, the resilience human beings are able to reach into, as nothingness descends and emerges into their reality, is remarkable. Through accepting nothingness, we can create something. *We* can create ourselves.

In moving to what can be argued as an even more accessible view of what existentially one is faced with through trauma, we turn to the work of Viktor Frankl (1905–1997). Frankl, an Austrian neurologist and psychiatrist, was the founder of a form of existential analysis he called 'logotherapy'. He described in detail in his best-selling book *Man's Search for Meaning* (1984) his experiences of the Holocaust as a prisoner in numerous concentration camps, including Auschwitz. During his incarceration he witnessed first-hand the importance of finding meaning in one's life, even in the direst of situations. Frankl writes how the underlying grasp of a sense of hope played a major role in whether his fellow inmates survived or withered away. As he alludes to from a famous quote of German philosopher Friedrich Nietzsche (1844–1900), 'Those who have a "why" to live, can bear with almost any "how"' (Frankl 1984, p.56). It is this very same sense of hope and 'why' that we find missing in those that we have worked with that have suffered trauma.

In the search for meaning there is a call to question the very significance of one's life (Krippner and Paulson 2007). Issues of choice, freedom, responsibility, meaning, tragedy, aloneness and alienation (all prevalent when grappling with the aftermath of traumatic suffering) are an essential source of self-exploration, where there is the possibility of restoring and authentically coming to terms with life. An arduous but freeing journey.

Kierkegaard, Heidegger, Sartre and Frankl are all proponents of the notions of authenticity, truth and the importance of meaning. But, for the trauma survivor, these ideas can often be somewhat abstract in relation to their continued struggle. What they are often more closely concerned with, or have come to face, can be found through the work of American existential psychiatrist Irvin Yalom (1931–), who offers an exploration into four pertinent and accessible areas of struggle that can help them find the words to form their story.

Yalom (1980, p.8) poses 'certain ultimate concerns, certain intrinsic properties that are a part, and an inescapable part, of the human being's existence in the world', that can be described as the 'givens of existence'. These facts of life, from which there is no escape, are *death, freedom, isolation* and *meaninglessness*, and they offer a route into finding the existential narrative that a trauma survivor needs to both confront and embrace.

For Yalom, the first core existential conflict is the tension between the new found awareness of the inevitability of death, and the wish to continue to exist in the world, creating death anxiety. What is even more challenging however, is the fear of *ceasing to be*, or as Yalom (1980, p.43) describes, 'obliteration, extinction, annihilation'. Out of this 'One dreads (or is anxious about) losing oneself and becoming nothingness' (p.43). The depth of death and annihilation anxiety in trauma is profound. An embodied 'dread' that Kierkegaard describes as a fear of *no*-thing. The dread of losing oneself and becoming nothing 'attacks us from all sides' (May 1977, p.207). The sufferer is consistently plagued with this intense anxiety that makes no sense and thus cannot be confronted, which creates further anxiety and a sense of helplessness. Without exploring and making sense of such intense feelings the trauma narrative is missing a vital part of the authentic story.

Yalom's second existential given is freedom and responsibility. That is the responsibility that we are free to choose what we do and don't do – authorship – and create our own life. We are free and responsible for how we relate to given situations, events, people and our struggles. Critically, as we move into a new era of understanding through neuropsychological research, Caruso and Flanangan (2018) explore how the development of neuroscience plays a major role in existential thinking about freedom and responsibility, challenging who actually is in charge – our left and right hemispheres, with their interrelated neural networks and systems, or our mind that crafts a narrative and sense of self in a social world. Research and debate will continue for some time to come, but ultimately, we need to recognize that the taking of responsibility for ourselves is crucial in our life if we are to live authentically. If I make a mistake, it was me that did this, be it through my brain's neural systems creating the feeling of anxiety, or being distracted by somebody else. If I reacted in a certain way, it was I that did the reacting.[1]

This taking of responsibility for oneself can be challenging to explore. In trauma there is often the encounter of being anchored into a position of intense justified anger, as what happened was not one's fault, versus feeling profound guilt because of over-responsibility, versus a sense of bewilderment for it not being possible to apportion responsibility or blame to anybody at all. However, as an adult we *are* choosing *a* position and could in fact choose another. We also need to acknowledge that we need to take responsibility of the present, reclaiming oneself to be responsible to and for our own existence, free to search for our own meaning. As Yalom (1980) writes, responsibility means authorship 'of one's own self, destiny, life predicament, feelings and, if such be the case, one's own suffering' (p.218).

The third ultimate concern for Yalom is that of isolation, identifying three different types. First, interpersonal isolation where we experience the loneliness of being disconnected from other people (for a variety of different reasons, such as geographic location or lack of social skills); feeling alone during the trauma, in the aftermath, and later on feeling isolated because of the awareness that no one else can ever really know how it felt and feels. In trauma there is often a withdrawal from people, which perpetuates further isolation.

Second, the intrapersonal isolation where Yalom alludes to the

---

1   It is important to say here that a child should in no way be held responsible for any kind of abuse they have suffered, or how they reacted to what was happening at the time. Physiologically, psychologically and emotionally, children are not 'response-able' for any trauma that is experienced.

partitioning off of parts of oneself. Often the trauma or parts of the trauma itself are segregated, or the person who experienced the trauma can be separated, creating a feeling of 'it happened to someone else', or there is the partitioning off of aspects of life, such as work life and personal life. Van der Kolk (1993, p.221) describes this positioning, as trauma is 'split off from conscious awareness and to be stored, instead, as visual images or bodily sensations'.

The third type of isolation underlying both these, and belonging to our existence, is known as existential isolation. Yalom (1980, p.10) refers to this as the

> unbridgeable gap between self and others, a gap that exists even in the presence of deeply gratifying interpersonal relationships. One is isolated not only from other beings but, to the extent that one constitutes one's world, from world as well.

When we are confronted with death and with freedom, we inevitably meet existential isolation, connecting with the reality that we enter this world alone, and we leave it alone, yet in the middle we are free to choose. Trauma and its aftermath open us up to this vale of aloneness and it is hard to shake off, once met. There is a need to acknowledge, understand and find peace with this, something that other approaches may omit.

The final existential concern, is the idea of meaninglessness, and Yalom's belief that this existential conflict arises because we have been thrown into a universe that fundamentally has no meaning, a notion gleaned from the earlier philosophers such as Kierkegaard, Heidegger and Sartre. In trauma we are jolted into the questioning of 'What does anything mean any more... Does anything actually really matter?'

Kierkegaard noted this struggle within human beings: on the one hand knowing we are alive can bring great joy, yet we are constantly troubled by the realization that we, as all living things, eventually die, and so what is the point?

This and all the other givens that trauma exposes us to can be somewhat terrifying. Indeed, as the founders of 'terror management theory', Greenberg, Solomon and Pyszczynski (2004) explain, 'Human beings are thus, by virtue of the awareness of death and their relative helplessness and vulnerability, in constant danger of being incapacitated by overwhelming terror' (p.16). Here we see why it is important for the trauma survivor to be privy to the philosophical vocabulary to explain their experience in a way that fully un-conceals the deep and true rich terror of their ordeal, so they can face the reality of their existence, *affirming* that they are indeed alive.

This is the sheer power of being able to create a narrative from within the existential domain, reforming a new worldview, where the sufferer becomes the survivor, the defeated emerges victorious and makes sense of and adjusts to what they have experienced. In turn they become able to connect to a new sense of meaning, aware of the fragility of life, but more resilient to live in the face of it. As Greenberg et al. (2004) further remark, this yearned-for worldview provides them with 'a sense of enduring meaning and a basis for perceiving oneself to be a person of worth within the world of meaning to which one subscribes' (p.17).

In finding the language to describe trauma, we are taken to the very nature of the existential and with this the beginning of a rich descriptive ability. The question arises now about how then do we delve deeper into the experience that trauma has taken us to. May (1969) states that the only way of resolving how one is, is to transform by means of deeper and wider dimensions of consciousness; and it is here that we need to look to non-ordinary states of consciousness.

Non-ordinary states of consciousness and trauma

Stanislav Grof (1931–), one of the world's foremost researchers into non-ordinary states of consciousness, describes how his work through holotropic breathwork is designed to help people at a deep preverbal level to find the images and vocabulary of trauma. 'Holotropic' (meaning wholeness-orientated) states are where 'consciousness is changed qualitatively in a very profound and fundamental way' (Grof 2000, p.2), and it is this that can enable us to access inner stories that previously appeared to have been locked away.

Grof and Grof's (2010) work describes two different forms of trauma. The first is *trauma by commission*, which occurs through external experiences such as physical or sexual abuse, scenarios that have been fear producing, or through destructive ongoing communicative patterns, such as being criticized or ridiculed. The second type of trauma, which highlights the need for a narrative creation, is *trauma by omission*. This can be the result of a distinct lack of positive and nourishing experiences essential for the healthy emotional development of an individual. This is more often found in developmental trauma or complex PTSD, where the environment has involved prolonged abuse or neglect from a young age. Here the narrative is quite empty and incomplete, because you don't know what you don't know. Grof (2000) advises that the 'only way to heal this type of trauma is to offer a corrective experience in the form of supportive physical contact in a holotropic state of consciousness' (p.194).

Medication and traditional trauma-based cognitive behavioural therapeutic techniques look to suppress or manage symptoms and/or intellectualize what has happened. However, if we can engage in the purposeful accessing of non-ordinary states of consciousness we can go beyond, behind, and above what has happened, opening into the depths of the existential narrative.

Non-ordinary states of consciousness are states that can be accessed in a wide variety of circumstances both in and outside of the therapeutic endeavour. They are experiences that bring about an altered state of consciousness. These may be found in the person who is intoxicated, ingesting mind-altering drugs, suffering from a raging infection where hallucinations take place or has experienced a cerebral trauma, where profound mental changes occur. Additionally, we can access these altered states through the consumption of psychedelics, engaging in mystical experiences, meditative states, yoga, shamanic journeys, and religious ecstasies, as well as through hypnosis.

In our trauma work, the use of hypnotic states to access non-ordinary states of consciousness plays a major part in existential narrative creation. This is where greater embodiment, imagery, and words combine for processing and healing.

> ...nonordinary states, when used therapeutically, seek to bring the deeper realms of the psyche into consciousness in order to expand self-knowledge and to integrate memories and experiences from which we have been cut off or which affect us through their actions outside of awareness. (Ablon et al. 1993, p.369)

Hypnosis allows a deeper psychological and embodied level to be reached than talking-based therapies, creating images that can access one's truth. Hypnotic techniques also give us powerful methods of working with the often explosively emotive power of trauma, in a way that is safe and manageable.

Hypnosis is perhaps the classically structured nonordinary state of consciousness, for it comprises both verbal and nonverbal techniques to facilitate and organize the emergence of affectively laden memories and to control the regressive intensity of the investigative and therapeutic processes. (Ablon et al. 1993, p.360)

A client remarks in one of her sessions, 'There is a block right here (pointing to her abdomen area). I don't know what it means but it is something fundamentally important to who and how I am.' We visit her narrative, sitting with being alone as a child and the traumatic events that shaped her and impacted her thinking and feelings about herself, but still this block holds firm, preventing us from even glimpsing at its meaning. There was now a need to connect at a deeper bodily level.

We explored the block through the use of hypnotic imagery, to assist her journey into the depths of her being. It was nothingness. Totally and utterly. The block was protecting her from the awareness of the self-disintegration and annihilation that Yalom speaks of. Through continued work we were able to explore the isolation, death of herself as she *could* have been, and reveal the deeper questions around meaning, purpose and authenticity, that were calling her to question.

What then enables this rich journeying into one's inner world? The moving into a hypnotic trance, which can be through a vast array of methods (Battino and South 2005; Hunter 2010), facilitates two very important shifts in relation to the kind of therapeutic work that opens somebody to their creative self. First, the brain's frequency slows down to 'theta' state where creativity and intuition are at their most potent. Additionally, the conscious 'critical faculty', the part that analyses, solves problems, makes decisions and is critical of the content that it is processing, is quietened. Without this critical factor in full flow, you feel less self-conscious and become more open and able to connect with an embodied creative imagination through heightened awareness of your sensory experiences. In this we are able, safely and with fresh perspective, to revisit experiences of the past.

In Table 10.1 we summarize the various brain states, showing how the lowering of frequencies (via hypnosis) impacts states of consciousness and assists in the accessing of existential material.

Table 10.1: Brain states during hypnosis (reproduced from Barber and Westland 2018)

Brain State	Frequency	State of Consciousness
Gamma	Typically around 40Hz	**The Unity State** Gamma waves can link information from all parts of the brain and are associated with bursts of insight, high-level information processing, and cognitive functioning (learning and memory).
Beta	14–40Hz	**The Conscious Realm** Generally associated with normal waking consciousness and active for effective functioning throughout the day at tasks such as critical thinking, reading, writing, socialization, left-brain thinking activity, logic and reasoning. Also, prone to nagging doubts and self-criticism.
Alpha	8–13Hz	**The Subconscious Gateway** The gateway to the subconscious mind, at the base of conscious awareness. This is relaxing, daydreaming, and in light meditation. Generally associated with right-brain creative thinking activity – a key state for relaxation and mind programming for success and the heightening of imagination, visualization, memory and learning.
Theta	4–8Hz	**The Subconscious Realm** Deeply relaxed, daydreaming, and restorative sleep, with access to insights and deep and raw emotions. The mind's deep-rooted programs are at theta frequency, with experiences of bursts of creativity, insights, vivid visualizations and intuitive ideas. This is the realm of the subconscious that is experienced when drifting into sleep from alpha, and awakening from deep sleep (delta). This is the hypnotic trance state. Theta is a key state for 'reality' or narrative creation through vivid imagery.
Delta	0.5–3.5Hz	**The Unconscious Realm** Is experienced in deep sleep and deep transcendental meditation. Dreamless and associated with no thinking. Delta provides a key state for healing, regeneration and rejuvenation. It is also involved in unconscious bodily functions such as regulating heart beat and digestion.

In summary, our brainwave patterns influence our experience of consciousness. In lowering our brain waves to theta state, we are able to connect with creativity and inspiration, and access the ability for vivid visualizations and embodied feelings. This allows the awareness of different 'lenses' of the narrative, fostering an expansive and richly healing experience, opening to deep learning in relation to the creation of the existential narrative of trauma.

Imagery and the existential narrative

In theta state, a client describes walking along a path in a forest, feeling like their legs are as heavy as lead. They see that ahead, also walking on the path, but quicker in their stride, is their authentic self. They see a cave to the side, and hear a child calling out for help from within the cave. They feel intensely the need to go to the child, and thus meet head on what has happened, as the child is him. He knows this has to be done alone, and that no one else can go there with him. In this we are helping him create the existential narrative that speaks of his *isolation*, being *responsible* for this very action and the meeting of himself and the potential drowning in *meaninglessness*. This profoundly shows the existential narrative forming, illuminating what now needs further exploration.

Such therapeutic use of imagery is well documented (Casement and Sawnson 2012; Hall et al. 2006; Krakow and Zadra 2010; Lu et al. 2009). Our own work (Barber and Westland 2010), has enabled deep insights for clients into the story of their inner struggles, when they have been unable to recognize what it is that is niggling away at them. Well-established methods of psychotherapy that utilize hypnagogic imagery, such as Shorr's (1972, 1974) psycho-imagination therapy (PIT) and Leuner's (1969, 1977) guided affective imagery (GAI), provide wonderfully rich imaginary scenarios with which to access and connect with a person's lived world. In a session of GAI we document in *Thinking Therapeutically* (2010), we guide Anna through a structured visualization of climbing a mountain. Imagining a path leading to the mountain, the journey of climbing the mountain and encountering various obstacles along the way, and then exploring what it is like at the top. This symbolic situation is suggested as relevant to the client's ability to master life challenges, aspirations and the meaning and achievement of life's goals.

For Anna, in this session, we uncovered aspects of living that she struggled with, in particular her disillusionment with life (meaninglessness). We connected her to a story of her traumatic past, and the intense difficulties she has faced. As we processed the imagery session, we connected most to what she felt was missing in her life and her feelings of isolation and her felt inability to connect with herself, others and the world.

Alex, in another imagery session, realized through the exploration of a dream that contained a garden full of statues, that she had learnt as a child not to be emotional and that she should 'swallow' her emotions (and thus herself). She found her story within the dream through dialoguing with the statues and by allowing the dream to unfold through her tears. In being able to describe how her life experiences had impacted her, a new sense of freedom was beginning to take on life. She was able to release her tears and begin reconnecting to her emotional self, lessening her feelings of isolation and her frustrations about her life, thus enabling her to meet and refine her existential narrative.

The way we access imagery and the exploration of each person's world and existential narrative are as richly diverse as the stories that unfold. As well as GAI, PIT and dream exploration, we can utilize other methods. Inner child work offers the opportunity to embody a younger self's existential narrative, a narrative that commonly describes isolation, loss and meaninglessness (in childhood trauma), but which is being falsely lived as 'not being good enough' or 'being unlovable' (for example). In revealing and re-writing, expressing and embodying a more authentic story, there is the reconnection with the emerging self and a new found sense of meaning and potentiality in life.

In parts therapy, where we may utilize imaginary scenarios such as sitting at a table and heading a meeting or being at a party with all our conflicting parts in attendance, we can begin an existential exploration. In bringing forth the voice of each of these parts we can illuminate the once concealed *givens of existence*, and offer access to new understanding and fresh perspective as to the source of our internal turmoil, which we had not previously been consciously connected to.

Exploring in this way offers a powerful source of insight, 'opening up new avenues of experience and initiating a whole new area of creative potential' (van Deurzen and van Deurzen-Smith 2018, p.107). Indeed, van Deurzen and van Deurzen-Smith (2018, pp.107–108) sum up succinctly the potential that using imagery in healing and narrative creation holds:

> Working with images enables us to stray from the verbal narrative that we are used to reciting and that tends to keep us on the straight

and narrow well-known paths. It helps us to stop and ponder and can then take us into new territory. As we grapple with images, we learn to express ourselves in a new language which brings with it new insights and possibilities. When we leave behind our pre-defined, rehearsed stories about our lives, we create a space to really explore what is going on beneath the worn-out narratives and to uncover tacit knowledge about our situation.

Towards belonging

In delving deeper into our inner worlds through non-ordinary states of consciousness, recognizing and embodying the unique experience of the human condition, and in finding new language as we engage in the deepening of ourselves through imagery, we not only reach and embody the internal processes that perpetuate our struggle, but we access who and how we experience life and living, and the meaning we live *by*.

It is only in this that we discover the existential narrative of trauma, re-find our inner resources, find meaning in life and begin the ever-unfolding journey towards authenticity. For survivors of trauma, this equates to *living* and finding a sense of belonging in the world once again, or for some, for the first time. To come home, belong and find a place within oneself, with others and with the world is a place of peacefulness, purpose and possibility. A place where we can live with courage, connection and vulnerability. A place of continual learning and transformation. A place where we can knowingly and authentically *be*.

References

Ablon, S.L., Brown, D.P., Khantzian, E.J. and Mack, J.E. (1993) *Human Feelings: Explorations in Affect Development and Meaning.* London: Routledge.

Barber, T. and Westland, S. (2010) *Thinking Therapeutically: Hypnotic Skills and Strategies Explored.* Carmarthen: Crown House.

Barber, T. and Westland, S. (2018) *Healing from the Other Side.* London: CCTS Publications.

Battino, R. and South, T. (2005) *Ericksonian Approaches: A Comprehensive Manual.* Carmarthen: Crown House.

Caruso, G. and Flanangan, O. (eds) (2018) *Neuroexistentialism: Meaning, Morals and Purpose in the Age of Neuroscience.* New York, NY: Oxford University Press.

Casement, M.D. and Swanson, L.M. (2012) 'A meta-analysis of imagery rehearsal for post-trauma nightmares: Effects on nightmare frequency, sleep quality, and posttraumatic stress.' *Clinical Psychology Review 32*, 6, 566–574.

Dezelic, M.S. and Ghanoum, G. (2016) *Treating Trauma: Healing the Whole Person.* Miami, FL: Pesense Press International.

Du Plock, S. (2010, 17 April) 'Trauma in the relational world: An existential perspective.' Paper presented at the British Psychological Society, Division of Counselling Psychology Conference: Approaching Trauma.

Frankl, V.E. (1984) *Man's Search for Meaning: An Introduction to Logotherapy.* New York, NY: Simon & Schuster.

Greenberg, J., Solomon, S. and Pyszczynski, T. (2004) 'The Cultural Animal: Twenty Years of Terror Management Theory and Research.' In J. Greenberg, S.L. Koole and T. Pyszczynski (eds) *Handbook of Experimental Existential Psychology* (pp.13–34). New York, NY: Guilford Press.

Greening, T. (1997) 'Posttraumatic Stress Disorder: An Existential-humanistic Perspective.' In S. Krippner and S. Powers (eds) *Broken Images Broken Selves: Dissociative Narratives in Clinical Practice.* Washington, DC: Brunner/Mazel.

Grof, S. (2000) *Psychology of the Future: Lessons from Modern Consciousness Research.* New York, NY: State University of New York Press.

Grof, S. and Grof, C. (2010) *Holotropic Breathwork: A New Approach to Self-exploration and Therapy.* New York, NY: State University of New York Press.

Hall, E., Hall, C., Stradling, P. and Young, D. (2006) *Guided Imagery: Creative Interventions in Counselling and Psychotherapy.* London: Sage.

Hunter, C.R. (2010) *The Art of Hypnosis: Mastering Basic Techniques.* Carmarthen: Crown House.

Jacobsen, B. (2006) 'The life crisis in an existential perspective: Can trauma and crisis be seen as an aid in personal development?' *Existential Analysis 17*, 1, 39–54.

Joseph, S. (2010) 'Working with psychological trauma.' *Healthcare Counselling and Psychotherapy Journal 10*, 2, 135–138.

Krakow, B. and Zadra, A. (2010) 'Imagery rehearsal therapy: Principles and practice.' *Sleep Medicine Clinics 5*, 2, 289–298.

Krippner, S. and Paulson, D.S. (2007) *Haunted by Combat: Understanding PTSD in War Veterans Including Women, Reservists, and Those Coming Back from Iraq.* Westport, CT: Praeger Security International.

Krippner, S., Pitchford, D.B. and Davies, J. (2012) *Biographies of Disease: Post-traumatic Stress Disorder.* Santa Barbara, CA: Greenwood Press/ABC-CLIO.

LaFond Padykula, N. and Conklin, P. (2010) 'The self regulation model of attachment trauma and addiction.' *Clinical Social Work Journal 38*, 4, 351–360.

Leuner, H. (1969) 'Guided affective imagery (GAI): A method of intensive psychotherapy.' *American Journal of Psychotherapy 23*, 1, 4–22.

Leuner, H. (1977) 'Guided affective imagery: An account of its development.' *Journal of Mental Imagery 1*, 1, 73–91.

Lu, M., Wagner, A., Van Male, L., Whitehead, A. and Boehnlein, J. (2009) 'Imagery rehearsal therapy for posttraumatic nightmares in U.S. veterans.' *Journal of Traumatic Stress 22*, 236–239.

May, R. (1969) *Love and Will.* New York, NY: W.W. Norton.

May, R. (1977) *The Meaning of Anxiety* (Rev. edn). New York, NY: W.W. Norton.

May, R. and Yalom, I.D. (2005) 'Existential Psychotherapy.' In R.J. Corsini and D. Wedding (eds) *Current Psychotherapies* (7th edn, pp.269–298). Delmont, CA: Brooks/Cole.

Norman, S.B., Tate, S.R., Anderson, K.G. and Brown, S.A. (2007) 'Do trauma history and PTSD symptoms influence addiction relapse context?' *Drug and Alcohol Dependence 90*, 1, 89–96.

Ratcliffe, M. (2016) 'Existential Feeling and Narrative.' In T. Breyer and O. Müller (eds) *Funktionen des Lebendigen.* Berlin, Boston: De Gruyter.

Richert, A.J. (2010) *Integrating Existential and Narrative Therapy: A Theoretical Base for Eclectic Practice.* Pittsburgh, PA: Duquesne University Press.

Sartre, J.P. (1943) *Being and Nothingness.* New York, NY: Philosophical Library.

Serlin, I.A. and Hansen, E. (2015) 'Stanley Krippner: Advocate for Healing Trauma.' In J.A. Davies and D.B. Pitchford (eds) *Stanley Krippner: A Life of Dreams, Myths, and Vision.* Colorado Springs, CO: University Professors Press.

Shorr, J.E. (1972) *Psycho-imagination Therapy: The Integration of Phenomenology and Imagination.* New York, NY: Intercontinental Medical Book Corp.

Shorr, J.E. (1974) *Psychotherapy Through Imagery.* New York, NY: Intercontinental Medical Book Corp.

Stolorow, R.D. (2007) *Trauma and Human Existence: Autobiographical, Psychoanalytic and Philosophical Reflections.* New York, NY and London: The Analytic Press.

Vachon, M., Bessette, P.C. and Goyette, C. (2016) 'Growing from an Invisible Wound: A Humanistic-existential Approach to PTSD.' In G. El-Baalbaki and C. Fortin (eds) *A Multidimensional Approach to Post-traumatic Stress Disorder: From Theory to Practice.* Rijeka, Croatia: IntechOpen.

van der Kolk, B.A. (1993) 'Biological Considerations about Emotions, Trauma, Memory, and the Brain.' In S.L. Ablon, D.P. Brown, E.J. Khantzian and J.E. Mack (eds) *Human Feelings: Explorations in Affect Development and Meaning.* Hillsdale, NJ: The Analytic Press.

van der Kolk, B.A., van der Hart, O. and Marmar, C.R. (1996) 'Dissociation and Information Processing in Posttraumatic Stress Disorder.' In B.A. van der Kolk, A.C. McFarlane and L. Weisaeth (eds) *Traumatic Stress: The Effects of Overwhelming Experience on Mind, Body, and Society* (pp.303–327). New York, NY: Guilford Press.

van Deurzen, E. and van Deurzen-Smith, S. (2018) 'Existential transformative coaching: Working with images, feelings, and values to revitalize the life-world.' *Existential Analysis 29*, 1, 105–122.

Yalom, I. (1980) *Existential Psychotherapy.* New York, NY: Basic Books.

POST-TRAUMATIC GROWTH, RECOVERY AND COMMUNITY

11

Image and Narrative Interventions in a Personality Disorder Specialist Service

Therapeutic Community Dynamics – Tracking the Trend Creatively in a Journey through Experiences

Sheila Butler

Storytelling or telling a story?

There's a difference! There are so many ways to tell a story. This same story could be reported, described and written in so many ways. It is like painting a picture with words. It is not just about weaving a lot of information into the telling, but it is to frame experience in a story so that you can see it a little differently on all its complex levels.

This chapter tells a story through an overview of a Personality Disorder Service and a snapshot of a Clinical Outcome Project. It illustrates and explores the work within the service and the key themes that emerge from the perceptions and experience of service users and therapists. The story, told from a variety of viewpoints, demonstrates the way a therapeutic community model leads to a different kind of therapeutic process and culture, one that has significant value in containing, motivating and improving service users' lives.

The therapeutic community model

A therapeutic community constitutes a managed social setting where relational expectations from the past rekindle in the present and can be challenged, understood and adapted to current reality. Some people when referred to a Personality Disorder Specialist Service in the NHS have no map to guide them or any sense of a direction. The impact of early life trauma and interpersonal difficulties are common presenting features and manifest themselves in complex and ambivalent relationships with professionals. Increasing engagement in the social life of the community shifts the individual's focus away from a state of self-absorption and preoccupation with internal dynamics towards shared co-operative endeavour. In the process of this engagement with others, within a culture of inquiry, members begin to feel increasingly defined and less fearful and avoidant. Interpersonal communication becomes clearer and more intentional. There is an increasing understanding of the role of emotion and its management and the importance of sharing feelings with others. As the capacity for concern and caring develops, members come to know themselves and to know others, better tolerating unwanted destructive aspects of the self and of others. The use of image and narrative is seen as an integral part of the therapeutic community model. The group is considered as the main tool of intervention – a space where people feel heard and seen.

In the Personality Disorder Service in question, the staff group represented a considerable mix of experience and expertise. They came to see that pattern and form will emerge from apparent chaos if there is trust and safety for the process. Establishing and maintaining this containment has been a core component of the therapeutic endeavour; elements include working closely as a team through a weekly facilitated staff support group, a peer supervision group to explore shared thinking and debriefing sessions. Promoting awareness and understanding is a key element of therapeutic work.

Understanding the interface between context, process and outcome

For a number of years now we have been developing the Clinical Outcome Project and collecting data about our service users in an attempt to better understand their condition, their needs and the effects of our evolving therapeutic work. Trying to deduce and identify what is at work in the complex interplay of intentional and accidental processes in the daily life of the therapeutic community is probably unachievable but we can distinguish certain salient elements:

- The structure of the day, when it starts and ends, the breaks dividing sessions where different activities take place is internalized as a primary model for mental organization.

- The benign, consistent and supportive milieu promotes a positive attachment to something good – perhaps for the first time. An attachment relationship with something good increases self-esteem as well as offering a model for identifications.

- The micro-society with its rules of engagement encourages opportunities for the exploration of maladaptive and self-defeating behaviour and promotes more positive and self-affirming interactions. It socializes.

- The dynamics of small and large groups improves self-confidence, openness and connectedness to others leading to insight and empathic development.

- Increasing self-awareness and recognition of the impact of our behaviour on others reduces the impulse to act out with self-harm and demands for care.

We designed the Clinical Outcome Project to take into account the complex psychological and emotional needs of the people referred to the service and it is informed by the current developments in the debates about mental health strategy (Department of Health 2011). For example, in the UK, these include the National Service Framework for Mental Health, the NHS Five Year Forward View (NHS England 2016), which identified improved access to psychological treatments as a key objective, and the New Horizons initiative (Department of Health 2009) setting a vision for the next ten years in mental health to improve the mental health and wellbeing of the population and improve services for people with mental health problems. In addition, the details of the various NICE clinical guidelines, published, or in development, in the area of mental health and wellbeing (i.e. depression, anxiety, borderline personality disorder), including recommendations on interventional procedures, encourage the implementation of guidance and highlight the importance of systematically investigating the outcome of the interventions to support improvements in care across the UK.

The project has a naturalistic framework, utilizing data gathered in 'real-world' practice settings, using practice research-based tools to provide greater understanding of the range of therapeutic community provision and treatment for people with personality disorders. The project also highlights the importance of understanding the interplay between context, process and outcome in therapeutic community practice. It explores the experience and impact of therapeutic intervention and the underlying processes of change using a multidimensional approach to understanding outcomes. The project integrates standardized clinical measures, used at different stages of the clients' contact with the service – from referral to follow-up – and qualitative outcome analysis, providing additional information and insight into the depth and scope of therapeutic practice.

Therapeutic community dynamics: Tracking the trend creatively

When analysing responses from the section of the project that asks about clients' expectations and aspects that they would like to change, it was found that a high proportion felt that they would like to change some aspect of their life to enhance its quality and to develop better coping mechanisms. Most reported that they felt denied a 'normal' life and would like to feel better about themselves but this was not possible due to the enduring, complex and severe emotional and behavioural problems they were experiencing. This issue is important, as this group have been seen in different mental health services for long periods.

The following brief snapshot of people's expectations of therapy encapsulates the wish 'to put life back in order' (in a phrase from a service user):

'Give me an understanding of why I do things the way I do. Improve my self-esteem. To break the cycle of depression and to develop better coping mechanisms.'

'Come to terms with myself, feel integrated into society. Accept the reality of the way things are and get a more realistic idea of how others perceive me.'

'To help me find out the reason why I feel I have to self-harm, then perhaps explore other ways I can cope in a more normal way.'

'My thoughts and feelings to become more positive and for me to feel *that life is worthwhile. To be able to make any major decisions which need making. To gain control back.'*

'Help me develop new coping skills. Help me control my life better. Give me support.'

Community members attend all parts of the therapeutic programme together: The participative group programme

At the end of the therapeutic community (TC) programme, community members joined the Leavers' Group. During their participation in the Leavers' Group, they were interviewed and asked to reflect on their experience of the programme and the changes they experienced during their participation and engagement with the programme.

Qualitative data analysis (Angus and McLeod 2004; McLeod 2000) was systematically carried out to understand how participants have constituted meaning and what TC means to them. This begins with awareness, appreciation and critical analysis of the variety of information available. The interviews present an in-depth description of their experiences, rich in detail from their point of view. The systematic analysis of the data took place in different stages and a thematic analysis was also carried out. Some of the main themes and domains are briefly reported here. Service users' accounts of personal change after TC are presented (at post-treatment). These provide differentiated descriptions of the impact of therapy and reflect separate processes and nuances of people's experiences of their therapeutic process.

Their accounts also indicate the ways they feel they have continued to make changes since ending the TC programme; for example, changes in the way they think about themselves, in the way they relate to others, in the way they behave in different situations or in the way they feel, compared with when they started and ended the TC programme.

Experiencing the 'in-between' and exploring the therapeutic landscapes

We present here an illustration of some of key themes that emerged from the analysis of the interviews (Figure 11.1), and a brief account, in their own words, of ex-members of the community, now in the Leavers' Group, reflecting on their experience of the TC setting and what made a difference for them.

1 The structure of the programme
Organizational and structural factors within the programme, and the structure of the day, provided by aspects of containment and safe boundaries and a primary model for mental organization and self-management.

2 The therapeutic milieu – promoting a positive attachment
Developing trust and hope and feeling safer. The supportive relationship, the respect offered and felt and the perception that someone believes in you.

3 The micro-society with its rules of engagement
Collaborative work, sharing day-to-day tasks, sharing social time together. The experience of being immersed in experiential learning intrinsic to therapeutic community everyday practice. Opportunities for exploration of maladaptive and self-defeating behaviour and promoting more positive self-affirming interactions.

4 TC dynamics, the TC everyday experience and the experiences that have made each participant who they are
The dynamics of small and large groups having an impact on self-confidence, openness and connectedness to others. An understanding of the dilemmas, the suffering and struggles, leading to insight and empathic development.

5 The experiences of the journey – the conditions the community creates and the chance to explore new ways of being oneself in relation to others
The TC culture in practice, the psychosocial environment – working therapeutically with complex problems. The creative potential and the experiential component that takes place.

6 The Change process, increasing self-awareness, insight, self-understanding
The perception of increase in positive feelings and expression of a welcomed state of wellbeing.

Figure 11.1: TC dynamics – key themes

The structure of the programme

This concerns the organizational and structural factors within the programme, and the structure of the day, provided by aspects of containment and safe boundaries and a primary model for mental organization and self-management.

'I think every element in this programme was helpful. From having small groups, to art therapy to the day a week large group and

studio time, these are all fundamental elements to the programme which help and encourage members to interact with each other in a therapeutic and social way.'

'I think the flat authority structure and the encouragement of socializing between members outside the unit mean that I did not feel that I was an alien in the world.'

'Regular reviews to update progress.'

'I think all elements were helpful and they are put into the programme for good reasons. Some elements that you may at first think are not going to be helpful are the ones which you struggle with e.g. social interaction with others. By having these elements with the programme enable you to build up confidence and self-esteem.'

'Small group and amazingly art therapy where you had more time and space.'

The therapeutic milieu

Comments here are about developing trust and hope and feeling safer – the supportive relationship, the respect offered and felt and the perception that someone believes in you.

'Finding other people who understood where I'm coming from.'

'I am more real with people, and surprisingly, people understand that and respond in a genuine way. I express my emotions more freely when I need to.'

'I have a lot more confidence, self-worth and feel that I am someone.'

'I feel that attending the Unit has enabled me to let go of my identity as a service user and to make changes in my life such as being in full-time employment, continuing my education, moving into my own place, driving again and being in a healthier relationship.'

'I will never forget it. The great courage I've seen cannot fail to inspire me for the rest of my life.'

'Therapist who had a wealth of knowledge and understanding about the condition.'

'The therapists who really cared and challenged.'

'Relating to other people's problems.'

'There are people with same condition that understand.'

'Meeting people who had the same experience as you.'

The micro-society

Another key theme emerged from comments about collaborative work, sharing day-to-day tasks and social time together. This included the experience of being immersed in experiential learning intrinsic to therapeutic community everyday practice, and the opportunities for exploration of maladaptive and self-defeating behaviour and promoting more positive self-affirming interactions.

> 'Without the Unit I don't know where I would be today. It offers exactly what I needed: the time and space to build up the trust in others to then be able to deal with issues which have been a struggle. It is not easy, and you have to be 100 per cent committed to the programme. But if you put the work in you will benefit completely.'

> 'I am a lot more confident around others and find it very easy to speak in front of others.'

TC dynamics

Participants commented on the TC everyday experience and the experiences that have made each of them who they are. The dynamics of small and large groups have an impact on self-confidence, openness and connectedness to others. An understanding of the dilemmas, the suffering and struggles leads to insight and empathic development.

> 'The therapy has helped me to recognize that a lot of my self-harm goes back to my upbringing. It has allowed me to open up and share with others my experience throughout my childhood, and how my behaviour reflected that.'

> 'The therapy has helped me to regain my confidence and self-worth. Before starting therapy I felt a complete waste of space, but now I feel I have a right to be here as much as anyone else.'

The experiences of the journey

This theme arose from comments about the TC culture in practice – the conditions the community creates and the chance it provides to explore new ways of being oneself in relation to others. Participants welcomed the psychosocial environment – working therapeutically with complex problems – and the creative potential and the experiential component that takes place.

'Challenging my thinking.'

'Drip, drip feed of this. Ability to look at your behaviour in a new way and not respond in all the old ways.'

'The Unit is amazing! In the middle of it I didn't think so but now I do.'

'It has definitely helped me making me understand and recognize why I felt the need to self-harm. Though very complex I have been able to unravel a lot of thoughts and confusion I had going on. And recognize now that self-harm only offers a temporary fix.'

'Maybe! The Unit gave me the tools to change my life for the better, combined with my willingness to make changes, things are now much better.'

'Art therapy, very useful medium for experiencing things you do not really know, can articulate.'

The Change process

One of the main themes briefly reported here explored service users' accounts of personal change, self-awareness, insight and self-understanding. Comments showed a perception of increase in positive feelings and expression of a welcomed state of wellbeing.

'Changed my life!!!'

'Given up destructive – but marvellous to me for coping for all those years (over time anorexia, self-harm, drinking, bulimia, psychiatric drugs, unhealthy relationships, obsessions of many kinds, on and on and on) – behaviours and instead relating to other people (humans of all kinds).'

'I now have a better understanding of my condition and the impact that it had on my life.'

'Have learnt to react to situations in a different way.'

'Has allowed me to look at areas of my life which I had been unable to before.'

'More real.'

'Helped me being able to see myself from others' perspective and being able to accept that.'

'Take opinions and ideas different to my own into consideration.'

'Socialize, develop social skills.'

'Ask for help, this ability is new and strange but important.'

'Check things out, if I am worried or unsure about things I can check them out with others on the group, friends, etc., instead of turning them into massive obstacles.'

'Able to see reality more closely.'

'I never thought I would but I do feel more positive about what the future may bring. Since leaving the Unit I've thought about work and do want to make something of my life.'

These comments are from the same members whose expectations of therapy at time of referral to the Unit were briefly reported earlier and encapsulate the wish 'to put life back in order'.

The Leavers' Group

After completing the main community programme, members are invited to attend a weekly post-community Leavers' Group. The Leavers' Group is an opportunity to continue the work started in the therapeutic community and gain the building blocks to cope in the outside world. Ending, separation and 'letting go' are important milestones in therapy. It has been shown that the transition between the community and the Leavers' Group is hard for members.

Members participating in the Leavers' Group report the way they value the chance to express any concerns, issues or behavioural patterns in a safe space with the support of the group and the feedback they receive. Sometimes issues and feelings within the group can seem overwhelming, and it is important to address them as and when they occur; the safeness that is present within the therapeutic community is carried through to the Leavers' Group.

Members of the Leavers' Group report what the group means to them.

> 'It may take a few weeks to settle in but it is here for a reason and it is special.'

> 'Feeling safe with the people that you know and have shared with and vice versa.'

> 'Sometimes getting into heated debate and discussion, knowing it is safe to do so.'

> 'Keeping the momentum going on what you have learned and practised.'

> 'To continue with unresolved issues.'

> 'Somewhere to check things out when you feel uncertain and struggling.'

> 'Somewhere that honesty is respected and respectfully given.'

> 'Taking responsibility, deciding for yourself what you want from the group and how you want to use the group and how you want to commit (I think this is different for everyone).'

Experience of art therapy and psychodrama: Integrating image and narrative
Art therapy

We were interested in discovering how members of the therapeutic community experience the process, and what their relationship was with the creative process through the art therapy groups. We found that the ways the themes were being expressed in both large and small therapy groups may be mirrored and reflected pictorially in the art therapy, image-making and group process.

> 'I find it incredibly helpful. It challenges my tendency to want everything to be perfect and encourages me to try new things and

interpret things in a different way, while allowing me to express things that I would have trouble communicating out loud. Having a visible prompt makes it easier to communicate to others how I am thinking and feeling about something.'

'Is good I feel it helps me get my feelings out.'

'The prospect of art was terrifying. However, I have really enjoyed the process, allowing myself to be messy. I look forward to art.'

'Invaluable. It helped me access and express inner horrors and torments – truly hellish ones...it helped get the "inside" out...'

'Art therapy helps me greatly to find my feeling and emotions. It helped me to express them safely and in a more calm and controlled way.'

'Before I started Art therapy it was difficult for me to even find and open my thoughts and feelings.'

Psychodrama

Members reported their experience of psychodrama, and the experience of relating in a TC group setting – the phases, the matrix of identity, the beginning of the recognition of the I and the other, experiencing relating and separation (social interaction vs. social isolation), gaining insight and understanding (feelings being externalized and processed).

'My experience of psychodrama is that it is a really important part of therapeutic work at the Unit, not only for those chosen to do the work but to all those involved, often times being a part of someone else's psychodrama can awaken parts of your own story, your own feelings. Seeing your emotions in a story you form in the moment can be so helpful in opening up feelings and memories long hidden.'

'Emotional, a bit scary very real reliving scenarios and healing.'

'Really powerful!!! A way to look back safely or look forward.'

'Brilliant, intense, thought-provoking, gave me the foundations in which to build myself back up as "me".'

'Incredibly emotional, immediate and provoking. Perhaps the most challenging and revealing aspect of therapy to date.'

The origins of the trauma appear to evolve from complex trauma in early life through the clients' voices. The place of the body in this process is referenced not only as a source of affect. Art therapies and psychodrama help in the process of regulating affect through expression and communication. It is possible to see how image and narrative can help clients represent what has happened but then re-story it.

These accounts suggest that to best capture the dynamic quality of this way of working it is important to systematically consider the interface between context, process and outcome of TC practice and take a closer look at culture.

Through the lens of the therapists

In an intersubjective, relational approach, the therapist and client co-construct the idea/sense of an intermediate area between inner reality and external life. The therapeutic community model provides a space where people with long-standing and complex emotional problems explore a culture of belonging, a culture of openness, a culture of safety, a culture of participation and a culture of empowerment (Haigh 2013) (Figure 11.2).

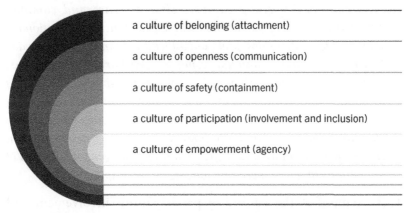

a culture of belonging (attachment)

a culture of openness (communication)

a culture of safety (containment)

a culture of participation (involvement and inclusion)

a culture of empowerment (agency)

Figure 11.2: A culture of five experiences

Through the analysis it has been possible to capture the quality and intensity of therapists' experiences working with complex clients in a group setting and to tap into the complexity of clinicians' reactions. The co-construction of therapeutic landscapes highlighted in the experience of therapists and the importance of an epistemology and methodology to capture the implicit intersubjective dynamics of the clinical interaction in group therapy is hugely challenging and demanding but also hugely rewarding.

Making a difference to people's lives?

'I have seen some impressive and important changes to people's lives – behaviourally, emotionally and relationally. A better understanding of past experiences and their impact can allow a greatly improved sense of self and an increased confidence in the ability to challenge repetition of unhelpful responses and destructive life choices.'

'An experience of being with others and finding acceptance and understanding can have a profoundly positive influence.'

'An atmosphere of openness and respect.'

This exemplifies the culture of openness (communication).

Key themes explored in the groups?

'The community group explores shared issues and common experiences. Some of the themes include past abusive or emotionally unavailable relationships, profound difficulties in managing everyday life, inappropriate emotional responses, self-harming behaviours, intense lack of sense of self, repetition of destructive/negative patterns of relating and behaviours and unbearable feelings of longing and entitlement. The difficulty members have in relating to others is made clear in the group – familiar feelings of exposure, self-preoccupation, shame, fear of failure and the expectation of judgement. Themes of abandonment, greed, need and longing are very apparent.'

This exemplifies the culture of participation (involvement and inclusion).

What changes?

'The more extreme and destructive elements of borderline features are often diminished. The supportive and non-judgemental atmosphere

of the Unit allows, sometimes for the first time, an open and honest discussion of painful and difficult experiences and feelings – which can lead to dramatic adjustments to previously destructive and sabotaging responses to events and interactions.'

'Most notable improvements to impulsive behaviours and affective instability.'

'From suspicion, mistrust and acting out to containment and attachment. The development of responsibility for self and others.'

This exemplifies the culture of safety (containment).

A positive outcome?

'Ability to explore and better understand past experiences and their impact.'

'Improved ability to make and maintain appropriate and satisfying relationships and to engage with everyday life/tasks. Improved sense of self and growth in confidence. Cessation of self-harming behaviours and suicidal attempts/ideation.'

'Reduction in acting out, less isolated, more socialized (improved social skills) improved affect regulation, improved personal and collective/ social responsibility.'

'Conscious understanding of past behaviours and defences, improved personal narrative and autobiographical competence.'

This exemplifies the culture of empowerment (agency).

What contributes to these?

'The support, containment and validation of group members. An opportunity to disclose feelings and experiences, sometimes for the first time, without judgement or rejection. The chance to acknowledge, explore and work through past experiences and current difficulties to gain a perspective and understanding that allows a growth of self and challenges the negative expectations of self and others.'

This exemplifies the culture of belonging (attachment).

Therapeutic change lies in members discovering a new sense of self-agency and what they can do for others. People feel a profound sense of belonging and links to that of a 'secure base'. The strengthening of the sense of self allows the members to be less anxious about potential fragmentation and loss. In any therapeutic process, all of the tasks/factors may be in action simultaneously with facilitated relational processes and new relational experiences.

Co-constructing a different type of narrative, narrative seen as a dialogue, highlights a crucial aspect of this process – the co-construction of shared meaning, which with relational processes facilitates the development of self-agency. So, 'self-agency is always at the heart of psychological growth and development, and it follows a developmental trajectory' (Knox 2010, p.9).

A commitment to the therapeutic process: An innovative and creative therapeutic space

What difference did these reported experiences from service users and therapists make to our findings? The answer is a lot, in terms of richness and complexity.

The community provides intensive psychosocial experience and the therapeutic environment is seen as the main factor for making change. It is a democratic, user-led therapeutic environment (i.e. members are active participants in their own and others' mental health treatment, and they are involved in the daily running of the TC, influencing service development and delivery).

Therapeutic work is always embedded in the cultural and social context. Thoughts, feelings and experiences are communicated through language (verbal or non-verbal) and interpersonal contacts that are informed by culture. Taking a closer look at how those cultural and social factors influence therapeutic process and therapist interventions highlights the nature of this way of working in different cultures and also highlights some essential common aspects across cultures.

It is interesting to think of cultural experiences as a place that involves the in-between space necessary for cultural exploration. Experiencing the 'in-between', building on the idea of the transitional area, demonstrates the importance of the environment in the therapeutic setting (Winnicott 1971).

It is important to realize how we experience the space that

exists between outer (objective) reality and our inner (subjective) understanding, a way of thinking that goes beyond crucial binaries. Seeing them no longer as two separate categories, but as two complementary aspects that are inseparably connected and interdependent, creates a network (Capra and Luisi 2014).

We have come to realize that the subjective dimension, our inner experiences, becomes an integral part of the intersubjective, which is the interactive social process within our world of experiences informed by culture.

The therapeutic community provides a living/learning experience where thinking and emotions can be safely explored. The TC creates a network of supportive and challenging relationships between members encouraging both individual and group responsibility. An experience of being with others and finding acceptance and understanding can have a profoundly positive influence. These are some of the factors that serve to moderate outcome and help to reduce the emotionally harmful impact of trauma on physical, emotional and mental wellbeing.

The therapeutic programme provides a conducive environment that is structured and helps to develop members' skills and fosters the use of creativity. There is an attitude of acceptance and an atmosphere of trust, which makes people feel respected, valued and hopeful. Through the developing network of relationships within the group, the unconscious influences by which past experiences affect current emotional experience can be explored.

So the process is to notice one's feelings and reflect on them, with support from structures, procedures and other minds. A full understanding is reached when we approach it through the interplay of different levels – the context, the process, the outcome and the non-linear dynamics of complex systems.

Therapeutic community interactions are here seen as a dynamic system, a complex, highly non-linear dynamics, from which a sense of culture arises. A culture through which values, belief and rules of conduct are continually communicated, modified and sustained. It emerges from a network of communications among individuals (Capra and Luisi 2014). The TC environment has the potential to create a sense of the wholeness of life and to provide the context for a potentially transformative learning experience.

The field of mental health is in an exciting period of growth and reorganization. Emerging interdisciplinary views enable us to further our understanding of lived experience, relational story, and interpersonal relationships that provide the framework for the exploration of new ways of working with people with complex needs, with a history of traumatic circumstances, in considerable psychological distress, severely troubled in areas of interpersonal and social functioning. The shifting priorities towards developing the creative potential of individuals who are adaptive, capable of changing and evolving is taking shape.

Today, as the transitional experiences of the individual self and its relationship with the outside world are constantly changing, to find a way of accessing the lost sense of interconnectedness and interdependency, developing a sense of belonging and connectedness, is more urgent and topical than ever before. The therapeutic community is one shining example of successfully developing this sense of belonging and connectedness.

A sense of connectedness...

- the underlying connectedness

- creating communities with shared values and practices that become the basis for the culture – the landscape

- the values we collectively choose to live by.

Figure 11.3: Image and narrative – finding a common ground.
Photograph by Sheila Butler (see online colour plate)

Acknowledgements

I am grateful to all my colleagues and service users who participated and contributed to the development of the project. And many thanks to my family and co-authors of this book for their encouragement and creative insight.

References

Angus, L.E. and McLeod, J. (eds) (2004) *The Handbook of Narrative and Psychotherapy: Practice, Theory, and Research*. Thousand Oaks, CA: Sage.

Capra, F. and Luisi, P.L. (2014) *The Systems View of Life: A Unifying Vision*. Cambridge: Cambridge University Press.

Department of Health (2009) *Recognising Complexity: Commissioning Guidance for Personality Disorder Services*. London: Department of Health/Mental Health Division. Available at https://lx.iriss.org.uk/sites/default/files/resources/dh_101789.pdf

Department of Health (2011) *No Health Without Mental Health: A Cross-government Mental Health Outcomes Strategy for People of All Ages*. London: Department of Health.

Haigh, R. (2013) 'The quintessence of a therapeutic environment.' *Therapeutic Communities: The International Journal of Therapeutic Communities 34*, 1, 6–15.

Knox, J. (2010) *Self-Agency in Psychotherapy: Attachment, Autonomy and Intimacy*. New York, NY: W.W. Norton.

McLeod, J. (2000, 23 June) 'Qualitative outcome research in psychotherapy: Issues and methods.' Paper presented as part of a panel on 'A qualitative inquiry into clients' experiences of change in brief experiential therapy for depression: From first session outcomes to six-month follow-up', Society for Psychotherapy Research Annual Conference, Chicago.

NHS England (2016) *The Five Year Forward View for Mental Health*. A report from the independent Mental Health Taskforce to the NHS in England. London: Author.

Winnicott, D.W. (1971) *Playing and Reality*. London: Tavistock Publications.

Further reading

Association of Therapeutic Communities (1999) *The Need for an NHS Policy on Developing the Role of Therapeutic Communities in the Treatment of 'Personality Disorder'*. London: ATC.

Bateman, A.W. and Fonagy, P. (2000) 'Effectiveness of psychotherapeutic treatment of personality disorder.' *British Journal of Psychiatry 177*, 2, 138–143.

Bion, W. (1991) *Experiences in Groups: and Other Papers*. London: Routledge.

Bowlby, J. (1969) *Attachment and Loss: Vol 1. Attachment*. New York, NY: Basic Books.

Bowlby, J. (1973) *Attachment and Loss: Vol 2. Separation*. New York, NY: Basic Books.

Bowlby, J. (1978) 'Attachment theory and its therapeutic implications.' *Adolescent Psychiatry 6*, 5–33.

Bruner, J. (1990) *Acts of Meaning*. Cambridge, MA: Harvard University Press.

Campling, P. and Haigh, R. (eds) (1999) *Therapeutic Communities: Past, Present and Future*. London: Jessica Kingsley Publishers.

Castonguay, L.G. and Beutler, L.E. (eds) (2006) *Principles of Therapeutic Change that Work*. New York, NY: Oxford University Press.

Davies, S. and Campling, P. (2003) 'Therapeutic community treatment of personality disorder.' *British Journal of Psychiatry 44*, 524–527.

Fonagy, P. (2001) *Attachment Theory and Psychoanalysis*. London: Karnac Books.

Kernberg, O.F. (1992) *Aggression in Personality Disorders and Perversions*. New Haven, CT: Yale University Press.

Kernberg, O.F., Selzer, M.A., Koenigsberg, H.W., Carr, A.C. and Applebaum, A.H. (1989) *Psychodynamic Psychotherapy of Borderline Patients*. New York, NY: Basic Books.

Lanius, R., Vermetten, E. and Pain, C. (2010) *The Impact of Early Life Trauma on Health and Disease: The Hidden Epidemic*. Cambridge: Cambridge University Press.

McLeod, J. (2000) 'The Contribution of Qualitative Methods to Psychotherapy Outcome Research.' In S. Goss and N. Rowland (eds) *Evidence-based Care and the Psychological Therapies*. London: Routledge.

McLeod, J. (2000) *Qualitative Research in Counselling and Psychotherapy*. London: Sage.

McLeod, J. (2010) *Case Study Research in Counselling and Psychotherapy*. London: Sage.

Meares, R. (2005) *The Metaphor of Play: Origin and Breakdown of Personal Being*. London: Taylor & Francis.

National Institute for Health and Care Excellence (2009) *Borderline Personality Disorder: Treatment and Management*. Clinical Guideline 78. London: Author.

National Institute for Mental Health in England (2003) *Personality Disorder: No Longer a Diagnosis of Exclusion: Policy Implementation Guidance for the Development of Services for People with Personality Disorder*. London: Department of Health.

National Institute for Mental Health in England (2003) *The Personality Disorder Capabilities Framework with Regard to Training Professionals in Working with People with Personality Disorder*. London: Department of Health.

Schore, A.N. (1994) *Affect Regulation and the Origin of the Self: The Neurobiology of Emotional Development*. Mahwah, NJ: Lawrence Erlbaum.

Schore, A.N. (2003) *Affect Dysregulation and Disorders of the Self*. New York, NY & London: W.W. Norton.

Stern, D.N. (1985) *The Interpersonal World of the Infant*. New York, NY: Basic Books.

Yalom, I.D. (2005) *The Theory and Practice of Group Psychotherapy*. New York, NY: Basic Books.

12

Frame by Frame

Stop-frame Animation with Trauma and Chaos Narratives

Tony Gammidge

Introduction

I met Irene, a woman in her sixties, when I started an animation project in a day centre for people with a diagnosis of personality disorder. Her therapist recommended me to her. When we met, I showed some films from my previous projects. She was a bit intimidated by the thought of making a film herself but keen to give it a go. I said that she could make a film about anything she wanted, but she was clear she wanted to make one about the abuse she suffered as a child. She seemed more than ready to do this having been in therapy for the last 18 months, and so she dived straight in, wasting no time. The first thing she did was make a couple of naked figures out of clay, which she said were her mum and dad. Under her direction, we went on to animate them being stabbed with a craft knife. From this start, Irene and I worked together (with the support of her therapist) over the next few months to make the film 'Just Like a Rag Doll' (2013).

This film was one of many that have been made in the animation projects I have run since 2010 in mental health settings, secure hospitals and prisons and with asylum seekers. I understand this work as an emergent practice that falls between art therapy, 'art as therapy' (Springham 2008) and arts in health.

This chapter tells the story of some of these projects, describing and exploring what I have observed from the process and in particular how participants often use this medium as a way of telling difficult and traumatic stories. I will primarily explore the film by Irene but will also refer to other animation project films, as well as taking an auto-biographical perspective reflecting on the experience of making my films ('Tim' and 'Norton Grim and Me') using personal and family narrative.

Trauma theory (Fisher 2017; van der Kolk 2014) has provided an invaluable lens through which to understand and make sense of the way many participants made work in relation to traumatic experiences. Arthur Frank's (2013) writing around illness and storytelling has also been an inspiration.

Irene's 'Just Like a Rag Doll' is a film in two halves; it starts with the story mostly 'as it happened', whilst the second half is a reflection, a deconstruction and essentially a re-write of events to how Irene would have liked them to be. It tells the story of Irene as a six-year-old child who was repeatedly sexually abused by her father. After ten years she eventually reports this to the police, who arrest him. Irene then endures the humiliation and added trauma of a court case, which is convened almost entirely by men. This section of the film ends with her father being found guilty and sentenced to (only) seven years in prison. The second part of the film starts with Irene talking about the judge whilst stroking his (the puppet's) head, 'he was the kindest man I ever met' she recounts. It then cuts into a far uglier scene with two naked figures in a bedroom with Irene's voice instructing them to 'get into bed, I'm in control now'. They are then forced into a bed filled with thorns and violently pushed onto them by Irene's real hand whilst they scream in pain. This is followed by another court case presided over by woman rather than men. Irene gets a chance to have her say and this time both her parents are sentenced to life and Irene is awarded a month's holiday in the Seychelles with her dogs.

Van der Kolk (2014) says: 'We have discovered that helping victims of trauma find the words to describe what has happened to them is profoundly meaningful, but usually it is not enough' (p.21).

I want to explore the idea that using animation is not about describing an event or experience but more a re-telling, re-imagining and re-creating. It frequently results in a new story being told using the traumatic memory as a starting point. Words largely come from a mental head space, whereas stop-frame animation could be described as a form of *embodied narrative*, in that it is a physical, hands-on process that involves making, building, manipulating and performing. It comes from the body, as well as the memory and imagination. I propose that a story is dependent on the form in which it is told, so that the same story will be different according to the medium in which it is told.

The animation process opens up a series of storytelling opportunities and possibilities that go beyond verbal narrative, namely:

- it is a physical, hands-on process

- it gives order to chaotic narratives

- it requires attention and the need for being present moment by moment

- it is a process that gives control to the storyteller and directorial authority; the director can play with fact and fiction, change details and change the ending

- it is a transformative and aesthetic process; using this medium to tell a story from a traumatic experience will create something new

- the final film can provide an enduring account that can be shared and witnessed repeatedly and beyond the context in which it was made.

It is these processes that I will explore throughout the chapter.

The physicality of stop-frame animation

Stop-frame animation is a simple technique in which a photograph (frame) is taken of a puppet, object or drawing that is then moved very slightly, another photo taken, then moved again and another photo taken, and so on. When the photos are shown one after another (via software on the tablet or laptop), there is the illusion of the puppet moving. There are traditionally 24 frames to a second of film (though I do far less to save time), so it is an extraordinarily time-consuming process that needs patience and focus.

Whereas commercial animation can be done purely digitally just using a computer, stop-frame animation is more hands-on. It requires something to animate, an object, puppet or drawing, as well as backgrounds, sets and props that create the world where the action takes place. These mostly need to be made, drawn and/or painted by hand. In the animation projects we have animated all sorts of things, including puppets made from clay/modelling clay, shadow-puppets (black card), cut-out puppets (paper and photos), drawings, shoes, furniture and soft toys (teddy bears).

For her film, Irene made all the puppet characters from modelling clay. It was notable how she built a physical relationship with them both through the making and the manipulation. After we had animated the first harrowing courtroom scene, Irene started talking about the judge whilst at the same time lovingly stroking his (the puppet's) head. She communicates something important using both words and touch (Figure 12.1). In contrast, the puppets of her parents she responds to in an aggressive way, attacking and stabbing them with a knife. Words have not been enough for her to express her rage but with the puppets she can enact a more staged and object-based revenge.

When we interviewed Irene for the project evaluation, she said that through making the film she could give back the scars she had for the last 40 years to her parents (a very literal somatic metaphor). Whilst speaking, she held the puppet of herself as a child, tenderly soothing, stroking and mothering it. It felt like she was soothing that wounded, vulnerable part of herself as a form of physical empathy, perhaps hard to conceptualize and enact using just words. Fisher (2017) talks about the need for people to befriend parts of themselves that have been cut off in attempt to survive ongoing trauma. Irene in stroking and soothing her childhood puppet seems to be doing this. As Fisher (2017, pp.77–78) notes:

> In order to unconditionally accept ourselves and 'earn' that resilience, we need to develop a relationship to all of us: to our wounded and needy parts…the parts we love, the parts we hate, and even the parts that intimidate us.

By developing a physical relationship with her puppets, Irene tells an embodied narrative, one that comes from the body as well as the mind, and in so doing she tells a new story.

Figure 12.1: Still from 'Just Like a Rag Doll' by Irene Balaam (2013) (see online colour plate)

Trauma as chaos

Fisher (2017) referencing van der Kolk (2014) comments that 'when the autonomic nervous system is repeatedly activated, the hippocampus (the part of the brain responsible for putting experience into chronological order and perspective preparatory to being transferred to verbal memory areas) is suppressed' (p.36). This means, the memories are not able to be processed into a particular time frame and so instead of belonging to the past they feel like they are still in the present, held in the more primitive, emotional parts of the brain and not able to be processed. Van der Kolk (2014) recognizes the difficulty of the task of processing past trauma: '...the experience of trauma itself gets in the way of being able to do that, no matter how much insight or understanding we develop, the rational brain is basically impotent to talk the emotional brain out of its reality' (p.47). Irene's early and sustained abuse led to high states of chaos and confusion that would play out throughout her child and adulthood. She was overwhelmed by her traumatic experience, and as a way of coping she became addicted to alcohol, was involved in several abusive relationships and regularly self-harmed through cutting and overdosing.

Frank (2013) writing about illness identifies three key narratives that people experience when they are ill: the restitution narrative, the chaos narrative and the quest narrative. He says about chaos: 'Those living in chaos are least able to tell a story, because they lack any sense of viable future. Life is reduced to a series of present tense assaults. If a narrative involves temporal progression, chaos is anti-narrative' (p.xv). Thus, in both chaos narratives and experiences of trauma, a similar lack of narrative progression can be found, i.e. a lack of beginning, middle and end. It is more a 'series of present tense assaults' (Frank 2013) or, from a trauma perspective, 'flashbacks' in which 'the sensory fragments of memory intrude into the present' (van der Kolk 2014, p.66). The right side of the brain, the intuitive, emotional, visual part, is unable to communicate properly with the left, the analytical and sequential part. It is very hard to tell a story from chaos, make sense of things in the eye of the storm, and this in turn creates more chaos.

Frank (2013) proposes: 'If a chaos story is told on the edge of a wound, it is also told on the edges of speech' (p.101). It seems that through the very gradual, methodical, frame-by-frame telling of a story allowed by stop-frame animation a way of ordering and organization becomes possible. Reflection and distance from the chaos emerges. If a participant animates a traumatic event, the process slows it right down, breaks it down to one micro-movement at a time. It is in extreme slow motion, perhaps in contrast to the original event, which can often happen or be recalled in a blur of fragments. It offers a chance for reflective distance.

For Frank (2013) this offers hope: 'The chaos that can be told in a story is already taking place at a distance' (p.98). For example, the initial animation Irene made, where her parent puppets were being stabbed, felt like it was coming from chaos and revenge rather than storytelling. However, as the project proceeded, she slowly started to think of the film as a way of telling her story with a beginning, middle and end. The storytelling was painful but not chaotic, rather something far more reflective, considered and processed. She seemed to become more able to work from the sequential, organizational parts of her brain (the prefrontal cortex).

The importance of the present moment

We now know that, as important as it is to acknowledge the past, it is even more crucial for traumatised individuals to stay connected to present time.

(Fisher 2017, p.39)

As described, animation is methodical, time-consuming and immersive. It requires great patience and presence of mind. I have found that even if a traumatic and upsetting event was being animated, the filmmaker could still maintain focus on the practicalities of what they were doing and not become triggered and emotionally dysregulated by the past trauma. They might even enjoy the process.

Fisher talks about the role of mindfulness in trauma work and how 'it also facilitates the capacity for "dual awareness" or "parallel processing" allowing us to explore the past without re-traumatization by keeping one "foot" in the present and one "foot" in the past (Ogden et al. 2006)' (Fisher 2017, pp.78–79). She goes on to say: 'When the client can stay present in a mindfully aware relationship to both present moment experience and implicit or explicit memory connected to the past, he or she is in dual awareness' (p.78). Despite the horror of Irene's film, my memory of the work was that we had great fun, with much humour, inventiveness and problem-solving.

Each scene is under the director's focus and control, and this seems to protect against triggering a traumatic flashback. One reason for this could be that the filmmaker is caught up in the technical and aesthetic process and not the event, so is firmly in the present moment operating from the prefrontal cortex. This may prevent them from becoming lost in the past event that they are re-creating. There is also a sense of distance from the event, the filmmaker can see that these characters are not real, that they are made of modelling clay; as Springham (2008) describes, 'the art is felt to be real but known not to be' (p.71). I am careful to keep participants focused on the task at hand, particularly when animating a difficult scene. I encourage attention on the methods and process and away from the emotional impact.

I worked with Gary, a man in a category B prison, to make his film 'Thamesmead Forever' (2015), which tells his story from his childhood home, into care, onto the streets and into prison. When it came to animating the scene in which he comes home from school and finds his mother dead from an overdose (Figure 12.2), I worried that this might upset him and even be triggering for him. He was keen to do the scene, though, and he did it with his usual humour and banter, commenting afterwards during the evaluation that 'if it is too serious I probably wouldn't have come' (Gammidge 2016). However, when we did the voiceover for this scene, there was far less distance from this traumatic event and less of a sense of play, and so it felt far more raw and emotional. As a result, Gary by his own admission avoided the group for a few weeks. I wonder if with the animation process, Gary was able to hold on to a 'dual awareness' (Fisher 2017) and so stay present and safe, but with the voiceover it was too close and he was triggered into trauma he had never really confronted before.

Figure 12.2: Still from 'Thamesmead Forever' by Gary (2015) (see online colour plate)

Directorial control and re-storying

Stories have to repair the damage the illness has done to the ill person's sense of where she is in life, and where she may be going. Stories are a way of redrawing maps and finding new destinations.

(Frank 2013, p.53)

In its methodical process, animation gives the participant control over what happens. I don't set a theme for the projects and participants can choose what story they want to tell. I encourage participants to think of themselves as the director of their film and story. The puppets will do what the director wants and the story will go as the director chooses. This can mean that participants choose to fictionalize their story. Sometimes taking this agency can be a challenge for people who feel disempowered and are not used to being in control of their narrative. However, some relish the opportunity and take full advantage of it. Irene did this right away in the first session when she attacked her 'parent puppets'; in the next session she reported that she had had the best night's sleep in ages. It seemed for her it was a relief to be in control of the story at last.

Irene wanted to reimagine the courtroom scene as convened entirely by women so that she could save herself from the terrible humiliation of the first all-male courtroom. She also re-wrote the prison sentence so that her father and also mother were both given life sentences. Finally, her dogs, which she saw as her loyal protectors, were present in court and could show their disapproval of the wrongs of her parents by growling and peeing on their bed.

'Living in Darkness' (2011) was made in a medium-secure hospital by Kerry and tells the (mostly fictional) story of Amy, whose mother commits suicide when she is a child following a visit from a mysterious man. She later discovers that this man is her father and her mother's uncle who had raped her mother. Her father, Tony Davidson, runs an escort agency, and Amy tracks him down, goes to visit him and shoots him dead. She ends up in prison where she self-harms and eventually gets transferred to a secure mental health unit. She becomes a participant of a film group on the unit and makes her own film. The final scene of 'Living in Darkness' shows Amy screening her film at a film festival in which two figures, one called 'Life' and one called 'Death', are in a boxing match (Figure 12.3). It ends when Life knocks Death out and wins.

*Figure 12.3: Still from 'Living in Darkness' by
Kerry (2011) (see online colour plate)*

This is a film made some years before Irene's and was the first film I worked on in which we consciously used re-storying. In Kerry's original screenplay the film ends by Amy killing herself in the prison. After some weeks of working with Kerry, I carefully asked her if she really wanted to end the film in this way or whether there was an alternative she wanted to consider. I made it clear that it was her choice, but I wanted to open up other possibilities. On the ward, she was considered a high suicide risk and frequently self-harmed. She eventually decided on changing the ending to Amy surviving, getting better and becoming a filmmaker herself.

This change in the narrative turned out to be a portent of the future, as not long after she finished the film Kerry was discharged from the ward and went to college to do a theatre design course. She now herself runs animation projects with 'looked after' children.

> The goal of treatment is to find a way in which people can acknowledge the reality of what has happened, without having to re-experience the trauma all over again. For this to occur, merely uncovering memories is not enough: they need to be modified and transformed, i.e. placed in their proper context and reconstructed into neutral or meaningful narratives. Thus in therapy, memory paradoxically becomes an act of creation, rather than a static recording of events... (van der Kolk, van der Hart and Burbridge 1995, p.2)

It seems 'Living in Darkness' contributed to Kerry's ability to find new meaning and hope for herself and imagine a more hopeful future.

Arthur Frank (2013) makes the case that people who are ill need to find a way to reclaim their story from both the illness and the medical profession. He argues that people who are ill can lose their voice and their story can be superseded by the medical model. 'Seriously ill people are wounded not just in body but in voice. They need to become storytellers in order to recover their voices that illness and its treatment often take away' (Frank 2013, p.xx). Through making her film, Kerry managed to find an ending beyond the poor prognosis and diagnosis she had on the ward, beyond the narrative of the suicidal self-harmer with a borderline personality disorder.

Self as super-hero and avenger

One of the advantages of fictionalizing a story is that participants will often use characters based upon themselves who then act as superheroes or avengers able to intervene and fix the situation. Irene used herself (with her real hand) as 'the intervention' that pushes down the cage door on her father during the first court case, then in the second half of the film it is her hand that forces the mum and dad figures onto thorns in the bed. Kerry's character, Amy, takes matters into her own hands by killing her father and mother's abuser, Tony Davidson.

In both there is a desire for revenge, which, according to Horowitz (2007), is common in people suffering from trauma and PTSD. In animation, the revenge can be enacted in a way that is metaphorical, safe and empowering. Sometimes it is not even revenge and more a disowning of the pathology and the violence that has been forced upon them. When Irene says, 'I knew that it [making the film] would make me feel better about myself and by handing back all the scars that I gave myself over the 40 years of my life I could give them back to my parents' (Balaam 2013), it is not a violent act but one of choice and heroism. It is perhaps another aspect or form of befriending and looking after the parts that have been disowned.

Likewise, in my own film 'Norton Grim and Me' (2016–2019) about my early experiences of boarding school, I use a comic book character, 'Norton Grim', that I created in my early twenties and took his form in handmade books and comics: 'Norton Grim was conceived when I was about seven, on that first night in boarding school and he was born some years later, on a scrap of paper ragged and torn' (Gammidge 2016–2019; see Figure 12.4). He took on the role of an alter-ego and seemed to express an unconscious self-destructive, self-harming and masochistic part of myself. Through making the film I understood that this character (in art form) I had lived with for most of my life was expressing my childhood distress in a way that I couldn't: 'He self-harmed so that I didn't have to' (Gammidge 2016–2019). He subsequently went on to 'become an unlikely super-hero for me as he endeavoured to rescue me from my captivity. He was the only one to recognise that my captivity was not normal and that it was wrong' (Gammidge 2016–2019). I realized that Norton Grim (i.e. the art-making part of me) was not only expressing something that had long been buried but could also retrieve something valuable from this lost state.

The nature of animation means that one can play with and experiment with themes such as revenge, violence, aggression but also power, empathy and gentleness all in a way that is metaphorical and safe.

Figure 12.4: Still from 'Norton Grim and Me' by Tony Gammidge (2016–2019)

The aesthetics of animation

Another project participant, reflecting on their mental illness noted that because images of self-harm were depicted in a controlled and creative way it turned something destructive and painful into something surprisingly beautiful. In telling a story through making an animation film, there are aesthetic decisions to be made (amongst many others); for example, what is going to be the style of the film? What will it look like? What will the main character be wearing? How should the lighting be? Whilst many of the people I work with, particularly those who have little experience of art-making, give this consideration very little thought, the process still requires them to make at least cursory decisions as to the look of their film.

In my own work the aesthetic is a major consideration; it is far more important that something looks right than it is accurate about how things were. I will re-animate and re-make a scene many times before I get the look that I am going for. There is something about circling around an event, playing with it, reflecting on it, re-jigging it that leads to an alchemical transformation.

It was after I had done a few animation projects in secure hospitals that I was inspired to make some films that directly addressed my own personal and family history. The first of these films, 'Tim' (2011), tells the story from my mother's perspective of how my elder brother was killed (some years before I was born) in a car accident. My mother speaks of what she remembers of the accident, its aftermath and how she was abandoned and left totally alone with her grief. She was seriously injured during the accident and as a result missed Tim's funeral (see Figure 12.5). The second part of the film (work in progress) addresses how when she found where he was buried under a shrub and in the shade, she demanded that his body be moved to a spot in the cemetery where he could get some sun. She writes to the bishop, gets permission, they move him and have another funeral, 'the proper one'. In this most desperate of moments my mother regains some agency.

The project started when my mother agreed to tell me what had happened and I recorded her. I wondered how I was going to tell this story about something so close and traumatic and do it justice.

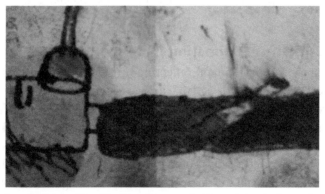

Figure 12.5: Still from 'Tim' by Tony Gammidge (2011) (see online colour plate)

When it came to animating the scene of the actual accident in which Tim is killed (and its immediate aftermath) I had to actively imagine something quite unimaginable and then re-create it, bring it (and him) back to life. I had to consider every detail: what each of the characters looked like (before and after the accident), what they were wearing, where they were standing, etc. These are strange and disturbing things to imagine, but that did not mean it was a purely upsetting process. It wasn't, I mostly enjoyed it; making the puppets (see Figure 12.6), the backgrounds, the props, getting the lighting right, the depth of field, the focus, the blur, the sound, the music. I wanted to turn something awful and heartbreaking into something beautiful and heartfelt. Even with such a sad story, there was vitality in piecing it all together.

Figure 12.6: Still from 'Tim' by Tony Gammidge (2011)

Part of the enjoyment was based in the aesthetic, sensory pleasures and decisions I made. I enjoyed the colours, the forms, the shapes, the textures, and yet the story it was telling was tragic and painful and not beautiful. How to make sense of this contradiction? I wondered if there might be something wrong with me. I also wondered if this is what Fisher (2017) calls 'dual awareness': one part of me is focused in the here-and-now, the aesthetic decisions that needed to be made, and the other part is focused on my family's traumatic experience.

I remember attending a talk given by the graphic artist Nicola Streeten, who made the graphic novel *Billy, Me and You* (Streeten 2011). This was about her son who died from heart complications when he was two years old. During the talk, someone asked her if the process had been very painful, and she replied, 'On the contrary it was an absolute joy.' She expands subsequently in an email to me: 'For me there grew a delight in the process of working out ways to visualise emotions, using mark-making, metaphor, and incorporating external "real" materials such as photos within a framework that was recognisable as "comics". The contradiction makes sense because making a piece of work that is based on tragic and traumatic events is not the same as the event. Fisher (2017) suggests: 'Rather than remembering what happened, once thought to be the goal of trauma treatment, we know now that resolution of the past requires transforming the memories' (p.40). Neither 'Tim' nor *Billy, Me and You* is about digging up painful memories and describing them (van der Kolk 2014), but instead more of a re-making. Through this transformative process they get alchemized, turned into something new, a film, a graphic memoir, a piece of art.

Lemma and Levy (2004) note: '…trauma always involves loss. The losses may be actual such as the loss of a loved one, of one's home and country, or they may be more symbolic, the loss of identity, meaning or hope' (p.xv). For my mother and Streeten, it was the loss of their sons; for Irene, it was her childhood; for me being sent away as a small child, it was my family. Streeten wrote to me: 'I do know with absolute clarity that in my case, the worst experience of my life took me on a path to the best experiences of my life.' This seems to echo Ogden's (2002, p.117) reflection on the work of mourning:

> Mourning is not simply a form of psychological work; it is a process centrally involving the experience of making something adequate to the experience of loss. What is 'made' and the experience of making it – which together might be thought of as 'the art of mourning' – represent the individual's effort to meet, to be equal to, to do justice to, the fullness and complexity of his or her relationship to what has been lost, and to the experience of loss itself.

To make art works from these events is not just about making sense of something, though this is important, but also compensating for the loss, making something worthwhile and beautiful that in part makes up for it.

Final film as an enduring account

The films that are made have a life, long after each project ends. There is often an initial screening in the setting where it was made, then the films are shown elsewhere at conferences, symposiums and art galleries.[1] The films often provide the 'voice of the service user' (e.g. at forensic mental health events where service users are notably absent). The films have also been used to train a range of staff and offer new insight into why the project participants might have ended up in the situation they have. An ex boy-soldier from Somalia with whom I worked in 2010 was able to give a copy of his film 'Chester' (2010) to clinical staff so that he did not have to repeatedly go through his story and trauma.

At her request, I have screened Irene's film many times over the years. At the Ortus Centre in London in 2014, we screened all six films made as part of this particular project and at the end of the screening there was a standing ovation from the audience. Most of the filmmakers (including Irene) agreed to sit at the front and answer questions from the audience. Irene spoke saying that she was very proud of the film that she had made, that she considered herself to have become an artist and that she had not self-harmed since making the film. Irene had not only made a piece of art from something ugly and traumatic, but was both changed and validated by the process.

Conclusion

Irene's therapist at the start of the project had commented to me that she was an extraordinary person, and I quickly understood what he meant. She had spirit, warmth and humour that were infectious. That is not to say there were no tricky moments; she did get upset after we had animated the scene of her as a child being dragged from her bed by her father, but she could also differentiate her upset at such disturbing memories from flashbacks.

When it came to doing the voice of her father, Irene asked her therapist if he would do this. He agreed, also doing those of the judge and policeman. I think this enabled her to navigate the potential for re-traumatization. Her therapist represented safety for Irene and helped hold the balance between past and present.

---

1   These have included, for example: British Association of Art Therapists (BAAT) International Conference, London, 2019; Tate Exchange at Tate Modern, London, 2017; Royal College of Psychiatrists Rehabilitation Conference, Cardiff, 2016; International Association of Forensic Psychotherapy (IAFP) Conference Keynote Presentation, Belgium, 2016; Pallant House Gallery, Chichester, 2015; IAFP Conference, Yale University, USA, 2015; Bethlem Gallery, London, 2014; and Ortus Centre, London, 2014.

For me, my relationship with Irene was that of a collaborator, someone facilitating an important story that needed to be told. She was passionate about her film being seen as widely and frequently as possible, as she did not want her experiences hidden and denied any longer. She particularly wanted her film to be seen by other people who had suffered similar experiences in the hope that it would help them speak out and come to terms with their trauma.

I cast my mind back to my mother's words when she told the story of her isolation following my brother's death: 'I was dreadfully left alone, because people didn't want to come, so they just left me…they didn't know what to say…and talk, people don't talk' (Gammidge 2011). I have long been passionate about the stories that struggle to be told, stories that are lost, forgotten, ignored, disbelieved and buried, stories from particularly those who are stigmatized and marginalized. Perhaps this is why Irene and I had such an easy and fruitful creative collaboration. We both understood the importance of this story being taken back into ownership and being remodelled, witnessed and acknowledged so that she could at last forge some sense of justice and peace for herself.

Thanks to Joanna Stevens and Mario Guarnieri.

In Memory of Irene Balaam and Ann Gammidge.

References

Fisher, J. (2017) *Healing the Fragmented Selves of Trauma Survivors: Overcoming Internal Self-alienation.* New York, NY: Routledge.

Frank, A. (2013) *The Wounded Storyteller: Body, Illness and Ethics* (2nd edn). Chicago, IL: University of Chicago Press.

Gammidge, T. (2016) 'Story to Tell: Stories from Animation Projects in Secure and Psychiatric Settings.' In K. Rothwell (ed.) *Forensic Arts Therapies, Anthology of Practice and Research.* London: Free Association Books.

Horowitz, M.J. (2007) 'Understanding and ameliorating revenge fantasies in psychotherapy.' *Treatment in Psychiatry 164,* 1, 24–27.

Lemma, A. and Levy, S. (2004) 'Introduction.' In A. Lemma and S. Levy (eds) *The Perversion of Loss.* New York, NY: Brunner-Routledge.

Ogden, T.H. (2002) *Conversations at the Frontier of Dreaming.* London: Karnac Books.

Springham, N. (2008) 'Through the eyes of the law: What is it about art that can harm people?' *Inscape: International Journal of Art Therapy 13,* 2, 65–73.

Streeten, N. (2011) *Billy, Me and You.* Oxford: Myriad Editions.

van der Kolk, B. (2014) *The Body Keeps the Score: Brain, Mind, and Body in the Healing of Trauma.* New York, NY: Viking.

van der Kolk, B.A., van der Hart, O. and Burbridge, J. (1995) 'Approaches to the Treatment of PTSD.' In S. Hobfoll and M. de Vries (eds) *Extreme Stress and Communities: Impact and Intervention.* NATO ASI series. Series D, Behavioural and Social Sciences, Vol 80. Norwell, MA: Kluwer Academic.

Films

Balaam, I. (2013) 'Just Like a Rag Doll.' www.tonygammidge.com/films-from-secure-psychiatric-setti and https://vimeo.com/309657709

Chester (2010) 'Chester.' https://vimeo.com/139122177

Gammidge, T. (2011) 'Tim.' www.tonygammidge.com/my-films and https://vimeo.com/101714412

Gammidge, T. (2016–2019) 'Norton Grim and Me.' www.tonygammidge.com/my-films and https://vimeo.com/199346613

Gary (2015) 'Thamesmead Forever.' www.tonygammidge.com/films-from-prisons and https://vimeo.com/131591966

Kerry (2011) 'Living in Darkness.' www.tonygammidge.com/films-from-secure-psychiatric-setti and https://vimeo.com/143017547

13

Mapping Addiction, Describing Trauma, Building Hope

Martin Weegmann

This chapter begins with etymology and explores some historical idioms of addiction and excessive consumption. All societies have intoxicants, and we all have a relationship with drugs, whether we or society judge them beneficial or detrimental. The 'trauma' word is excavated next, and whilst psychological trauma is a particularly 20th-century concept trauma in some form or another has a long pre-history. Turning from the historical to the clinical, in the next section I describe the use of personal maps in groups with addicted individuals, which help people gain a fuller picture of their life-spaces. Finally, Angie, an ex-patient, describes aspects of her journey from addiction and trauma into recovery, after which I consider the process of change more widely as a symbolic rite of passage.

Addiction: Idiom and image

'Addiction' (*addicere*) traditionally signified being 'given over to something' and in Latin and Roman law, *addico* and *addictus* had positive and negative connotations, positive in the sense of, say, a person given over to civic devotion, or negative in the sense of, say, a person given over as a slave to a master or creditor. As for the slave association, the notion of '*enslavement*' reverberated in subsequent concepts of addiction, particularly in 19th-century temperance movements with its language of 'slavery to drink' and of giving up alcohol as a symbolic 'breaking the chains' (Crowley 1999).

In English contexts after around 1500, addiction signified a form of 'surrender', to a habit, penchant or occupation (Walton 2001). The concept of 'devotion' was a somewhat similar expression then in wide circulation, with connotations of earnest attachment. There were approved forms of devotion and indebtedness, such as spiritual and scholarly addiction, or addiction to fellowship, but these had downsides if carried to the extreme (Lemon 2018). Surrender had positive connotations within certain contexts, Lemon (2018, p.42), quoting Protestant sources, refers to those 'addicted to praiers', and to 'the meaneynge of the scripture'; as for their rival community, Catholics were blamed for 'addiction to superstition'. On a less positive side, in Shakespeare's *Henry V*, the Archbishop of Canterbury comments on the king's misspent youth, when, 'His addiction was to courses vain, His companies unletter'd, rude, and shallow, His hours fill'd up with riots, banquets, sports' (Act 1, Scene 1). This emphasis on excessive consumption and the misuse or squandering of time is common in the history of addiction, as in Shakespeare's reference to power, luxury and indulgence or, say, in 18th-century reflections on the excesses of the urban crowd or mob. McKendrick, Brewer and Plumb (1982) trace the birth of 18th-century consumer society with a commercialization of life reaching revolutionary proportions by the end of that century. We all now live in a culture saturated by consumption, where it becomes hard to draw the line between what is healthy and what is excessive – use of food is a clear example of this. Some psychologists view addiction as misplaced consumption and excessive appetite (Orford 2009).

People describe suffering and illness in a whole host of ways, often using everyday metaphors and analogies in so doing. Bury (1982) refers to the 'disruptions' of normal resources (cognitive, material, social) and of biographical continuity that illness brings in its wake, prompting explanations that are brought to bear in response to it. There is a lived, cultural and discursive aspect to physical and mental disorders that is powerfully influential over and beyond its actual aspects. In the case of addiction, it was always (and remains) a disorder bound up with wider cultural dimensions, which we might characterize as 'stigma'. Whether regarded as penchant, excess, sin, disease, deviance or defiance, substance misuse is overlayed by a wide range of moral and symbolic meanings. These are linked to how a given society or era views unruly appetites and desires and judges appropriate or inappropriate use of a given substance and how its sets norms as to what or who is considered normal or otherwise.

Marlatt and Fromme (1987) link addiction to classical myths and stories, such as those of Bacchus, Pandora and Icarus. I had a patient who compared himself to the figure of Sisyphus, endlessly trying to change his feelings through drugs and forever falling back to a lower starting point. The analogy made a lot of sense to him and was the basis of extended clinical conversations between us. The cultural load applied to substances is wide-ranging, with Derrida (1991, p.20) suggesting that the drug has its 'power of fascination…both beneficent or maleficent'. The imagery of panaceas (from the Greek goddess Panakeia, representing a universal remedy) and elixirs (with roots in alchemy) representing substances that are elevated, runs alongside the converse of bad, malignant potions, poisons or drugs. Sigma is extended to the users of substances, who personify its malignant role, users seen variously as inebriates, habitual drunkards, junkies, habitués, dope-heads, crack-heads, and many more.

In the literary realm, countless authors have described their real-life struggles with substance use, be it the image of 'living under the volcano' (Malcolm Lowry), interruptions to temporality as in Charles Jackson's 'lost weekend', having the seductive 'John Barleycorn on the shoulder' (Jack London), or as, William Burroughs claimed speaking of his heroin habit, 'Junk is not a kick. It is a way of life.' In the first 'drug confessional' of its kind, De Quincey (1823/2003) beautifully captures an exalted relationship to opium, his 'portable panacea' that could be 'bought for pennies and carried in a waistcoat'. Likewise, in an era of science fiction, Huxley (1932/2007) invented the 'perfect drug', which allowed citizens to take a holiday from reality whenever they chose. My own favourite playwright, Eugene O'Neill, lived with and wrote about the shadow of alcoholism (his own and that of family members) throughout his work, even though he established long-term abstinence. He called writing, rather like the alcoholism that had affected him, his 'vacation from living' (Gelb and Gelb 1960).

Listening out in narrative terms to how clients describe addictions, one witnesses many graphic, evocative communications, for example: 'I'm going round and round in circles', 'It's a roller-coaster that's gonna crash', 'Like fighting demons all the time', 'It's my way of hiding and running away', 'Drink is my best friend, or rather, it was...', and so on (Weegmann 2017c). Shinebourne and Smith (2010) provide further examples of addiction metaphors and analogies. People use other tropes besides metaphor, such as metonymy (one thing standing for another), like 'brown' for heroin, 'the bottle' for alcoholic drinks, 'scripts' for prescribed methadone. Their effectiveness as a coinage in particular contexts, such as the street or clinic, is that 'everyone knows' what they mean. 'Struggle' and 'conflict' metaphors are common, as clients tell us how they are 'torn', behave 'just like Jekyll and Hyde', 'hold on for dear life', and so on. In narrative expressions such as these, the person presents multiple or contradictory versions of who they are or wish to be (Shinebourne and Smith 2009). When invited to talk about their histories then, clients seldom report bare accounts or chronologies but instead present vivid accounts that include an implied picture of who they are, descriptions of what they have done, the 'story so far' as it were. Thematically, such accounts often take the form of a story of decline; although if the person does not see problems associated with their use, they may convey a sense of glamour and bravado, which could be typified as 'romance', 'war' or 'status' stories. I worked with a client in detoxification who in a therapy context presented one image – that of his life 'falling apart' – but, in another, with his ward peers, reverted to boasting about his drug antics.

Trauma: Idiom and image

Human disasters have always been with us, but 'psychological trauma' is a particularly 20th-century concept, shaped as it has been by a succession of major wars, displacements and the 'discovery' of abuse at the heart of family or in relationship life. Some argue that trauma has become an over-extended term to cover all manner of phenomena, others suggest that PTSD is decontextualized from social and political conditions and others still contend that terms like *trauma*, *stressful events* and *crises* are all-too-easily conflated (e.g. Furedi 2004; Summerfield 2001; Tedeschi and Calhoun 2004). In the words of one leading expert on PTSD, 'The subject of trauma attracts passionate advocacy and passionate scepticism in a quite disproportionate measure' (Brewin 2007, p.15).

The origins of the word *trauma*, at least in Western contexts, are mostly surgical: meaning injury or wound. In ancient Greek society it had additional connotations of physical (visible) disfigurement

(Meineck and Konstan 2014). Surgical and damage metaphors continue to carry force in our times, as when people say things like, 'I'm wounded by the experience', 'I am scarred by what happened', 'She's completely shattered', 'He is damaged goods.' I worked with a refugee patient whose principle self-narrative was that of being 'a broken man'. In models of psychological therapy, analogies and metaphors are frequently used to help people to reframe what has happened to them and to envision progress, such as the image of the 'messed-up linen cupboard' or 'untidy filing cabinet' to explain intrusive memories, a 'faulty fire alarm' to explain hyperarousal or the notion of a 'broken vase' to help people to picture recovery – putting oneself together again – in the aftermath of trauma. What some clinicians call 'mutative metaphors' (Cox and Theilgaard 1987) have an important role as creative responses to the troubles that people experience and, as a shared resource, help a given story to gather meaning (as in thicker descriptions) in the process of being told.

Trauma has social context even when and if the traumatic event is natural. In Ancient Greece, for example, a key feature of the social context was the omnipresence (and normalization) of war as a means of settling disputes and vanquishing rival states. Dominant warrior traditions, including those that evoked particular masculine ideals, would have powerfully influenced how soldiers fought and viewed the consequences of so doing, including death and injury – clothed in a language of glory, heroism, strength, valour, endurance, and so on. Wounds were all around, including the symbolic wounds associated with loss of pride, national standing and status. The hero of Homer's *Odyssey* experiences profound disruption of memory and continuity in the aftermath of the fall of Troy; his sense of a once-familiar place and world is completely ravaged as a result (Crowley 2014). It is very much a soldier's journey.

Wounded minds cannot rest, and in Germanic and Nordic folklore the nightmare is sleep disturbed by an evil spirit (Old Norse *mara*; Middle English *mare*) who rides oppressively on the chest of the victim. These are the souls of living people, or witches, who are able to leave their bodies and who travel with the intent of tormenting others. In the Icelandic Sagas – and commonly in myths and holy books – nightmares are portents or warnings of events to come. Similarly, in Shakespeare's references to 'troublous dreams', many have natural/supernatural, divine/diabolic significance. In *Macbeth*, Lennox complains, 'The night has been unruly, Where we lay, Our chimneys were blown down, and, as they say, Lamentings heard i' th' air, strange screams of death, and prophesying with accents terrible' (Act 2, Scene 3). The disturbance in question relates to the death of King Duncan, on that same night. Graphic imagery of 'dire combustion', apocalyptic confusion, tumult, storms, rebellion and turmoil were common ways of describing disorder in pre-modern times, with Providence usually serving as the principle of explanation.

The notion that ordinary rest and memory are disrupted by trauma – and the individual disoriented as a result – is common in Renaissance literature, with its cultures of melancholy and references to the 'wounds' of love and diseases of life, including those not visibly borne. Scholars have also examined the literary imagination of the Romantic period, with its own stock of images, such as 'infirmity of the mind', the 'wounding of honour' and, as in Renaissance times, 'wounded hearts', that are literary versions of the later concept of psychic trauma (Schönfelder 2013).

Notions of nostalgia (from *nostos*, return to one's native land and *algos*, pain) returned from the classical world to that of the 17th century onwards to explain the distress experienced by mercenaries (oddly, Swiss soldiers were highlighted) and all those considered broken and unfit for further fighting (Rosen 1975; Sedikides, Wildschut and Baden 2004). Listless, solitary and melancholic, such soldiers were stricken by a form of homesickness. As a concept, nostalgia soon travelled beyond the confines of Swiss mercenaries and was considered a proven clinical entity by the end of the 18th century. And by the end of the next century again, nostalgia was linked to nervous disorder and melancholy. In the killing fields of the American Civil War nostalgia was a common diagnosis, some doctors emphasizing its psychological aspects and others its physiological. One notable medic, working with Civil War veterans, considered those disturbances to the cardiovascular system said to be implicated and coined what became popular expressions, 'soldier's heart' or 'irritable heart' (also, in honour of its founder, Da Costa's syndrome: Da Costa 1871). Trauma and sickness symptoms were increasingly diagnosed beyond the theatre of war, this time associated with industry and accident, 'railway spine theory' and 'concussion of the spine' more generally were amongst the new categories of trauma. Terms like 'commotion' and 'concussion' were used, the latter derived from Latin *con*, meaning together and *quatere*, meaning to shake, strike or dash, and had contextual relevance in terms of the potential 'shocks' of modern, industrial life. The end of the 19th century and beginning of the 20th witnessed an epidemic of nervous disorders, such as hysteria and neurasthenia, with entire psychiatric and psychoanalytic empires being based upon them. Trauma was often implicated, and the focus less on industry than the occurrences of 'private', domestic life.

If interest in trauma dipped at the start of the 20th century, interest was soon, and urgently, revived. War encourages psychiatry and with World War I a new picture and social context thrust itself onto the stage; visible and invisible injuries were all around, and by 1915–16 the idea of 'shell-shock' was established. Charles Myers, a British psychologist employed by the army as consultant and nerve specialist, was the first to officially use the expression (Babbington 1997; Weegmann 2006). I will not trace this fascinating history, but note that Myers was called upon to explain those shell-shock symptoms originally seen as caused by unobserved molecular damage, the result allegedly of proximity to bombardment. His discovery was to find that many of the men in question had not been near a bomb, and so it was not a question of physical but of mental injury and the wounded mind. Meanwhile debates about its true causation raged with many contributing to the debate. The celebrated contribution of W.H.R. Rivers at Craiglockhart Hospital and his 'talking treatment' with war poet Siegfried Sassoon has been fictionalized in Pat Baker's (1993) novel (and film) *Regeneration*.

Addiction and trauma: Close cousins, travelling companions, different beasts

In American psychiatric terminology, substance addiction figures within a range of substance use disorders, whilst trauma figures within post-traumatic stress disorder. As a psychiatric society, these forms of classifications and demarcations are highly influential ways of seeing things, even if they are not the only way of seeing things; increasingly, patients apply such language and classifications to themselves, in a process that Hacking (1995) calls 'cultural looping'. Appreciation of these and other cultural contexts of meaning-making is still an essential component to an understanding of such disorders (Brodie and Redfield 2002; Maercker, Heim and Kirmayer 2018).

There are potential crossovers and overlaps between the two disorders in that someone with PTSD might resort to substances to cope, and those with substance misuse histories may have experienced traumatic life experiences, even if this does not have a predictive value *per se*. People may sometimes meet criteria for more than one disorder, as in dual diagnosis and multi-morbidity. It is important to underline that addiction is itself a traumatizing disorder, with substance misuse repeatedly exposing individuals to experiences of loss of control, accidents and the cumulative damage that is often life-shortening if not life-ending (Khantzian and Wilson 1993). Although trauma does not necessarily lead to substance misuse, there are similarities in the phenomenology, with individuals feeling less in control of their lives and less able to activate good self-care, and left compromised in terms of hope. Both addiction and trauma involve repetitive patterns: intrusions in the case of trauma and compulsion in the case of addiction. There remains an interesting difference between the disorders, insofar as an addicted person actively seeks their object of consumption whereas the traumatized person avoids situations that remind them in any way of the trauma, but traumatic memories force their way back. By contrast, in addiction the memory is often distorted by euphoric recall and an ingenious editing out of negative consequences. In short, whilst addiction has invited objects, trauma has feared objects.

Mapping addiction

The influential relapse prevention model of Marlatt and Gordon (1985) regards addictive behaviours as maladaptive, over-learned (over-practised) behaviours whose short-term benefits are compelling to the user. The use of a substance, at the time of use, seems to be able to solve certain problems and to lift subjective feelings, becoming an ingrained pattern or habit. For those embarking on change, relapse prevention aims to interrupt the problematic, self-reinforcing patterns of substance use whilst at the same time building new, alternative skills of coping. Unlike approaches that are mainly concerned with persuasion, motivation or challenging people to 'admit' their problems, 'break down denial', and so on, relapse prevention is a social learning model that considers *how* people are addicted and the need to create an alternative repertoire of responses. The relapse prevention model is a pragmatic and evidence-based approach to addictive behaviour, helping to build the confidence or the self-efficacy, and the skills, that are required to forge a viable path of recovery.

I ran a weekly Relapse Prevention Group for many years and

incorporated a range of creative exercises. Amongst these was the construction of maps or sketches, consisting of drawing a bird's-eye view of a person's situation, sites of drug/alcohol use, alternative social activities and resources (Weegmann 2005b). Consider two examples:

Julie's resource

As she was in her first year of abstinence from substances, Julie sketched what she called a 'recovery map', resembling a spider diagram. A regular group member, people believed that they knew Julie well, but as she put detail to her map we learned new aspects about her life and social connections. Not far from her home on the map, which she labelled 'Safety', she drew a church and a group of people nearby, labelled 'Resource'. Julie at first spoke with hesitation, being worried that the group would not be interested to hear about 'private beliefs.' Instead, other members were curious to hear more and so Julie explained the centrality of church activities to her recovery, including a church walking group. Taking courage, she said more about the role of her beliefs. Julie shared a parable of King David, who spots beautiful Bathsheba bathing from the vantage point of his palace. The King believed he could take anything – or anyone – he saw, and so the story of Bathsheba represented a tale of complacency, power and temptation. Julie used the parable as a reminder, adding, 'I think of that story every time the thought of having a drink passes my mind.'

In response, others too spoke of a complacency that creeps in with recovery, marked by temptations to drink, nostalgia and other memory distortions. One person said, 'I can spot when the drinker starts to romanticize what I did, and forgets where I ended up.'

Ian's drinking holes

In contrast to Julie, Ian struggled to remain abstinent from alcohol for more than a month or two before 'falling off the wagon', his expression for relapse. He was demoralized, feeling defeated in his efforts to achieve change. As Ian sketched his map in the group, populated by various pubs, another person said, 'Well, your drinking is hidden in plain sight – it's all around you!' Although Ian played this down, retorting that public houses were 'common landmarks', he soon acknowledged how easily they became the very centres of his life. Ian entitled his map, 'My neighbourhood', whilst another member suggested the alternative 'Ian's drinking-holes'.

There is a useful contribution for a sociology of drinking places (and other leisure spaces), conceived as 'third places' beyond home and occupation with distinctive conventions and opportunities for social bonding (Jenkins 2007; Oldenburg 1991). They are characterized by informality, playfulness, social contact, and more. All were relevant to Ian's lifestyle, pubs being his main option and preference for spending time, rewarding himself and mixing with various 'regulars'. Giddens (1992) says that addiction is a form of 'time out', and if one's culture is centred around the idea that alcohol is reward and a natural way of meeting people, it is easy to understand the role and allure of pub to some people. Ian had little by way of an alternative notion of sociality, and there was powerful sensory familiarity to the pub, as he described their 'homely sounds' and the visceral, positive anticipations of 'popping inside'. Asked about the converse place of the relapse prevention group on his map, Ian replied, 'That's me looking for a new way.' Ian was indeed looking for a new way but had no real conception or imagination about what that could be. He wondered if moving away from his neighbourhood could help, but another person said, 'but you'll only take your problems with you, unless you do something about them'.

Comment

The use of maps, as illustrated by Julie and Ian, helps trace the sites and territory of substance use, highlighting the social contexts involved. They have the advantage of increasing the visibility of connections and activities that might otherwise not be spoken of. Maps point to the importance of an 'ecological view' of addiction (Moos, Finney and Cronkite 1990). Wittgenstein (1953/2009) spoke about 'noticing an aspect' and 'aspect blindness', and relapse or recovery maps do invite clients to look again at their lives, to see differently, all of which happens in the group context of telling and retelling their story. A picture does indeed 'tell a thousand words' (Dansereau and Simpson 2009).

Case study: Angie's story

Angie is an ex-patient of mine who here describes some aspects of her successful struggle to overcome the effects of both trauma and addiction.

She gave me permission to quote from her account, originally published in a journal series called 'Life after addiction' (Weegmann 2017b) and previously in a chapter concerned with 'dangerous cocktails – growing up with addiction' (Weegmann 2005a).

Rock bottom or realization?

Angie's family was from a heavy-drinking culture, and both her parents were alcoholics. An adult child of alcoholic parents, in time Angie developed her own drug and alcohol problems, causing serious damage to self, relationships and hope. All in all it took Angie two spells in rehabilitation, an addiction day centre and commitment to Alcoholics Anonymous to establish secure sobriety, at which point she came into my psychotherapy group where she stayed for four years.

With the benefit of hindsight, I asked her to elaborate on what enabled her to change course. Angie spoke of a 'moment of clarity' with a *realization that drink was more powerful than me. It was the destruction I had caused myself and others and I just knew the game was up. I didn't know where I was going but I knew I didn't want to be where I was or where I was heading.'* Alcoholics Anonymous grounded her sobriety, one day at a time, which Angie redefined as her 'daily bread'.

A culture of violence

When I first met Angie for an assessment, she showed a worrying degree of delinquency and was caught in a violent relationship; she dismissed any links between her trouble and misuse of substances. Her parents had not themselves been violent, but were inconsistent and neglectful.

I assessed Angie again a few years later, by which time she was sober and she looked like a different person, albeit it with many fears. We agreed some family sessions, with her daughter, which was, *'help with emotional separation, as my daughter had taken on the role of "parent"'*, after which she joined my psychotherapy group for four years.

Experiences of group therapy

'I started using substances at a young age and came from a neglected background – my parents were both alcoholics. As a child I felt fearful and believed that the world was cruel and unsafe. I started smoking around eight and solvents around 11. I liked the feeling it gave me and felt a real sense of not being there, which I loved. I stopped using solvents but began to drink regularly in my teens. I believe I was an alcoholic from my first drink as I never

drank sensibly and got into trouble from the start. I started having blackouts from 14 where I couldn't remember the night. But drink helped me feel better and I was no longer this terrified little girl. I didn't give a shit. Each day I would drink and go into a fantasy world. My whole world was falling apart. I was in a dark, lonely, and desperate place.

Three years into sobriety I hit an emotional rock bottom as I became aware that I could not feel love for my daughter, and just felt numb, very frozen. I attended a psychotherapy group once a week for about four years. I felt uneasy with [the therapist] as I found him hard to read, I used to crack jokes about him and realize that I was testing him to see if he would react and hurt me. I projected a lot of negative stuff I had around men onto him, as well as my own negative feelings I had about myself, which he pointed out. I felt very nervous attending this group as they were people from all walks of life, but the group helped me to challenge my assumptions about people, i.e. it's not just addicts that struggle in life. Slowly I began to sit with these uncomfortable feelings and began to trust the group and realized the psychotherapist wasn't this scary person I projected, and that he was a nice man.

The group helped me grow, was a space where I first found my voice. I learnt that people can get angry but it doesn't have to end with violence, and I got in touch with some painful emotions around old traumas. The group expanded my life as I began to take risks, but positive ones. I used to attack people when challenged instead of responding, so have become aware of my defences. I have reclaimed my voice – actually I used to physically lose my voice, which was psychosomatic. I created fantasy parents as the neglect was too painful. I learned how to parent myself.'

Mourning the childhood she did not have and re-evaluating the childhood she did have, were central to the work she did in the group. As she commented (after one year in the group):

'In these last few weeks, I've had so many feelings from when I was small, so many small things which make me angry to think about. It's like with everything they [her parents] always put drink first – like if we were on holiday, it would be the pub all day and if I was ill that was a problem because they might be too hungover to look after me. So, I had to look after me. They were always in some kind of mood – loud when they were drunk, feeling sorry for themselves the day after, or guilty when they were off it for a few weeks, and then I was given a lot of freedom, but punished when they were back on it again. I did not know whether I was coming or going.'

As she spoke, Angie shook and would periodically glance at me. Because drinking was normalized, Angie had no evident means of 'seeing' the alcoholism at home during her growing-up years. She did, however, recall a dawning sense that her family was not 'like others' and an awkwardness when the topic of family life was discussed at school. It was only when she managed to stop drinking and face reality that she was able to re-evaluate her parents and see the problems, which, to outsiders, would have been all-too apparent.

Angie revisited many of the small details and patterns of family life, including sequences of behaviour, such as: drinking parent—intoxicated parent—withdrawing/sick parent—dry parent. There were corresponding affective patterns, such as: tension—disinhibition—moodiness—guilt. With the help of group discussion, Angie came to see how her own affective responses were tied in to the behaviour of her parents, as she learned the art of maintaining vigilance, scanning her parents for signs of the state they were in and, above all, maintaining safety. Her vigilance of me in the group, the nervous glance, was, I surmised, an expression of her need to maintain safety in the therapy and to anticipate my possible responses.

Comment

Angie taught me a great deal about the realities of growing up with addiction in the family and the depth and persistence of family wounds. Intergeneration is a critical dimension, with the transmission of risk and vulnerability, and her openness to family world was a hopeful sign. Angie used different resources at different stages of recovery – e.g. rehabilitation, AA (which is still there in her life), day centre, therapy group, and so on.

Angie was caught up in cycles of trauma and addiction, so mixed that they were hard to disentangle. She speaks movingly of the world of her parents – for whom alcohol came first – her own serious troubles as child and adolescent, and immersion in an abusive relationship. Psychotherapy, as Bowlby suggested (1988), is one way in which more protective developmental pathways can be built to counter and gradually weaken the effects of negative models and to 'disprove' the worse aspects of fear-based internal working models.

Violence came later – hers and that of a former partner – unleashed by new rounds of substance abuse in a compound of consequences – as she said, *'I continued to drink and the relationship worsened.'* Addictive behaviour is itself traumatizing, establishing closed circuits of behaviour so that a person's repertoire of responses becomes stereotyped and narrowed down. Having said this, addiction is reinforced as a result of its apparent short-term effectiveness in the killing of psychological pain and as way of coping with trauma, such as violence at the hands of a partner (Weegmann and Khantzian 2017). Khantzian and Wilson (1993, p.269) put it succinctly, in that drugs 'substitute dysphoria and a relationship with suffering they do not understand or control for one they do understand and control'.

The group was, it seems, an important staging post, which, Angie says, *'helped me grow, was a space where I first found my voice'*. Group therapy provides opportunities for mirroring, identification, support and reality testing, and is also a sober resource. I seemed to represent a compound of safety and danger and was aware that Angie did not just bring 'internal parents' but was herself a parent trying to provide a better foundation for her child. In time she was able to experience conflict or arguments between group members with less fear: *'I learnt that people can get angry but it doesn't have to end with violence, and I got in touch with some painful emotions around old traumas.'*

Recovery: Idiom and image

There are many ways in which people describe recovery from addiction and disorders such as trauma – recovering, 'pathway to normal living', growth, renewal, sober, strength, transformation, flourishing, breakthrough, pushing-on, spiritual awakening – to name a few. Angie also referred to turning points, another common expression for change. Robert Frost's 1916 poem *The Road Not Taken* was originally about a walk but has been taken up by many who use it metaphorically to characterize a road or journey of recovery.

Addiction represents personal trouble and social issues. Likewise, trauma represents personal trouble and social issues. One way of thinking about recovery from both disorders is to see them as defining forms of 'life-after', during which new paths are forged whilst the person concerned re-authors their experience. In a recent consultation with a client who experienced sexual abuse in childhood, they remarked, 'I don't want to live my life as defined by the past, I want to reclaim my future.' Addiction and trauma leave a trail of consequences and are stripping of health, purpose and hope. Recovery has to be well-founded, compelling enough and able to provide a viable alternative to the disorder that it leaves behind. A sense of future, a road less travelled by, has to be built.

Let us examine recovery further on the basis of three related notions, (a) rites of passage, (b) recovery narratives and (c) personal journeys.

Turner (1969) sees rites of passage as transitions from one state to another, traversing a betwixt and between or *liminal* period, which he defines as a passage 'through a cultural realm that has few or none of the characteristics of the attributes of the past or coming state' (p.94). Rites of passage are about status change, but unlike the rites of passage and ritual that surround established cultural and religious transitions, there is a looser way in which the term has come to be used, which applies to transitions more broadly, as, say, during a process of recovery. Each person who 'makes it' fashions a distinctive route from addiction and/or trauma, creates a personal idiom of recovery, even if this form is borrowed from existing cultural models of change, as provided, for instance, by Alcoholics Anonymous (Weegmann 2017a). Re-orientation, becoming oneself and knowing what one wants is slow and painstaking, made clear by Angie's story. Recovery is seldom only a matter of achieving psychic change but critically involves reconnecting and re-joining wider human resources, resources that support the migration of identity.

Narrative psychology starts from the assumption that we are 'story-creating animals' who continually make sense of our actions and reorient ourselves throughout life within narrative-like structures (Bruner 1987; Sarbin 1986). People who face serious adversity, such as alcoholism or PTSD, find means of accounting for their condition and reappraise themselves when they embark upon major change, such as committing to abstinence or overcoming fear. The shadow of any potentially chronic disorder is long, and recovery requires a remarkable re-adaptation and revision of personal identity. Transformations in narrative identity – how people speak and figure themselves – are critical to the recovery of a more coherent, ordered sense of self, of a viable autobiography, so that life can be rebuilt after devastation. Harré (1997, p.177) argues that it is through narratives that are expressed '"[the] sort of person one is, what one's strengths and weaknesses are and what one's life has been", and moreover, given that the self-concept is linked to the "stories we tell about ourselves", the actions one performs as oneself'. Rodriquez-Morales (2019, p.157) in her research on change, suggests that 'former lives in addiction were re-evaluated and so too were their "former selves"'. Angie, in her account, refers to the many steps involved in achieving change, each providing recovery resources or capital along the way, and found ways to integrate how she was and what she used to do with the confident, forward-looking identity as actively responsible for her recovery. She found membership of Alcoholics Anonymous, for example, a sustaining narrative community, amongst other things (Weegmann 2017b). From the perspective of resilience and post-traumatic growth (Joseph 2009), subsequent (new or renewed) relationships can improve and people may change their view of themselves and/or their wider outlook in life (White, Laudet and Becker 2006).

Many people use journey metaphors to describe recovery. Schultz (1944) argues that everyday reality provides people with a sense of continuity and security, with automatic recipes for action and 'practical knowledge' of what is likely to happen. What, then, when a person embarks upon a process of significant change, such as recovery from addition or trauma? 'Through passage to a new status (e.g. ex-drinker) or a new social world (e.g. a recovery network), persons may find themselves on the threshold of uncharted territory whose customs, contours and inhabitants are unknown' (Pollner and Stein 1996, p.205). The clinical example of mapping addiction and recovery is one small way in which a person can stop, pause, appraise their direction and envisage the territory into which they would like to move.

Conclusion

In tracing something of the etymology and imagery of disorders like addiction and trauma we can see something of importance about the contexts in which they are defined and their associated meanings. By extension, through listening to the everyday allegories and metaphors that clients use we gain important insights into the contexts and meanings of their life spaces.

The use of 'mapping' of substance use, risk and recovery resources helps clients to see, and to show to others, aspects of their living and physical spaces. As I hope Ian's and Julie's maps show, they allow us to home in on those details that are easily missed and overlooked – others too are invited to 'take a look' and provide their own feedback, especially if done in groups. People think and express themselves in narrative forms, by which they make sense of their lives and progress (or otherwise) through it. We 'author' ourselves and our lives in all kinds of interesting ways. Angie's story brings home a reconstruction of herself over many years. Recovery, in this respect, can be thought of as a complicated and non-linear 'rite of passage', in which narrative unfolding occurs.

References

Babbington, A. (1997) *Shell-Shock: A History of Changing Attitudes to War Neurosis*. London: Lee Cooper.

Bowlby, J. (1988) 'Developmental psychiatry comes of age.' *American Journal of Psychiatry 145*, 1, 1–10.

Brewin, C. (2007) *Posttraumatic Stress Disorder: Malady or Myth?* New Haven, CT: Yale University Press

Brodie, J.F. and Redfield, M. (2002) *High Anxieties: Cultural Studies in Addiction*. Berkeley, CA: University of California Press.

Bruner, J. (1987) 'Life as narrative.' *Social Research 54*, 1, 691–710.

Bury, M. (1982) 'Chronic illness as biographical disruption.' *Sociology of Health and Illness 4*, 2, 167–182.

Cox, M. and Theilgaard, A. (1987) *Mutative Metaphors in Psychotherapy: The Aeolian Mode*. London: Tavistock Publications.

Crowley, J. (ed.) (1999) *The Drunkard's Progress: Narratives of Addiction, Despair and Recovery*. New York, NY: Johns Hopkins University Press.

Crowley, J. (2014) 'Beyond the Universal Soldier: Combat Trauma in Classical Antiquity.' In P. Meineck and D. Konstan (eds) *Combat Trauma and the Ancient Greeks* (Chapter 5). London: Palgrave Macmillan.

Da Costa, J.M. (1871, January) 'On irritable heart.' *American Journal of the Medical Sciences*, pp.18–52.

Dansereau, D. and Simpson, D. (2009) 'A picture is worth a thousand words: A case for graphic representation.' *Professional Psychology: Research and Practice 40*, 1, 104–110.

De Quincey, T. (2003) *Confessions of an English Opium-Eater*. London: Penguin Classics. (Original work published 1823)

Derrida, J. (1981) 'Plato's Pharmacy.' In *Dissemination*. Chicago, IL: University of Chicago Press.

Furedi, F. (2004) *Therapy Culture: Cultivating Vulnerability in an Uncertain Age*. London: Routledge.

Gelb, A. and Gelb, B. (1960) *O'Neill*. New York, NY: Harper and Brothers.

Giddens, A. (1992) *The Transformation of Intimacy*. Cambridge: Polity Press.

Hacking, I. (1995) 'The Looping Effects of Human Kinds.' In D. Sperber and A. Premack (eds) *Causal Cognition* (Chapter 10). Oxford: Oxford University Press.

Harré, R. (1997) 'Pathological autobiographies.' *Philosophy, Psychiatry and Psychology 4*, 99–109.

Huxley, A. (2007) *Brave New World*. London: Vintage. (Original work published 1932)

Jenkins, P. (2007) *The Local: A History of the English Pub*. Stroud: The History Press.

Joseph, S. (2009) 'Growth following adversity: Positive psychological perspective on posttraumatic stress.' *Psychological Topics 18*, 2, 335–344.

Khantzian, E. and Wilson, A. (1993) 'Substance Abuse, Repetition and the Nature of Addictive Suffering.' In A. Wilson and J. Gedo, (eds) *Hierarchical Concepts in Psychoanalysis* (pp.263–283). New York, NY: Guilford Press.

Lemon, R. (2018) *Addiction and Devotion in Early Modern England*. Philadelphia, PA: University of Pennsylvania Press.

Maercker, A., Heim, E. and Kirmayer, L.J. (2018) *Cultural Clinical Psychology and PTSD.* Boston, MA: Hogrefe.

Marlatt, A. and Fromme, K. (1987) 'Metaphors for addiction.' *Journal of Drug Issues 17*, 2, 9–28.

Marlatt, A. and Gordon, J. (1985) *Relapse Prevention.* New York, NY: Guilford Press.

McKendrick, N., Brewer, J. and Plumb, J. (1982) *The Birth of a Consumer Society: The Commercialisation of Eighteenth-century England.* Bloomington, IN: Indiana University Press.

Meineck, P. and Konstan, D. (eds) (2014) *Combat Trauma and the Ancient Greeks.* London: Palgrave Macmillan.

Moos, R., Finney, J. and Cronkite, R. (1990) *Alcoholism: Context, Process and Outcome.* New York, NY: Oxford University Press.

Oldenburg, R. (1991) *The Great Good Place.* New York, NY: Marlowe and Company.

Orford, J. (2009) *Excessive Appetites: A Psychological View of Addictions* (2nd edn). Chichester: Wiley.

Pollner, M. and Stein, J. (1996) 'Narrative mapping of social worlds: The voice of experience in Alcoholics Anonymous.' *Symbolic Interaction 19*, 3, 203–223.

Rodriques-Morales, L. (2019) 'A hero's journey: Becoming and transcendence in addiction recovery.' *Journal of Psychological Therapies 4*, 2, 55–166.

Rosen, G. (1975) 'Nostalgia: A "forgotten" psychological disorder.' *Psychological Medicine 5*, 3, 340–354.

Sarbin, T. (1986) *Narrative Psychology: The Storied Nature of Human Conduct.* New York, NY: Praeger.

Schönfelder, C. (2013) *Wounds and Words: Childhood and Family Trauma in Romantic and Postmodern Fiction.* Bielefeld: Transcript Verlag.

Schultz, A. (1944) 'The stranger: An essay in social psychology.' *American Journal of Sociology 49*, 6, 499–507.

Sedikides, C., Wildschut, T. and Baden, D. (2004) 'Nostalgia.' In J. Greenberg (ed.) *Handbook of Experimental Existential Psychology* (Chapter 13). New York, NY: Guilford Press.

Shinebourne, P. and Smith, J. (2009) 'Alcohol and the self: An interpretative phenomenological analysis of the experience of addiction and its impact on the sense of self and identity.' *Addiction Research and Theory 17*, 152–167.

Shinebourne, P. and Smith, J. (2010) 'The communicative power of metaphors: An analysis and interpretation of metaphors in accounts of the experience of addiction.' *Psychology and Psychotherapy: Theory, Research, Practice 83*, 59–73.

Summerfield, D. (2001) 'The invention of post-traumatic stress disorder and the social usefulness of a psychiatric category.' *British Medical Journal 322*, 95–98.

Tedeschi, R. and Calhoun, L. (2004) 'Posttraumatic growth: Conceptual foundations and empirical evidence.' *Psychological Inquiry 15*, 1, 1–18.

Turner, V. (1969) *The Ritual Process: Structure and Anti-Structure.* Ithaca, NY: Cornell University Press.

Walton, S. (2001) *Out of It: A Cultural History of Intoxication.* London: Hamish Hamilton.

Weegmann, M. (2002) 'Growing Up with Addiction.' In M. Weegmann and R. Cohen (eds) *Psychodynamics of Addiction* (Chapter 11). Chichester: Wiley.

Weegmann, M. (2005a) 'Dangerous cocktails: Drugs and Alcohol Within the Family.' In M. Bower (ed.) *Psychoanalytic Theory for Social Work* (Chapter 10). London and New York, NY: Routledge.

Weegmann, M. (2005b) 'The road to recovery: Journeys and relapse risk maps.' *Drugs and Alcohol Today 5*, 1, 42–45.

Weegmann, M. (2006) 'The humanisation of trauma: Witnessing and social context.' *Therapeutic Communities 27*, 2, 163–175.

Weegmann, M. (2017a) 'Alcoholics Anonymous and 12 Step Therapy: A Psychologist's View.' In P. Davis, R. Patton and S. Jackson (eds) *Addiction: Psychology and Treatment* (Chapter 14). Chichester: Wiley.

Weegmann, M. (2017b) 'Life after addiction: Understanding recovery.' *Psychodynamic Practice 23*, 3, 293–304.

Weegmann, M. (2017c) 'Narrative Identity and Change: Addiction and Recovery.' In P. Davis, R. Patton and S. Jackson (eds) *Addiction: Psychology and Treatment* (Chapter 9). Chichester: Wiley.

Weegmann, M. and Khantzian, E. (2017) 'Dangerous Desires and Inanimate Attachments: A Psychodynamic Approach to Substance Misuse.' In P. Davis, R. Patton and S. Jackson (eds) *Addiction: Psychology and Treatment* (Chapter 5). Chichester: Wiley.

White, W., Laudet, A.B. and Becker, J.B. (2006) 'Life meaning and purpose in addiction recovery.' *Addiction Professional 4*, 4, 18–23.

Wittgenstein, L. (2009) *Philosophical Investigations* (P. Hacker and J. Schulte, eds). Oxford: Blackwell. (Original work published 1953)

14

How to Manage the Impossible?

Using Image and Narrative in a Psycho-anthropological Approach to Support a Parent of a Child with a Rare Chronic Disease

Tania Korsak

Parents confronted with rare and chronic illness in their child undergo an 'ontological collapse', a complete break with their previous psycho-cultural references. In order to cope with this kind of diagnosis, their daily lives are initially limited to home and hospital. The distress prevents them from establishing links between their past and future lives and from building meaningful connections between the shape of their own lives and that of their chronically ill child. Faced with distraught parents, doctors find it difficult to collect information related to the child's health and grasp the full nosological details. Dialogue with parents remains so necessary, both to provide ongoing care and in collecting vital information for appropriate treatment and further research. While some parents remain affected all their lives by this collapse, others wrestle with their new lives and engage with it through affirming new priorities. We modelled this process and created learning devices called 'sorting exercises', based on images and metaphors aimed at empowering the families.

I was trained in anthropology and specialized in psychoeducational tools. My clinical practice centres around Clean Language; a pre-linguistic tool that helps transform sensation into words through metaphors and vice versa. David Grove, the founder of this method, mentored me in his later years, in both trauma work and inner child therapy. In 2011 I began researching families facing severe chronic illness in their children under the tutelage of Professor Olivier Dulac (who at the time was the founder of the neuro-paediatric ward of the Necker hospital in Paris and was the director of the Institute of Rare Diseases). This ongoing research has been a challenging and humbling experience in which the psycho-anthropological and Clean Language approaches have proved to be invaluable.

Being faced with the diagnosis of a rare disease in one's child is a definitive reversal of the expectations of lived experience; in this sense it is catastrophic. Unlike the socially and culturally shared experience of mourning, with which it is sometimes compared, one of the challenges of facing the predicament of a rare disease in one's family is that it is largely unknown. It does not belong to the host of shared experiences. This results in a collapse of meaning and a struggle to put it into words, agree on future perspectives and define priorities. Moreover, unlike the process of mourning, the child is alive, seeking more attention as the situation becomes more complex with time. Parents are therefore forced to take on this horrendous and 'unshared' situation *alone*. It is *only within themselves* that they are likely to find the necessary resources. To date, very little research has been conducted in this field so parents negotiate the field poor of landmarks and tools to use.

Developing the psycho-anthropological approach

I have studied this traumatic experience for over seven years using a psycho-anthropological perspective. My clinical work focused on Dravet syndrome, a form of early and severe epilepsy, refractory to treatment.

First, I shadowed pediatricians at Necker Hospital, in their meetings with peers and in their consultations. Each consultation was con-cluded with a debriefing with the doctor to clarify what had happened between the parents and the doctor, followed by an analysis of what could be perceived of the parents' experience. This then led to informal discussion with nurses and parents in the wards of the hospital.

Second, for 30 months I facilitated individual meetings with approximately 40 parents as part of the Dravet Syndrome Alliance charity (ASD-France) using Clean Language as a means to understand what families were experiencing *from within*. Stemming from this understanding I then devised tools (sorting exercises) to support parents to model their life experience. In addition to these exchanges with parents I became directly involved in the charity's activities (round tables, workshops, events, mediation, etc.) which helped build strong bonds with some parents and enabled me to refine understandings of everyday struggles.

Third, in 2017–18 I conducted two qualitative studies in collaboration with ASD. This was a chance to present and improve a generic model of the predicament and experience the sorting exercises through monthly three-hour workshops with a group of eight parents. A semi-structured questionnaire followed by an in-depth interview with 20 other parents helped gain understanding of the conditions of announcing a diagnosis and the difficulties parents face when attempting to weave sense into their lives. The results of this study were presented to medical congresses in 2017, at the Journées Françaises de l'Épilepsie (JFE) in Marseille, and 2018, at the Société Française de Neurologie Pédiatrique (SFNP) in Bordeaux. I reshuffled the model into a more comprehensive tool for the caring profession and presented it in Vienna in 2018 at the European Congress on Epileptology.

Finally, throughout 2019 I focused my research on siblings of the sick children. The modelling and the sorting exercises proved invaluable. In 2019 I participated in two symposiums, the SFNP in Athens and the JFE in Paris. My objective is now to deploy the model and the sorting exercises to other rare diseases, as I believe that carers are in desperate need of this care.

Exploration and discovery

Post-colonial anthropologists do not have licence to reinterpret experience as if it was a separate reality, as if the other was an object of inquiry; knowledge is acquired through ongoing and dynamic inquiry into the ways we are part of and participate in different becomings (Barad 2007), we immerse ourselves in the experience and are transformed by it and by the people we meet. As with client-centred psychotherapy, anthropologists do not know ahead of the exploration, do not know better than clients, do not read minds or bodies. They simply discover what is perhaps already known by the other, or perhaps uncover something new as the collaborative exploration moves onward. This participant observation means both to experience and to be present to what is happening, free of intervention, free of interpretation, and yet to participate in untainted transformative immersion. In this sense, Clean Language is an anthropological tool that supports the inner symbolic journey of the explorer by not interfering with the images and the words of the client and nonetheless being so sensitively close that it may reveal something of the unexpected.

In other words, my practice is a licence to create conditions to let reinterpretation happen, from this untainted or 'clean' posture. As in Good's (2012) words, '[t]he way we learn about others' subjectivity depends on the place we ourselves occupy'; with the parents concerned with the predicament, it is essential not to fall into issues of ranking the 'knowing' of what the other may know differently. In brief, my psycho-anthropology journey has been an attempt to create conditions to collaboratively explore what resists this catastrophic situation, in order to generate empowerment for those concerned.

Metaphor – gateway to experiencing from within

Facing rare disease in one's child is like being thrown into the middle of the ocean, without any explanation as to why, without a manual, nor training, nor direction in which to swim, without hope of ever stopping, without a rescue team, nor resources, nor solutions, nor hopes, nor methods, nor models, without adult centres for our children, without arms, without legs, without dreams...[1]

In 2012, in response to my suggestions, ASD France found an office on l'Île de la Cité, Paris, via its network, to carry out individual sessions. It was a perfect setting, as the office overlooked the River Seine and had a view of Nôtre Dame. This opportunity provided a unique setting for exploring with parents a range of issues families faced, from the love for their child to the fear of their death. Subjects ranged from violence, despair, difficulties with the caring profession, the side effects of treatment, isolation and lack of career prospects to inadequate institutions and inadequate professionals. These exchanges, deeply personal and sensitive, were an opportunity to weigh the extent of the difficulties and to observe the diversity of associated behaviours.

---

1   Information collected in a group at the last AG 2018 of ASD; 185 parents were present at Imagerie Institute, Necker, Paris.

Using open questions, the parent was asked to build a metaphorical landscape to depict the complex situations of their experience in terms of single images or symbols. This psycho-anthropological approach, inspired by Clean Language, helped to understand from within what parents were experiencing without trying to suggest new ways of thinking. It became apparent that it was possible to develop a new kind of tool, 'sorting exercises', what came to be psycho-sensory devices that generate new insights and stimulate the parent's ability to reorganize internally, sometimes even rebuild an understanding of their condition. An opportunity for the parent to reclaim his/her history and his/her own solutions:

> As in a forest of thorns that should be clear to find the small path that leads to an objective. You[2] say, 'Stand there, there are brambles, what are you doing?' – Well, I take my gloves and I clear them, allowing me to move to another stage and to discover new perspectives, a different vision and different solutions that seem obvious because they are already in me.

It was thus possible to apprehend these new and poorly understood situations, to identify the path of the parent best suited to their experience and to create landmarks, specific 'sensitive' phases, exploring the best means of supporting them.

The phases of a psycho-anthropological journey

Facing this kind of diagnosis and its implications is like a rite of passage that asks the parent to pass through the conditions of initiation, which seem inevitably to entail some form of initial traumatic shock, namely a collapse of previous identifications, before being able to regenerate and re-appropriate new means of understanding (Van Gennep 1909).

Parents facing their child's illness are not in a state of unconscious regression. They are caught in an intense process of constructing and learning that calls upon all their imagination and intelligence. To support this movement, it seemed more appropriate to speak of a 'phase of appropriation' as in the ontological movement of humanity, which successively found means to dominate nature and to prevail in the world, rather than referring to the developmental phases in a

---

2   Tania Korsak as facilitator.

child, which would imply that the parent in this initiation would be in regression. The 'symbiotic, magical, mythical, spatiotemporal, individual and collective' phases is the nomenclature with which the author aims to echo the immensity of what these families face (Figure 14.1). The steps and phases are described in detail below.

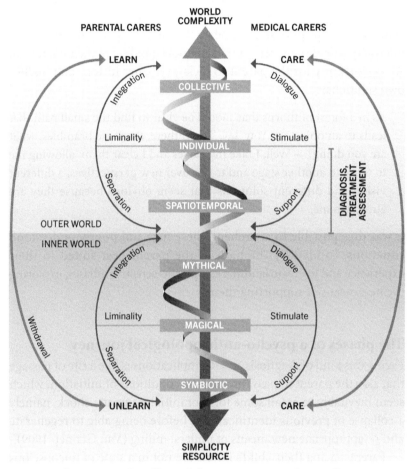

Figure 14.1: Capable model – a gateway to understanding complexities (Korsak et al. 2018)

1. The traumatic shock

Following the announcement of the diagnosis the parent experiences a real collapse. Every parent met in this study evokes a traumatic injury.

'It is as if the doctor had taken a bazooka and shot me in the legs.'

'I remained silent, unable to move, glued to my chair, frozen.'

'Since that day of the diagnosis, I drag a cannonball chained to my foot.'

Few people realize that this shock is only the beginning of a succession of recurring events, each more painful than the other. After this initial diagnostic shock, parents wander in a state of confusion, unable to find any kind of support due to the lack of available references.

'This is the third time he has had a heart attack, he is convulsing from the age of four months, the nurse told me that I would soon be able to go home. To go home? To come back to the hospital? When? Tomorrow? In a month? My husband doesn't want to know anything. I had to stop working. No one wants to keep the baby. At the nursery home, they all got scared. I do not dare do anything. And if he has a new heart attack?'

Initially, the parent will attempt to remain attached to the reality of their daily life before they realize that their habits and future plans have become totally unrealistic.

'I loved partying; before the arrival of our child, I used to go out all the time, we had a real group of friends, I liked a laugh and dance... now I do not see anyone, yet I did try in the beginning to keep going out, I tried by all means...'

These 'failed' attempts to escape the new constraints of the disease leave all concerned baffled, in an uncomfortable nebula; friends, family and the wider circle are frightened by the enormity of the symptoms. Medical staff are stripped of their resources to offer encouraging prospects for the child, as medical care is often ineffectual. The unarmed parent, upset by the magnitude of the requirements, is unable to locate or to engage their reactions in the maze of complex and intricate problems. This situation thrusts the parent into an almost unbearable state of emptiness and rootlessness.

'A door slams and I remain behind this slammed door, just the noise of the door slamming, nothing else, just the door slamming, slamming without a sound, without even the wind, without a door to push open...'

*'My life has been scooped out of me, what remains is just empty...
scooped.'*

The parent then seems to pass through a tunnel.

*'I have the feeling of skidding, not being able to attach myself to
anything.'*

Old references to what-was-once, some form of shared normality,
vanish. Life seems to be reduced to waiting for the next crisis.

*'We do not sleep, do not eat. Nothing is as it was before. I do not know
where I am. Who I am? What I do? ...our life is a crisis, then another,
and then another.'*

A rupture with the past and a deconstruction of the parent's 'habitus'
follows.

'I do not know where I live.'

The last expression of this process of collapse is a 'genuine uncertainty
about the future', which is nothing other than the awareness that there
will never be a return to previous normality. An embodiment of a
'before' and 'after' the diagnosis.

*'I have lived a clean break. I was not prepared for this disease, even
though I had always thought of it.'*

2. The process of appropriation of new living conditions

Parents' isolation facing the announcement of the diagnosis forces
them to build their personal future in a world where social references
disappear from their daily life, where the habitus[3] has collapsed. In
order to survive, the 'offbeat' parent is faced with the need to re-invent
themselves, to discover that there is a possibility of a new process of
'individuation'.

2.1. The personal processes of adaptation

Because the parents' suffering is immeasurable, they have difficulties
maintaining relationships with others other than their child. They are

---

3   Marcel Mauss (Hubert and Mauss 1950), followed by Bourdieu (1990), attempted to
    show that the culture in which we were born shapes our understandings but also our
    behaviour and the way we pay attention.

centred on the family and the attachment to their child, a curtailed perspective. This apparent and temporary confinement is constitutive of this appropriation process. In this sense, the three phases described below may be understood as appropriately 'narcissistic' in the sense of focusing on 'their' own ability to make sense of 'their' experience.

'At first, I did not come to the Association, I did not want to meet other parents, I could not imagine that we could have something in common.'

I. Symbiotic Phase

The parent is in a state of deep sleep, stunned, shocked by their situation, devoid of prospects. Life forms and possibilities of life are one, the past has been swallowed up, the future does not exist.

'I do not remember my life before, it's like a perfume of which we have forgotten the smell, I know it existed but I do not recall how [it was].'

The parents and child are undifferentiated, they form a single-cell family, united by a love fusion.

'I live for my daughter and my daughter lives for me, she is my sun.'

'My son and I we are a team, we are locked together [hands are clasped together to illustrate].'

Consultation: A young mother holds with pride a child in her lap. 'I have come only to make sure everything is well.' The child has a marked squint, her mouth permanently open, tongue hanging. She has great difficulty holding her plagiocephalic head when sitting. She was born prematurely, and, at birth, the medical record shows that the mother was informed that her child would definitely require special medical attention. Six months later, none of these therapeutic necessities have been put in place by the mother. According to her, all is well; the child is gaining weight and is learning to sit. The mother is clinging to any signs of progress, she is using the conversation to search for hope and reassurance. 'I tell my husband that everything is going well, the glasses will repair the eyes,' as she twirls the glasses in question in her hand.

II. Magical Phase[4]

The parent is motivated by a desire to transform the situation. Ungrounded anticipation can sometimes seem compulsive, as an enthusiastic bias can cause the parent to over-interpret and fall for an apparent link between several independent things.

> *'I'll bring my son home, in the village we have someone who can take this evil away.'*

The family is under the effect of conflicting emotions. The parent, still strongly associated with the family, answers to the most urgent call in a 'form of doing without knowing'; the important thing is to act. The family functions as a tribe, refocused on itself and its survival.

> *'In our charity, we have families who seek self-medication, some even travel abroad to find treatment that is forbidden in this country, some of these explorations have had dreadful consequences.'*

Consultation: A six-year-old boy comes into the consultation room with his mother. Her sentences are dominated by 'must' and 'it has to': 'It has to stop', 'The operation must be done quickly!' The mother does not listen to the nuances introduced by the neurologist, 'We need to specify the extension of the lesion to avoid a second operation, it is necessary to further our analysis.' The mother resists, she does not want to come to the hospital for further tests, the neurologist's request leaves her indifferent, she remains camped in her position. She thinks that the surgery will give her back the son she never had.

III. Mythical Phase[5]

The parent re-invents their narrative; this phase corresponds to the force of imagination, the heroic and sacrificial capacities of the parent. The parent begins to differentiate themselves from their family. The progressive internalization of a new reality is organized in opposition to outside realities. This internalization process helps contain and stabilize emotions.

---

4   For Marcel Mauss, 'Magic is essentially an art of doing…these gestures are sketches of techniques. Magic is both an opus operatum from a magic point of view and a technically inoperans opus' (Mauss and Hubert 1950, pp.11–12).

5   'Myth is the place where the object is created from a question and its answer – let's put it another way: myth is the place where, from its deep nature (Beschaffenheit), an object becomes creation' (Jolles 1972 quoted in Baros 2009).

'Sometimes I feel my heart aches seeing my sister's toddlers so free, far from suffering, and as a result, I hide from them how much I do not always manage to share their happiness, I feel awful (they are unable to imagine what I go through!).'

The ability to make associations to ideas, often rich in images and evocations, is woven into a narrative structure in which the components of the imaginary and reality combine to form one whole.

'I'm trying to change the world. The only weapon I have against this epilepsy is my pen.'

Parents start to endure their anguish. Evocations of the future have a sacrificial component: 'The day it comes to doing tests on my son [likely to put his life in danger] I will not hesitate to eradicate this disease from the world,' 'My wife has to stay at home, to keep our daughter, she does not want to, but she must know her life is like that.' Often projects appear to function in some narrative loop and do not happen because it is too internalized. 'Together, me and my son, we will live on a farm, I know I'll get there.' These early visions are essential but they sometimes lack realization because they are limited by the ability to integrate multiple perspectives and as such may seem somewhat self-centred or too focused on one cause.

Consultation: A mother brings extended files in a backpack, of information she has found in libraries, on the net. Somewhere in this stack of information lies the key to her daughter's healing.

2.2 Social integration process

When the parent begins to feel that they can identify their emotions and stabilize them, and is able to relate to their personal aspirations, it is usually a sign that they can begin to adopt different roles. The three phases described below may be understood as a social process of integration, the parent becoming a social actor of their future. The possibility of rebuilding one's habitus becomes foreseeable.

'I like coming to the Association, we share the same things.'

I. Spatiotemporal Phase

The parent is aware that time and space can be their allies, and they can finally mobilize their capability to self-organize as opposed to being permanently overwhelmed. Their life often appears as a mosaic built of separate worlds.

'One afternoon a week, I joined my sports club, where no one knows anything about my life, I am like the others.'

'To survive this misfortune it is very simple, you have to have two lives, a life with the child and a life on the side. My wife wanted to stay home with the kid, I told her no, it is important to work.'

'I work at home but my painting studio is separated, there is a nanny who takes care of my son, we have established emergency criteria [smile].'

Time and space punctuate lives.

'Wow, he just had a crisis, we have two hours of break.'

The parent realizes that time is running out, and the prospect of the future causes new concerns.

'I am no longer young, my other children that I fortunately have, will have to take up this responsibility.'

This phase is often characterized by a need for compliance and difficulty asserting one's differences.

'Our children do not look disabled, and when I push the pram, I often feel shame when others comment in the street that my child is too big to be pushed.'

The opinion of the outside or the expert is often called upon and is not always called into question.

'The drugs have evolved. I have two Dravet children, one who is 25 years old and one 15 years old. My eldest is bedridden, she no longer walks, it's because of the drugs, and my second, loves Michael Jackson, she danced with the Professor. He is an extraordinary man.'

Consultation: A young man bedridden, 16 years old, is pushed in in a wheelchair by his mother. 'So, you're happy, you have a little man now, the Department of Endocrinology worked well, the growth hormone has worked well, we now have reached standard growth.' The doctor examines the patient, 'You have grown up!' the doctor's face sketches a smile; the mother's face expresses weariness and sadness. Using what looks like a straw, she sucks from an opening in the young man's throat the surplus saliva. The consultation is short, a new prescription ends the session. At the end of the consultation, an aside contradicts the neurologist's satisfaction: 'Before this hormonal treatment I had to carry a little one; to put a diaper on a child is one thing, but to put a diaper on an adult with hair and erections is another! I also have to shave him now, as if I did not have enough to do! I dare not tell the doctor that it is all much worse.'

II. Individual Phase
The parent becomes aware that they have the right to a life of their own and a certain normality, but different from before the diagnosis. They manage to name specific targets and recognize the means to implement them.

> 'I love my child very much but I cannot see him this week.'

The parent envisages new projects that have nothing to do with the child.

> 'Honestly, I would like a new love affair. Not that the story with my child is not a story full of love, but I want to start a love affair with a man. I think I'll meet him on the subway or in the cafeteria. Very probably. And I will love his shoes.'

Their rapport to the medical authorities changes.

> 'Tired of finding our child bashed by the falls due to seizures, I had to insist [to the doctor]. I felt that we should not be swayed despite the resistance of scientific minds. I deeply respect the medical view and the research, but I think a mother has the right and duty to bring another dimension to health matters, one that is not palpable, one that is beyond the balance sheets, exams, crunching numbers...so I had the treatment for a month...and now our child is calm, radiant as ever, progressing apace.'

> 'If the goal is to make our children zombies, it's not a life, the doctor must understand that we do not require a prescription that eliminates all epileptic fits. We want to save the relationship to our children above all, how to say, how much medication for what quality of life?'

In this phase, the doctor's role is often that of an adviser, an expert in their art.

Consultation: A couple, somewhat shy, look at the disabled child. 'We love our boy but we would like a second. We want to live another experience. In our situation is this possible?'

III. Collective Phase

Now the parent realizes that in their process, they have gained expertise that can serve the community.

'When I see young parents, I see myself, I see that through which I have passed, and if they knew that this is possible, it would make all the difference.'

The parent is aware of the turmoil they have traversed and have the tools to help new families facing their child's illness.

'We [the parents], we are a bit of a family, we recognize we have this outlook on life, on things, what we have lived.'

The parent is part of a collective that has overcome certain difficulties. The board of the charity faces new challenges.

'In the Association, we have more and more families with older children, the institutions did not follow us, we must find ways to manage this problem.'

Relationships with the doctors are grounded in partnership.

'We have an appointment with the head of department to decide if it's a good idea that our daughter is part of the clinical cohort for the new molecule x.'

The parents become aware of the role they can play in society. They start to participate in the development of a common project, and become aware of the ins and outs of their role within the group. This participation is reflected in the ways the charity becomes more effective in achieving its goals whilst the burden of looking after older children becomes more difficult.

'We organized the Association in groups of people where everyone is invited to carry a project. We try, whenever possible, not to take over but to let everyone be responsible for their commitment. This is the only way to ensure that the Association does not implode mid-way.'

Role of the medical profession in supporting parents

The announcement of the diagnosis of a chronic and rare severe disease in children has a devastating effect on family systems but also, and more insidiously, on doctors and their healthcare team. Parents are as overwhelmed by the disease as doctors may be by their scientific technology. Everyone is speaking a different language. Everything opposes optimal communication, which is so necessary because of the confusing nature of drug-resistant rare diseases. Progress in this communication requires each player to acquire a clearer perception of their own operational mode and their interlocutor. Thus, the feeling evoked by parents 'of losing one's ability, of being emptied from the inside or being shell-shocked' constitutes a way of reacting to the shock of the disease and, unfortunately, it is often misunderstood by doctors: 'When I try to tell them about the disease, they may not understand me.' This disparity between the two parties is not always in favour of the child's health, and it makes consultations difficult to manage.

Without a model to understand the reactions of the parents, the doctor can only see the difficulties parents face. Both are caught up in the inability to take advantage of these medical consultations, which should be an opportunity to establish a dialogue to support the child, to gather information about the disease, to organize a strategy tailored towards care and education while allowing the parent and siblings to pursue their own life path. Moreover, beyond the care of the sick, the suffering expressed by the child and their environment also has consequences for the caregiver that result in psychological or somatic disorders (anxiety, burnout, sleep disorders). Doctors are poorly trained to handle so much suffering and it may lead them to close themselves to this reality.

A questionnaire to 20 parents in this study revealed a disturbing fact: only 55 per cent of the diagnoses were given face to face. This observation is symptomatic of the problem of the self-protective distancing doctors tend to develop. In addition, for 80 per cent of cases, no explanation of what the parent will face was expressed. Clinical observations of the study showed that the caregiver has neither the tools to manage all this suffering nor supervision or practical analysis that would allow them to manage the sequence of emotions that this constant exposure to such suffering engenders. The physician's role is essential and should not be not limited simply to medical care for the child's illness but should also include the implications of disease (impact on the parents' lives, impact on the future of the child and their quality of life – as progressive deterioration is manifested for some in the medium and long term). The recognition by the doctor of the phases likely to be experienced by the parent may lead to the possibility of adapting one's speech appropriately to each phase. This step would constitute real progress and a paradigm shift in the care of these families.

Conclusion

It is possible to accompany parents to let their own strategies emerge and so overcome the experience of vacuity and rootlessness that follows the announcement of a diagnosis of a rare disease in one's own child. As one parent put it: 'So far I have associated these cycles with the disease. The work of the last session made me aware of the constructive aspect of this method, of how we can bounce back on these phases, that they are not only those of the disease but of a new way of approaching our life, its organization.'

The parent can seize their own means to acquire autonomy and, in this way, feel able to make decisions in line with their life choices: 'This session was an opportunity to realize how much we can evolve and change the situation by the strength of mind.' To begin with parents' emotion and experience, and to build and refine the references for parental and medical carers, is essential. Today, thanks to this psycho-anthropological study, the future of these families can be evoked as a model (phases of appropriation) and a supportive method (sorting exercises) that can generate a constructive dialogue between family, doctors and social partners.

References

Barad, K. (2007) *Meeting the Universe Halfway: Quantum Physics and the Entanglement of Matter and Meaning.* Durham, NC: Duke University Press.

Baros, L.M. (2009) 'À la recherche d'une définition du mythe.' *Philologica Jassyensia 5*, 1, 89–98.

Bourdieu, P. (1990) *The Logic of Practice.* Stanford, CA: Stanford University Press.

Good, B. (2012) 'Theorizing the "subject" of medical and psychiatric anthropology.' *Journal of the Royal Anthropological Institute 18*, 3, 515–535.

Hubert, H. and Mauss, M. (1950) 'Esquisse d'une théorie générale de la magie.' In M. Mauss, *Sociologie et anthropologie* (pp.10–137). Paris: PUF. (Original work published 1903)

Korsak, T. et al. (2018) Poster presented at the 13th European Congress on Epileptology, Vienna, 26–30 August.

Van Gennep, A. (1909) *Les Rites de Passage.* Paris: Dunod.

Wolfe, J. (2013) '"The Ordinary" in Stanley Cavell and Jacques Derrida.' *Minerva: An Internet Journal of Philosophy 17*, 250–268.

15

Image, Narrative and Migration

'Najma', Tania Kaczynski and Jon Martyn[1] and Emma Hollamby[2]

This chapter considers how art-making and exhibiting can offer opportunities for those who have become alienated by trauma and migration, enabling them to form connections with their sense of self, others and society. It contains an interview with a member of the New Art Studio, a therapeutic art studio for asylum seekers and refugees, as she reflects on her experiences exhibiting at Ben Uri Gallery and Museum in North London.

Introduction

Identity is a major concern for asylum seekers; they are often faced with an intense sense of separation from their past: family, friends, culture, faith, language, careers and homeland. Many will have endured the trauma of violence, perhaps in the form of gender-based and human rights violations, imprisonment, violence, torture or military conflict. The psychological impact of such violence shatters the sense of self and capacity to feel safe with others. As well as this, the asylum seeker is made to feel unwelcome in the UK where there are multiple legal, social and economic barriers put in place by their new and often hostile host country. Asylum seekers and refugees exist in the margins of our society. They are often placed in substandard accommodation, excluded

---

1   New Art Studio.
2   Ben Uri Gallery and Museum.

from most education and not allowed to work, forced to live on £37.75 a week in state support (Refugee Council 2019). This enforced poverty and exclusion from mainstream society further erodes one's identity. They are neither at home, nor able to build a new life for themselves. The asylum seeker exists in limbo, usually waiting years for their legal case to conclude.

At the time of writing the prospects for a person seeking asylum have continued to deteriorate, as migration continues to be used as a political scapegoat for economic disparity (Dorling 2016). The most current manifestation of this is the 2012 hostile environment policy, a set of legislative measures designed with the intention of reducing immigration figures in the UK.[3] One action undertaken as part of this policy was the use of advertising vans that used the slogan 'In the UK illegally? Go home or face arrest.' 'Go home' is a slogan linked to racist and far-right groups. This incident is part of a long history of blame and denigration placed on migrants, asylum seekers and refugees (Grayson 2013).

The combination of migration, trauma and social-political hostility can lead to a profound sense of alienation. This situation leaves the person unable to own a sense of personal narrative, being cut off from their past – their life has become a story that is both painful and subject to intense scrutiny. During the frequently long legal battle to be granted political asylum many have felt humiliated and dehumanized (Refugee Action 2018). In turn, this leaves the person unable to engage in their future. It is difficult to consider a narrative for one's future when excluded and at risk of detention and deportation.

The New Art Studio

The New Art Studio ('the Studio') offers its members the opportunity to rebuild their sense of self through art-making in a communal environment. The basic ethos of the studio is that of inclusion, personal agency, authentic discourse and creativity. Art-making in a social environment offers an opportunity to rebuild connections with oneself as well as forming relationships with others. The atmosphere of the studio allows for creativity and relatedness; essential elements to counteract the hostility and disintegration so often experienced

---

3   See https://en.wikipedia.org/wiki/Home_Office_hostile_environment_policy

by multiple losses and severe trauma. In parallel to the therapeutic environment, members are offered the opportunity to exhibit their artwork to the public, presenting ways to develop an artistic identity and form positive relationships with the public and wider society.

The New Art Studio was established in 2014 as a therapeutic art community for asylum seekers and refugees. It is a place of solace, creativity and personal agency. The group runs once a week for six hours a day, has 12 members and was founded by art therapists Tania Kaczynski and Jon Martyn. The group is based in a community arts centre in North London. Its location reflects a conscious decision to give members the opportunity to make connections with the local art community.

There is no time limit to membership, and some members have been a part of the group for several years. Long-term relationships are an integral part of our ethos, and when members decide to leave, they are welcome to rejoin, visit or contribute to exhibitions. For people who have lost family connections the Studio offers a secure base, a place that is familiar, welcoming and safe. This is in contrast to both the precarious housing endured by asylum seekers as well as the time-limited services that currently dominate psychological therapies.

The group is facilitated in a way that makes members feel welcome. Food and drink is available and the day is largely unstructured, with members arriving and leaving when they please. Art-making and conversations are unstructured and spontaneous. At the end of the day a 30-minute 'talking time' is held, where the group sit together, look at the day's artwork and talk, though not every member chooses to attend. The studio also organizes group shows on- and offsite, seeing exhibiting as part of its therapeutic remit.

The ethos

The ethos and philosophy at the core of the Studio is influenced by the writings of R.D. Laing and by The Studio Upstairs, a therapeutic community for people with mental or emotional difficulties. Ronald Laing (Laing 1990, 2010) not only challenged conventional interpretations of madness, but also challenged the diagnostic labels that are designated by others. Such labels easily become pejorative. Similarly, the designation of 'asylum seeker' has become a persecutory one, and the Studio is concerned that this can be internalized into a denigrated sense of self, and further damage the relationship with the self and others.

At the Studio everyone makes art together, therapist and member alike. This approach is in keeping with approaches developed by The Studio Upstairs. Art-making is seen as an opportunity to address a sense of alienation; making art is a universal need, which can communicate beyond the limitations of language. By making artwork together we address the profound feeling of otherness that asylum seekers experience. The relationship for Studio members is not only as therapist and client but as mutual artists.

Art-making also offers the opportunity to reconnect with one's imagination and allow opportunities to explore parts of oneself that may have been forgotten or repressed. When all is lost, imagination is the only place of true freedom. By being with others and developing a creative practice, one can reconnect with oneself and develop a new sense of self. With asylum seekers and refugees, the need to make a mark in order to confirm one's existence is apparent and urgent.

Exhibiting

Exhibiting is part of the Studio's culture and boundaries, being something that members desire and value. Exhibiting can present an 'opportunity for the collaborative reauthoring of personal narratives' (West 2018), and the Studio sees its exhibitions as an integral part of its approach. Exhibitions present opportunities for members to explore and develop their relationship with society (Martyn 2019). For some, being in public is not easy, and the act of exhibiting can bring up painful past experiences. The Studio's approach offers members the opportunity to face the public as a group and allows them to explore their experiences when they return to the therapeutic setting after an exhibition. The exhibition offers an opportunity to change how a person is seen and how a person may see themselves and the chance to develop an artistic identity. Exhibiting may bring challenging feelings of inadequacy and inequality, but if those feelings are held, heard and acknowledged there is much room for personal development. Seeing an artwork can offer something human and personal, in turn challenging denigrated and reductive notions of asylum seekers. For the member, the process of framing, hanging and seeing the artwork in the gallery presents the artwork in a new (and often elevated) light.

A narrative of the art-making experience: How we come to exhibit

Art-making starts as a solitary experience but becomes an increasingly social one. The process of exhibiting can be seen as a natural conclusion to making art. It is useful to break down this process in order to understand the additional complexities raised for members of the studio. The journey from the first mark to the gallery wall is explained below.

1. Image imagined

First the image may exist only in one's imagination. Executing that image is the first step in the journey, and often remains unconscious until it's on the page. Members of the Studio may struggle to make the initial mark. There is bravery and vulnerability in exposing oneself on the page, and the first mark, like the first step, is often the hardest.

2. Image on the page

Often members of the Studio are surprised by their marks; the unconscious surfaces act like a dream remembered. Even if a concrete idea started the process, surprises are still present. After making an image, it is as if people awake and return to conscious thinking. During the process of making, members are quiet, internalizing and processing their own personal journeys.

3. Image in the group

At the end of the day, members stop engaging in the making and sit together to look at and discuss the day's creations. The members take their images from the flat surface of a table to the upright position of the wall. We display the artwork on a wall for all to see. This a major step in the journey of creating artwork. Although this experience remains within the safety of the studio and with familiar people it can still be exposing, albeit contained in a safe space. This could be seen as a form of exhibiting.

The images take on a different significance when they are viewed away from the maker and by other people. Often members find it challenging to articulate the meaning of the image. This can be partly due to language limitations, cultural differences, shame and the need for privacy. Groups make us look at ourselves through the eyes of others. The group acts as a mirror.

During the 'talking time', when there is time and space for reflection, extreme emotion can be present. The members of the group can therefore support and assist each other. The journey continues.

4. The image after time

Often the group reviews a member's work after a set period of time, maybe months and in some cases years. The feelings that gave birth to the image may well have changed. External circumstances may have changed for the better, and the member may now feel distant from the image. Although themes are often repeated, there is always some movement. It is important to recognize the changes that occur, however small and seemingly insignificant.

5. Image in the gallery

There is much excitement and anticipation during the lead-up to a show. Members review their work and choose images that they are comfortable to show publicly. There are 12 members of the group, and each of them experiences this process differently. There is often an initial sense of achievement and pride.

Members are no longer simply asylum seekers, they are artists in a public space. For some this is significant as they want the world to see their story in order to relay a better understanding of their own experience. There are many common myths and misrepresentations offered by the media, and exhibiting represents a chance to show the world that these people are not simply asylum seekers, but creative people with individual experiences and imaginations.

As a culture, we are bombarded by statistics pertaining to the migrant experience, and some members feel a sense of relief that they can share their experiences in a visual form with a sympathetic audience. For others, it is a different experience. Some members have internalized the hostility to such a degree that they are ashamed of being an asylum seeker. They want to move away from that identity, and by showing work in an exhibition that is clearly work made by asylum seekers they feel exposed and uncomfortable.

These experiences highlight the inherent difficulties of a dynamic identity; not only in terms of how people see themselves but of how others see them. The experience of being an asylum seeker is so intense and disturbing that people may remain traumatized for many years after the events that brought them here. Within this context, imagination and creativity take on profound meaning.

6. Image after the show

Some members experience a sense of disappointment if their work isn't chosen for display, if it wasn't displayed as they had imagined or if they did not sell their work. These experiences may be felt by any artist after an exhibition, but for asylum seekers the need for approval and public acceptance is heightened.

For many members the experience of showing work can be a positive one. Even to be in a public space away from familiar asylum environments can be an uplifting and hopeful venture. Exhibiting opens up worlds previously unknown.

New Art Studio at Ben Uri Gallery and Museum

Ben Uri Gallery and Museum originally approached New Art Studio for a project called Starting with Art. In this collaboration, the Gallery was able to offer the Studio a trainee art therapist on placement for one academic year. The student would use replicas of the Gallery artworks in their sessions as a stimulus to their therapeutic work. Ever open-minded in its approach, the Studio welcomed both the trainee and the introduction of artworks, representing in effect a reversed collaboration, in which the Gallery enters the Studio. The group therefore had an awareness of Ben Uri.

Ben Uri Gallery and Museum is a public art gallery based in St John's Wood, North London. Founded in 1915 as a Jewish art society by Russian-Jewish émigré artist Lazar Berson in Whitechapel, London's East End, it provided support for Yiddish-speaking, Jewish immigrant artists and craftsmen who were working outside the cultural mainstream. Poets, musicians, artists and creatives of all kinds met to find solace and companionship in a new and unfamiliar place through Ben Uri.

Ben Uri then focused its efforts as a Gallery and Museum and over the past century, new waves of migration have contributed to its collection, comprising predominantly British and European art reflecting the work, lives and contributions of émigré artists and their journeys to London. This culminated in a renewed focus, not as an expressly Jewish organization, but one representing core themes of identity and migration, and in turn the extensive contribution of migrant artists to British culture since 1900.

Operating as an independent, non-national museum, Ben Uri

receives no core government funding but operates as a registered charity. Compared with larger London galleries, its charm lies in the sense of intimate connection and ownership engendered in visitors from minority communities, represented by the collection. Given the strong themes and history of the collection it was felt the two organizations had a natural affiliation.

Following the Starting with Art collaboration, New Art Studio were invited to exhibit at Ben Uri Gallery to mark Refugee Week. The studio responded to this invitation by curating the exhibition 'Thirty Six Pounds and Five Pence', which ran from 13 to 18 June 2017, accompanied by a programme of events. Politically motivated in its provocative title (the amount of weekly state support given to asylum seekers in vouchers at that time), the exhibition also represented great sensitivity in its aim to bring greater awareness to the real lived experience of being an asylum seeker. In an opening speech Tania stated, 'We see endless images of refugees but rarely do we get a chance to see work *from* refugees', going on to reinforce with: 'This highlights the continuous need to understand, educate and expose the immigrant story – usually one of loss and hope.'[4]

Works were for sale, and the response from the Gallery audience was sincere and supportive. Many of Ben Uri's supporters have experience of forced migration, be it first or second generation, and so a sense of empathy and community was expressed by visitors. Sales were positive and attendance at the private view event was good. The public were keen to speak to the artists, seeing the studio members foremost as artists rather than asylum seekers or refugees. People were keen to better understand the emotive, accomplished and at times challenging artworks on display.

The following year, New Art Studio returned to Ben Uri, featuring in the exhibition 'Using Art Differently; Art and Wellbeing at Ben Uri Gallery and Museum', which ran from 26 September to 15 October 2017, again with a programme of accompanying events. Works were not for sale via Ben Uri on this occasion (for clarity, given the presence of other work which was not for sale). Some visitors to the Gallery recalled seeing the work of the Studio earlier that year. The theme of this exhibition was more closely linked to the restorative, healing and empowering nature of art-making.

4   See www.youtube.com/watch?v=_MFrNueRZqU

On both occasions staff from the Gallery visited the Studio to select work for the exhibition, and a group of Studio members came to private views and to visit the exhibition in situ. The Gallery was keen to ensure both exhibitions were regarded with the same professionalism and respect afforded to any other exhibition, and so terms such as 'community arts' were avoided, lest they unintentionally diminish those aims. Ben Uri has a long-standing tradition of showing works by great artists who are perhaps lesser known or for whom circumstances outside of their control had an impact on their trajectory and ultimate success.

Interview with a member of the New Art Studio

In this interview Najma (a pseudonym) will explore both her experiences of the studio and exhibiting her work with Ben Uri Gallery and Museum. In keeping with the ethos of the Studio, this chapter represents an opportunity to give a voice to the Studio members.

Najma has been a member of the Studio since 2015. She had little prior experience of art-making, and no prior experience of exhibitions. She was living in the UK on a work visa. When her experience of domestic violence and blackmail in the UK led to death threats from her family, Najma found she was no longer safe to return to her home country and was forced to claim asylum in the UK. She is well educated and a practising Muslim. Najma had a seven-year wait for her claim for asylum to go to court and had just been granted refugee status at the time of the interview. During this time, she lived a double life – she felt intense shame from her experiences and asylum claim. She did not tell her friends what had happened, or that she was claiming asylum. She was encouraged by her family to take her own life, as a way of ending the shame bestowed upon her and her family. There have been times when she considered suicide as her best option. Najma openly recognizes how her relationship with God and the relationships formed through therapeutic support have kept her alive.

Below are short selections from a 40-minute interview conducted in May 2019 with Jon Martyn, who has co-facilitated the Studio throughout Najma's time in the group. The conversation was largely unstructured. Najma was asked to think about her experiences as a Studio member, her experiences exhibiting at Ben Uri Gallery and how this may relate to trauma. Text has been added in square brackets to give context to the selected material so it may be fully understood. Najma's own words are in italics and indented in quotation marks.

Core themes

Continuing themes underlying the interview are the impact of violence and Najma's resultant claim for asylum, and the impact this has had on her identity and sense of self. She refers to her difficulty trusting others. She experiences, at times, an overwhelming sense of self-blame regarding her experiences, and refers to suicidal feelings, and her difficulty living under the asylum system for so long.

> 'After such a long time in this process [she could be referring to her claim for asylum and/or her psychological recovery] I lost the stamina to even fight to have a different life, this life. I was so tired, there were a few times when even I gave up. You're right, I was hiding. This was not what I wanted to show or to be.'

Being in the group:

She explores her experience joining the group, her difficulties in relationships, and considers previous experiences of individual talking therapy.

> 'When I joined this group I was in a very strange state of mind and I found comfort there [in the Studio]. Because I just didn't know how to go on with my life. One was this high-flying life, one was this asylum seeker life.'

> 'In therapy...I used to get angry. When people say "everything will be alright" you say no! Nothing will be alright because I have no idea whether [asylum] will be sorted or not, there was a lot of insecurity and uncertainty. When I used to get angry I used to get quiet, and I never used to talk.'

> 'In the art group, if I become angry I will make and draw stuff so it's still coming out. My anger, my thoughts are still coming out. That's why it's really helpful to me.'

> 'If you are angry that has to go through paper or through art because everyone is so stressed, you know, there was a point where I was scared to even share my point of view with anyone else because I thought it

*might hurt someone, it might make someone angry. In the beginning
what I learnt through art, is take everything out, whatever is inside
you, anger, sadness, happiness, whatever, on the paper, through art,
through paint. So this really changed me. And that was the way I jelled
with other people.* [I made art] *with everyone else, because that was
what everyone else was doing.'*

Her relationship with the Studio now:

'Whenever I go there [the Studio], *I'm naked, because whatever I
think, whatever I feel, I draw that. I feel like this, but obviously, it's a
bit scary when I go there, because I'm just myself. I put all my guards
down, I'm not defending myself. I'm just me.'*

*'I don't know if it's a good thing or a bad. For me, I only draw what
I feel and think. Being naked, normally I don't share my difficulties
with anyone, I will not ask for help. But in that group it's like going
to your mum,* [laughs] *you are being honest, you can tell everything,
this is what I feel there.'*

*'But this group actually comforted me, through this group I felt a bit
calm, I felt like it's ok. If you blame yourself, it's ok sometimes, it's ok
to be stressed. I mean, because in this group, because I had therapy
and everything and nothing worked. But this group really worked. I
felt comfortable… I think it's really helpful, I never knew before that
art is so powerful, never before, never.'*

Najma talks about her experience of sharing her art with other group
members. A theme emerges of a sense of alienation regarding trauma,
separation and seeking asylum.

*'…one they said it looks really pretty. And the other that it's really
claustrophobic. And I am thinking exactly the same, that I'm looking
very pretty from outside, and I am looking happy and strong, but
inside I am all messed up. So what they see is actually how it is. It
looked so pretty, it looked so neat, it looked so clean. But there is no
way out, and that is actually how I feel.'*

Exhibiting:

*'During my first exhibition I learnt one thing, I got this confidence, I'm
not just nobody, I'm not just a useless person. I can make art. I felt like*

I'm not just an asylum seeker. One thing I realized is that you can't just make art, you have to have a message, because there are people coming to see you. [As an asylum seeker] *that's the only opportunity you have to tell people. To explain what problems people have in their life, whether it is asylum, whether it is a health problem, whether it is a cultural problem. So I thought it is not just an exhibition, it is also a responsibility to deliver something which is important.'*

'It's not a pressure, because as an asylum seeker you know it's a golden opportunity, you know that there is no other way that you can express or show your feelings. It's like a pressure but also…I see it as a great thing. If I was [exhibiting] *alone, I would see it as a pressure, but because* [the group] *all are there, we all are working on it, it is not a pressure for me, because you know there's someone to help you, they're not going to let you fall.'*

The exhibition at Ben Uri Gallery was Najma's third exhibition. Being at Ben Uri offered specific experiences. The group first visited the gallery while migrant artist Eva Frankfurther was exhibiting. Frankfurther painted portraits and scenes of working-class London life. The exhibition informed the audience that Eva committed suicide in 1959 at the age of 29.

'[When we visited] *I realized that it's not just, you know how people say things like "people only come here to claim asylum because they don't have a good life" or "they just come here for a better life". But in BU gallery I find out that some people came here, left everything they had…to escape Germany and this was their life. They came here just to be alive. And then I thought, seeking asylum is not a bad thing, it is fighting for your life.'*

'…my ex took everything away from me, I had a beautiful life, I had this, that and that. And I think that I now realize that he couldn't take my life. That is the most valuable thing I could ever have.'

'There was a Jewish artist there… I found out that refugees are not only from Arab countries…they are from everywhere, even the rich people…and I could really relate to that…because living this life is really difficult…and I realized that I shouldn't be shameful of the life I'm living because there are other people who came from good families who had to leave everything and start again. It was very touching for

me. I didn't really know that Jewish people all left Germany and came here. They had to leave everything. They just came here to be alive.'

Najma participated in the group show 'Thirty Six Pounds and Five Pence' in June 2017 at Ben Uri, alongside 11 studio members. She attended the private view with other exhibiting artists. Najma sold a number of artworks that night and had conversations with several visitors, including those who had bought her art. As an asylum seeker, she was not legally permitted to receive the money from the sale. It was therefore decided collectively by the studio members that the money should be used to purchase communal art materials, in support of the work of the studio.

> *'When I went to Ben Uri I felt that it was my story* [meeting people who had bought her work]. *I was happy to meet them, and I felt that they were like me, there is no difference between us. A lot of people were there. I knew a lot of people were Jewish, and I was relieved that they knew what a refugee is, and what leaving your country and losing everything is. So I was a bit relieved when I was talking to them. That was a beautiful thing. It was like a flower in my life, it was like, "Wow!" I sold my work, it was really beautiful.'*

> *'When someone is buying your stuff, I was very happy, [as it] was that they believe what you are saying. Because for me everything has a message. I was going through certain things in my life. Somebody bought [my] sleeping picture* ['Dreams Are Like Ghosts'], *and I was actually going through that.'*

Relating to trauma:

> *'I have a serious sleeping issue, I can't sleep at night, and some people will not believe you, as it doesn't show on my face. When I exhibited [my] picture* ['Dreams Are Like Ghosts'], *I was scared [to show it], but I had a conversation with the guy who bought it; he said it was so powerful. Then I realized that this problem is universal, a lot of people are going through it, there was a realization and happiness.'*

> *'I was happy not only to be believed, but there were people there that have gone through asylum. I remember there was an old man, he said he fled from Germany, and he was very old, his wife had died, but he*

still hadn't forgotten. He was still coming to see these exhibitions and stuff. It was the nicest thing.'

'That's the most amazing thing, that people do actually believe that you are going through that problem. It's like people actually care about you. It's a mixed happy, because it's that people believe in you.'

'The person who bought my picture ['Dreams Are Like Ghosts'] *I wondered after buying the picture, I was thinking a lot about him. Does he have a problem with sleeping? I still think about him.'*

'[Exhibiting] *is a great opportunity for an asylum seeker, and if you get it you feel pressure, but if you don't get it, you get disappointment.'*

'As an asylum seeker I will be the first person to understand that life is not fair.'

On getting status:
Jon asks Najma if she thinks her relationship with exhibitions and art will change.

'I think one thing will change: I don't think I'm in that maze any more, I have a way out. I'm not a person who will just move on, I can't move on. This will always be in my mind. I know it's not easy for me to move on, because I'm still there, seven years ago, with what happened, I'm still there. I'm still crying about it. Even though asylum has gone, I'm still crying about what happened – it was a great loss in my life. It's hard to think differently, but I feel like that no one can treat me differently, because you get treated differently when you are an asylum seeker. Now I feel like I'm allowed to do a lot of other things. Before I got status, I was only given the opportunity to exhibit as an asylum seeker. Now I feel that I can exhibit as an artist.'

Discussion and conclusion

The common themes that emerge at the Studio are those of loss, exile, identity and the desire to belong. Najma's reflections illustrate how the experience of trauma, shame and separation leads to a profound loss of connection with oneself and others.

For Najma, and many asylum seekers like her, the therapeutic work of the Studio exposed how her sense of identity had been severed by external forces as she struggled to make connections with her past and present, whilst unable to consider a future. She was severed from vital relationships that contributed to her identity, struggling to cope with the loss and aggression of her family, finding it difficult to form trusting relationships with disbelief. Her interview indicates that these hostilities had been internalized – both the shame and self-blame imposed by her family, as well as the wider denigration from political and cultural sources.

The interview indicates how art-making in the therapeutic environment gave Najma an opportunity to reconnect with herself and others. Najma also indicates how an identity can be repaired by being part of a group, and how the development of an artistic identity can help to counteract denigrating experiences. Ben Uri exhibitions gave Najma a sense of purpose – a responsibility to communicate her experiences to the public. Within this we see how a narrative was being formed – both via her relationships in the Studio and her developing relationship as an exhibiting artist. She indicates how exhibiting and selling artwork gives her the opportunity to connect with the public and how she felt less isolated in her distress as she became aware that members of the public have had similar experiences.

The context of the exhibitions also added meaning. Exhibiting at Ben Uri gave Najma the opportunity to move away from social and political alienation as she was able to connect with histories of persecution and asylum that took place in Europe and the UK. The experience of exhibiting at Ben Uri gave Najma the opportunity to link with a different migratory narrative, moving away from the degenerate asylum identity to one where asylum is seen as an experience of resilience and respect.

The conclusion of the interview is significant, as Najma indicates that she continues to suffer the impact of trauma and loss. While we do not know if Najma will overcome these difficulties, what seems to have changed is her capacity to live with these experiences. We argue that they have become part of the narrative of her life, and something which she is able to accept and consider as part of her identity.

In keeping with the ethos of the New Art Studio the significance of connection is apparent and essential for all human survival. Trauma is magnified in isolation, and we see that the relationships in the New Art Studio together with the experience of exhibiting can help our members integrate trauma and understand that they are not alone with their difficulties.

References

Dorling, D. (2016) 'Brexit: The decision of a divided country.' *BMJ 354*, i3697.

Grayson, J. (2013) *Welcome to Britain: 'Go Home or Face Arrest'*. Open Democracy. Accessed on 7/11/2019 at www.opendemocracy.net/en/shine-a-light/welcome-to-britain-go-home-or-face-arrest

Laing, R.D. (1990) *The Politics of Experience and the Bird of Paradise*. Harmondsworth: Penguin.

Laing, R.D. (2010) *The Divided Self: An Existential Study in Sanity and Madness*. Harmondsworth: Penguin.

Martyn, J., (2019) 'Can exhibiting art works from therapy be considered a therapeutic process?' *Art Therapy Online 10*, 1.

Refugee Action (2018) *Waiting in the Dark: How the Asylum System Dehumanises, Disempowers and Damages*. Accessed on 23/7/2019 at www.refugee-action.org.uk/wp-content/uploads/2020/07/Waiting-in-the-Dark-Report.pdf

Refugee Council (2019) *The Truth About Asylum*. Accessed on 23/7/2019 at www.refugeecouncil.org.uk/information/refugee-asylum-facts/the-truth-about-asylum

West, J.D. (2018) 'Research, Epistemology and the Fee in Art Therapy Private Practice.' In J.D. West (ed.) *Art Therapy in Private Practice* (pp.323–325). London: Jessica Kingsley Publishers.

16

Everybody Has a Story, and Everybody Can Learn to Tell Their Story

Dan Milne and Jane Nash

We are two theatre and filmmakers who are the Directors of Narativ London, a company dedicated to the power of personal storytelling. The sphere of Narativ's work is personal development, creativity and leadership. Not being from the world of therapy, we examine this topic through our own experience. This experience tells us that spaces in which people share stories, whether they be 1:1 sessions, workshop rooms with a handful of people or live theatre events, become communal circles of understanding, healing and growth – are essentially therapeutic spaces.

In this chapter we explore some of Narativ's techniques designed to help people excavate and tell their stories. One aspect of the methodology uses the metaphor of a camera – the teller is encouraged to 'paint' the images of the story with words, *to say what the camera sees, to 'show' rather than 'tell' in their storytelling.* We will explore our observations about this technique, drawing on over a decade of working with individuals in diverse contexts, and examining what can shift and be illuminated in the distinct space between listener and teller. (For more on the work that informs our methodology, see Nossel 2018.)

We conclude by revisiting Narativ's origin story in conversation with our colleague and Narativ founder Murray Nossel, and in retelling the story discover new resonances in relation to the subject of this book.

*What is the story that wants to be told? Stories have some
kind of a mythical, energetic existence, almost like they are
outside of us. We are not our stories. We story our lives.*

(Murray Nossel, Narativ Founder)

Jane: 'I'll go next'. The circle goes quiet. There are 13 people, our first
workshop as Narativ in London. Me, Dan and the rest of the circle turn
to look at the woman with the round face. Her skin is pale with patches
of pink flaring in her cheeks. 'You, know what?', she says. 'I was going to
tell one story, but I've changed my mind. There is a different story I want
to tell.' She tells us a story of being in an emergency room somewhere in
Canada with her parents in the 1980s. Her brother is lying on a bed with
a ventilator in his mouth, wired up to machines monitoring his breaths
and heartbeats. The images – a large clock on the wall with a second
hand clicking slowly around the clock face. The teenager, now sitting
in the storytelling circle as an adult woman, watches the seconds on the
clock, watches her mother's face, watches her father's face, watches her
brother and his injured body. Our circle is silent, everyone watching the
storyteller, holding her with their gaze, or some with their eyes closed.
I look at my timer. Three minutes is up and I pick up my bell and ring
it. The woman exhales and wipes tears from her face, the people in
the circle shift in their seats. Dan says, 'Thank you.' At the end of the
workshop the woman says to the group, 'I have just realized something.
Telling my story like that – I get that I am not sad, that I don't have to
be sad. A sad thing happened to me, but I am not sad.'

Dan: In 2000 I was working as a director at the Young Vic creating
a piece of 'verbatim theatre' – this is a piece made from transcripts
of interviews, using the words of subjects to create a text, which is
then usually performed by actors. My subjects were a group of elderly
people living in sheltered housing in Southwark, and I was interested
in exploring empathy. I wanted to understand their perspectives on
the world now at the turn of the century exploring the similarity and
difference between how they viewed things and how I did, to question
that perceived gap that allows elderly people to be marginalized. Their
words were to be performed by teenage actors to see what interesting
resonances this revealed – what disparity, what commonality. What

I ultimately discovered was more pertinent to the power of personal storytelling than anything else.

A couple of times a week I visited this group for tea. I would meet them downstairs in their communal lounge, me in a high-backed armchair opposite a line of them on the chintzy three-piece suite, a tray on the coffee table between us, with white mugs, a chrome tea-pot and a plate of Lincoln biscuits.

On my second visit Cindy arrived late. The others tutted when I asked where she was – 'Oh, she'll be off gallivanting,' Henry said. 'Goodness know where...' Ten minutes later she burst in bringing the damp of outside with her, wheelie shopping trolley in tow. 'Where today?' Henry asked. 'East Street market, thank you very much, I needed new tights.' Joan rolled her eyes at the others, and they all smirked. Twenty minutes later I had been invited to record Cindy and was sitting in her small sunny room as she unpacked tinned salmon and washing-up liquid, my mini-disc recorder with its red light illuminated on the coffee table between us.

'I could never bear red,' she said. 'They made us wear red in the orphanage, and ever since then I could never bear red. I don't wear it, I avoid it at all costs. I can't abide red.' Cindy talked as she unpacked. I had a list of questions on my lap as prompts. Cindy responded, giving me glimpses into the workings of her mind, and into her story. 'I grew up in the orphanage you see. I hated it there. I mean they were nice enough, the staff, and I had friends an' all, but I hated being in an orphanage with all the rules and having to do this and having to do that. They were quite strict. Oh, they were terrors to us, some of them. Wicked.' I listened, my mini-disc red light glowing.

That evening my house-mate asked, 'How did it go?' 'Good. I have this one woman Cindy who loves to talk and we chatted for ages. She invited me back on Thursday – she's a real character. She talked a lot about growing up in an orphanage, but it's not really the material I'm after. I'm more interested in Now to be honest, not her history. I want to understand how she sees the world...'

I went back on Thursday. We had tea and biscuits, and Cindy talked again about the orphanage. 'I mean I know there's a bit of red in this top I'm wearing, but I can't abide red. I won't wear red. And that's because of the orphanage, that is.' I looked down at the mini-disc recorder on the coffee table capturing everything. I leant forward, pressed the button and the light went off. Cindy carried on talking. That night I told my house-mate that I had given up on recording that day. 'I'm just after material and I don't think I'm quite getting what I need... Cindy says the same thing over and over, telling me the same story about being in the orphanage. I'm asking her all these other things, but one way or another we always come back to that. "I never wear red, I hate red". It sounds terrible, but I sit there thinking, what am I going to do with this?!' My house-mate listened and then said, 'But those are the words you are capturing. Is there a way to think about it differently...?'

The next time I visited Cindy I placed the mini-disc on the table, turned it on and asked, 'Cindy, will you tell me all about the orphanage?' She turned. 'The orphanage? Oh, I hated it there,' she said. 'They were terrors to us.' As she talked, I leant in and listened acutely. She used many of the same words, the same phrases, revisited the same thoughts. I just fully listened. And then after talking for a while she suddenly said, 'You see, there were two halves to the orphanage, a girls' side and a boys' side. There was a big wall between us and never the twain! We never mixed with them, never even saw them. Girls on one side and boys on the other. That was the way they ran it. And you see the thing is...the thing is, I had a brother the other side of that wall and I never even knew it. They never told me. I never knew he was there. I had a brother just the other side of that wall and they never even told me. I found out much later when I was in my forties. I mean that was wicked, wasn't it? I would have loved to have had a brother.'

I am so grateful to Cindy – she taught me a few crucial lessons. For me, this has become an origin story for my work with personal storytelling. Why? Because this was the beginning of learning about the challenge we all have in listening to other people and the power that open listening has. Furthermore, I saw the hold that our individual stories have over us, how they can define us, for better or worse. The way we 'story' our experience is key to how we understand ourselves, defining who we are and how we operate in the world. As I sat with Cindy in those later sessions, I received an important insight into how the narrative of her 'trauma' at the orphanage had become the defining story that had to be told and retold, rehearsing the details of the clothes and the treatment, the nice people and the 'terrors'. And the wall, and what lay on the other side.

Listening is generative

In the theatre you become acutely aware of the listening of an audience, and the difference between one audience and another. Listening has an impact. In our story work at Narativ we see that listening is generative, it shapes what it is possible for people to say. We always begin with listening before we start looking at storytelling. The impact in a theatre is not that the listening changes the words, but it changes the energy with which you connect with the other performers and with the audience. However, when telling a story to someone, their listening has the ability to shape what comes out of your mouth. We say that there is a 'reciprocal relationship between listening and telling' – just as speaking creates listeners, so listening creates the space into which people speak. It is a rare and precious thing when we actually give someone else a genuinely open, non-judgemental listening. Ultimately it allows someone to speak their truth.

In everyday life our listening contracts and expands with different people in different circumstances. It expands when we have the time and inclination to give someone our full attention; it contracts when the opposite is true. This may be about time, it may be about interest, it may be that we are listening but only for specific things to be spoken. A good example of how our listening changes is with mobile phones. When your phone next rings, notice how your listening is shaped by seeing the name of the person come up before you answer it. Is it a name that makes your listening open with anticipation? Or does it close your listening down, making it narrow and uninviting?

Dan: At the outset, my listening with Cindy was narrow. How was I going to be able to use the words she spoke in my theatre piece? We would call this a major 'obstacle' in my listening, changing the 'shape' of it. *How good was this material for my needs?* I wasn't creating a space for her to tell her story for herself, to speak her truth. And when I realized this, I changed my listening and this meant that she told me her narrative, I heard Cindy's story. Then I was able to understand who she was from her perspective.

In our work now we always begin by identifying what 'obstacles' we have to being present. What are the things that might be getting in the way and taking us out of the that essential moment of connection?

Working with stories and Narativ methodology
The circle

Dan: During the mid-90s my work at the Young Vic Theatre introduced me to a number of key concepts that remain central to my work now. The Young Vic is famous as a theatre-in-the-round. When configured as it was designed and built, the audience are essentially sitting in concentric circles. It was my first experience of working in this way and it certainly changes your stage-craft as an actor. The kind of stage images that you create with the other actors are now '3D', every audience member receiving a different 'picture' at every changing moment. This is fascinating for both actor and director, as you can no longer control what each person sees as you do in the frame of a proscenium arch – there are *literally* multiple perspectives moment to moment as the drama moves.

One key shift is that you the actor have a different relation to the audience: they surround you, they create the space in which you tell the story rather than sitting outside it looking in. They become the container for the story rather than just being the observer. Standing in the middle of the circle you feel very powerful, you become the focal point. And having sat in the audience too, you feel that energy of connection – it feels harder to disconnect, to take your eyes away from the stage, than in conventional end-on theatre where everyone sits in the dark looking in one direction.

But I think the most interesting thing for the audience dynamic is that you are not only powerfully connected to the energy of the story onstage, you are also palpably *connected to the other members of the audience*. A collective communal experience takes place. You clearly see people's attention, their emotion, their connection to the story on the other side of the circle – you see them laugh, you see them cry. And you also see their lack of attention if it is not there. It can be unforgiving, as there is no escape from the contract you have made with your audience. Theatre at its best always seeks to create this charged, live experience, shared between a group of people – growing up playing in a theatre-in-the-round, I came to feel this very keenly. My job was to create that sense of communion, to connect people to a story and to connect people to each other.

And now at Narativ a workshop day starts with setting out a single circle of chairs for everyone in the group.

The image

The act of telling your story is always one of connection and empathy. Your story offers up your experience for the listener as an invitation to understand you, to understand what has happened to you. And the only way for the listener to do that is through *their own experience.* If I tell a story of standing on a beach barefoot with a melting ice-cream in my hand, your mind searches for similar experiences that you've had, in order to understand this. Connection. Empathy.

At Narativ we work with a methodology to enable people to tell their stories in a way that really connects and has impact for the listener. The most powerful stories are ones that transport us into someone else's experience, taking us to a real moment in time and space when something happened to them. When we work with people to explore their stories one of the first stages is something we call 'excavation' – uncovering the layers of a story that are buried under the surface, but that once uncovered can be used to bring a story to life and make it vivid for the listener.

This act of vividly transporting the listener is enabled by using all the senses to do it. We experience everything that happens in our lives through our five senses – if we can use them in retelling an experience, we activate the senses of the listener, allowing them to inhabit the experience themselves, to step into our shoes. As with the example of the ice-cream on the beach, if the teller spoke about the feeling of it melting and running over their fingers, it will light up the parts of your brain where you hold sensory memories of experiencing the same thing. Similarly, we know that referencing freshly cut grass or newly ground coffee will make an olfactory connection, allowing you to believe you are experiencing those smells anew; and descriptions of sounds and tastes work in the same way. And of course there is sight – the painting of descriptive pictures in words, full of detail and specificity, really serves to transport those listening to another time and place, into another experience.

Image in storytelling is so powerful and we encourage storytellers to 'paint pictures' as an important tool in communicating an experience. One key part of Narativ's methodology is 'show, don't tell'. In the end, it is the images you create that people really remember. We use the metaphor of a camera in telling a story – you ask yourself, 'What would the camera see?' Importantly, using this idea precludes all the internal processes, the thoughts, feelings and interpretations attached to a story

– the camera cannot see them. It can feel very counter-intuitive not to tell the listener what things mean, as it can seem that this is what is important in telling a story. When we tell stories we naturally want to control the experience of the listener so that they will really 'get' our experience. Conversely though, if you leave space for the listener to bring their own interpretation, through the filters of their own life experience, they will have a much more personal connection to the story and a more impactful experience of it. Also, evoking all the senses and painting vivid images enables the listener to step inside the story, connect to you and empathize with your experience.

Jane: It's 1983, in a youth club in Coventry. A room with different-coloured gaffer tape marking out a basketball court on the wooden floor, the basketball hoop on the wall next to the barred window. The room smells of sausage rolls, plimsolls and kids. Lawrence and I are on the stage area, a circular canvas floorcloth. In front of us are rows of teenagers on plastic bucket seats, laughing and leaning in to each other, pointing at Lawrence's sweaty face. Lawrence and I are shouting at each other now, 'Oh yeah, I know your game,' I say, 'feel sorry for me – I'm mentally handicapped.' The kids gasp, Lawrence says, 'I hate you,' and stomps off the stage.

Ten minutes later we are standing holding hands, bowing to the kids who are stamping their feet and applauding. 'Now you are going to get the chance to have a conversation with the characters from the play, this is called "hot-seating". So split in half, some of you go with Lawrence, and the rest come with me.' There's a scraping of chairs and a cacophony of voices and then I'm facing them, my group. They ask questions: 'Did you always know you wanted to be a nurse?', 'What's it like having a brother like that?', 'Why is your hair blue?' Then from the middle of the group I hear someone say, 'It's not right. The way that you talked to your brother in that play, it's not right.' I couldn't see who was talking, and the rest of the kids were shifting in their seats, turning round to have a look. The voice was slightly indistinct, a couple of kids laughed and nudged each other. 'It's not right,' he said again. I leaned in my chair so I could see who was speaking and I caught sight of him. It was a boy of about 15 years of age, with sandy-coloured hair and a wide pink face. My cheeks went hot, sweat breaking out on my top lip as I registered that he had Down's syndrome. Then he got up out of his chair, his voice booming across the whole room, kids from the other group turning to see what was happening. 'People talk to me like that sometimes. I don't like it.' I stared at him. 'Sometimes when I go to school and I'm standing at the bus stop, people slow down in their cars and they shout things at me. They say "mong" and "spaz" to me and I don't like it and it's not right.' The kids all around him were quiet. They stared at him or looked at the floor. And then I saw next to him there was a woman. She didn't look at him or at the floor but kept her eye-contact with me. Tears were rolling down her cheeks and dropping into her lap.

Half an hour later Lawrence and I were rolling up the floor cloth and taking our set and props out to the van. At the end of the room the boy and the woman were waiting. 'That's them,' I said to Lawrence, and we stopped as they came towards us. 'Hello,' the woman said, 'we just wanted to thank you for your play. I hope we didn't spoil it.' 'Not at all, we want people to speak up afterwards, that's what it's for.' I looked at the boy, who smiled at Lawrence, 'This is my son Joe,' the woman said, 'and I've never heard him say any of that before.'

Community

Narativ's work creates story spaces where individuals explore and tell their stories. The common thread is the dynamic connection between the listener and the teller, the shared experience, whether it is a 1:1 session, a group story circle, or a live storytelling event in a theatrical space. The two complementary aspects to this activity are always listening and telling. By listening we get to understand commonality through the connections we make with someone else's story. We listen, we witness, we connect. Through telling we get to hear our own story from our own mouths as we tell it, providing the opportunity to hear it anew and also potentially to hear other people's reflections on it. In this way, in these spaces the individual is able to integrate themselves into a *community* of listening and telling. This is an activity that allows us to see ourselves as part of a greater whole of human experience.

The ability to place a series of events from our lives in context is where the power in telling our stories lies. It allows us to see that there is a multiplicity of stories, that there is no single story that defines us. We also see that there are multiple perspectives that can be told about any one single experience, multiple meanings if you like. When we share stories with others this is reinforced – we hear and connect to other people's experience, and we hear varied reflections on our own.

Jane: Sitting in a group sharing stories last week, I heard someone say something we often hear on receiving reflections on a story. The man paused and said, 'I never knew that was in there!' The meaning is always in the ear of the listener.

So this act of sharing stories is a communal act of integration, an act of connection and identification. When we tell our story and listen to someone else's, we get to relate, to identify, to connect our experience to theirs and their experience to ours. We see that our isolated, solitary and subjective experience of being a human being can be understood in a wider context, in a tapestry of others' experiences, which can allow for perspective, understanding and acceptance.

I often tell the story of my encounter with Joe in workshops because for me it illustrates the power of theatre, of all storytelling, to connect – Joe saw his story being told and it empowered him to find his voice. That was his connection. What listeners reflect back to me is that it is a story about many things: advocacy; the capacity of humans to be cruel; the ability of children to hide things from their parents; the benefit of youth clubs; the experience of being intellectually impaired; etc. etc. There is a multiplicity of stories in one story. For those perspectives I'm grateful to our listeners for enriching my story and reminding me how storytelling creates a community of connections.

The origins of Narativ: In conversation with Murray Nossel

In looking at Narativ's work in relation to the subject of this book, we returned to the source to have a conversation with Murray Nossel about the origins of Narativ in his work at the AIDS Day Program in Brooklyn in 1994. These are Murray's reflections on storytelling, trauma and the creation of community.

I went to work in the AIDS Day Program in Brooklyn as part of my PhD. This was at the height of the AIDS epidemic and there were no treatments. Or there was AZT, but it really wasn't working. So the atmosphere was one of urgency, one in which people were dying. When we're dying there is a tremendous feeling of being alone. You are dying and all the other people around you are living. Nobody can be going through that for you, or with you. So if we just take that one little point and we zoom in on it – there was this existential reality that was going on in that programme. The second thing is that they were heavily marginalized in the community. In 1994 there was enormous stigma attached to HIV. And the patients on the programme were further stigmatized by the fact that many of them were gay and many of them were IV drug users, that's how they had contracted HIV. So a great number of the patients had been 'excommunicated' by their families. When the clients were coming into the programme those were the kind of burdens they were bearing. And now they are in this programme together. And the strange thing, if you want to talk about the creation of some kind of culture or community, was that it was in the basement of a building and it had no windows! So you have the creation of this little micro-culture in this basement and there is no connection to the outside world by virtue of the fact that there are no windows!

Every day they come to this place. There was a doctor and nurse, an acupuncturist – they were provided for medically. And there are recreational activities, including art therapy. It depended how many showed up each day, but there could be maybe 50 people, of all ages ranging from early twenties to forties, and all ethnicities, but mostly people of colour. The art therapy happened in the main space – there was a common room when you came in, and in the centre where everyone sat around and where meals were served, was a woman called Stella Dawson – the art therapist. The art was happening in the centre of everything.

In a sense there was the patina of community, in that you've got a group of people who are brought together by virtue of a common illness or diagnosis, and they are in the same place for the same number of hours throughout a day and doing the same things together. But does that constitute a community? No. It constitutes a group of people coexisting. What makes a community is something much more threaded with shared meaning. And I don't think that by virtue of those people being there together all in the same place that you could automatically assume there was going to be shared meaning.

People were dying, and life would just go on. For those of us who were still alive, we saw that that was what was going to become of us…next week. We saw that we would also just be a scant memory in everyone's mind, and we saw that our belongings would show up in these garbage bags which nobody would come to claim. So part of what created the atmosphere there, was that the death of each person presaged your own death. Not many of us have the opportunity to see what it is going to be like when we are dead, what it is going to be like after. But they did...

There was this absolute *crisis of meaning* on the most fundamental level. And that's when I tried therapy with them and that just failed miserably. Why? Because...things were racing. It was going so fast. When things are going so fast it's...well it can be a very bad time to sit and reflect, particularly also when you've got physical symptoms.

So I had no idea what to do! Firstly, I was stunned myself, faced with my own mortality – it was very confronting. And when you have trained as I was in a hospital and have been part of a private practice, the therapists, the doctors and all of that, they are venerated. There's a power dimension to the whole thing. You've got power and they don't. Well, in this programme the power relations were completely inverted. The patients didn't give a fuck who you were and what your status was, because the doctors were helpless, nothing was helping the patients! So the patients were furious with the doctors and they were quoting the *New England Journal of Medicine*, they became experts on what was going on and what they needed. They were going to tell you how you were going to help them, you were *not* going to tell them. They had nothing to lose! For someone who had been trained in a mental hospital in apartheid South Africa where power relations were very circumscribed and expert knowledge was very venerated, it was just all pulled out from under me! I felt – 'Who am I?'

I had nothing to do basically, because it didn't work to talk to these people one-on-one, that was useless! There were these big tables in the common room and that's where everyone made their art and I started hanging out there a lot, partly because I love making stuff myself. And I made a poster, and the poster basically said 'Write your own history!' I put a picture of Martin Luther King on it, and I put a picture of Gandhi... Everyone could see that I was making this poster, it was probably about eight feet long and about five feet high. So then I announced it – Friday at 11 o'clock! And one person came. One! And it was Sharon and she told me her story.

In a sense I had no choice but to just be myself, because you couldn't pretend in there, there was no hiding. That edge that I would usually have and that I had come to depend on didn't exist! And that's where I realized the only thing I can really do is *listen* to them. The only thing I can do is create a context for them to connect with one another, because what I have to say is pretty much irrelevant. So instead of it being about my input, it became about my capacity to create a context for them. And the input I could give them didn't derive from my therapeutic knowledge, it derived from my knowledge as a playwright. I had come to the States to learn playwriting and this idea of 'show, don't tell'. So basically my job was to teach them how to tell a good story. The therapeutic aspect came into how we listened to one another. It was about recognizing all those things that get in the way of our ability to listen to one another in order for those stories to be told.

So what was the Storytelling Group? It was really a way of *arresting time*. But instead of arresting time in an individual, you do it with a group, you bring everyone together. And for these people it really was a 'sacred space', because it was a moment to claim your life in the presence of other people, as witnessed by other people. It was literally that 'I am being witnessed in the fact that I am alive, I am being witnessed in the fact that I exist.' So it was beyond the fact that 'My story is being witnessed with all the pain that I went through.' It was 'By telling my story, I live; by virtue of being able to tell my story, I am alive!' It was like that.

The idea of stopping time is in the definition of a 'ritual' – a ritual is a way that you can stop time for a moment and reflect on or experience profound meaning. Some people would say individual one-on-one therapy is that kind of ritual. You go in for 50 minutes, you pay your money, these are all elements of a ritual. What happened in the AIDS Day Program was that this ritual, the one-on-one experience of seeing a patient as a therapist, was not sufficiently powerful to hold the gravity of their experience. It took a group, the energetic field of a group, to create that ritual. They became a community.

The biggest group was Christmas 1994, because Christmas is loaded with all this expectation about how families are going to be, and all this collapsed with this group of people when they were with their families. So there was this horrible feeling of isolation. And what happened? They all came. They came because there was a real need to connect. There were probably 30 people and they just poured in. They were all: 'I wanna go, I wanna go next!' That was 'witnessing' at its peak, Christmas '94.

What happens is that when you start to share stories in this way and you start to find all these areas of commonality, the areas of commonality bring you into a tremendous feeling of 'heart closeness' with one another. It's not an intellectual exercise of thematic consistency, seeing how many themes we can actually find that coincide. Your hearts feel connected by virtue of sharing these stories. And that's what creates *community*. So I think that is what happened to those people in that AIDS Day Program – it was that feeling of heart connection. Even though you are going through the biggest shit in your entire life, for those four minutes while that other person is telling their story, you are there for them in that room. So it really is that 'gift exchange' that we talk about at Narativ, where you are both receiving and giving the gift of listening and storytelling. To think that you are dying and that you are being rendered or deemed completely worthless by your family and your community and you can still give something that is of value to another person, is very acknowledging of your existence. Giving your listening in that moment is enough.

Reference

Nossel, M. (2018) *Powered by Storytelling*. New York, NY: McGraw-Hill.

TO BE CONTINUED...
THE WIDER CONTEXT
AND THE RETURN

17

Image and Narrative in a Changing World

Sarah Deco

What does it mean to be a therapist in these times? Every era has its traumas, there have never been shortages of wars or natural disasters. But the developed world today is experiencing, I would argue, psychological trauma with particular intensity. We seem at the moment to have a 'perfect storm' of conditions which, while challenging us in ways that demand unusual psychological resilience, also undermine our capacity for recovery and restoration.

There are many challenges facing us and each deserves a chapter of its own, but the biggest of these, the overarching story, is climate change and the irreparable damage we are causing to the natural world. Climate change or global warming is such a large problem it is perhaps almost unthinkable. It is a 'hyperobject', something beyond our capacity to fully comprehend, which has 'an extension in time and space…historically beyond the range of human cognition' (Manley and Holloway 2019, p.133). 'Hyperobject', a concept first used by Timothy Morton, refers to things that are 'massively distributed in time and space relative to humans' (Morton 2013, p.1). These vast, unthinkable things are both highly abstract and unable to be pinned down, but are also 'right here in my social and experiential space' (Morton 2013, p.27).

Things that are 'right here in my social and experiential space' of course form the background to any therapy that takes place, both individual and group, and are so ubiquitous and familiar that we may overlook their effect on us and our clients. That doesn't mean we should ignore them. And questions many of us are asking ourselves now are:

how do we live and work in ways which are congruent and appropriate to the emergency we are facing? How do we properly face the realities of it and behave accordingly?

Some years ago I experienced an epiphany. I remember it with an eerie clarity. I was sitting in a café drinking coffee and reading a newspaper. I turned the page and saw a headline which said that, for the first time in human history, ice was on course to disappear entirely from the North Pole. I felt deeply shocked. I looked around the café at people chatting, reading, etc., a scene of normality. But I realized that nothing could ever be normal again. Climate change was real, it was happening now, we were responsible for it and it was going to change all of our lives. Both before and of course since that moment I have read countless articles about climate change, but at that particular moment the usual padding of denial fell away and I felt the full force of what it really meant.

Since then I have tried to explore how the knowledge I've gained from training and working as an art therapist and group analyst over the years might contribute in some way to understanding this new context in which we now all live and work. This has led me down various paths. The most enduring and meaningful of these paths for me has been storytelling, particularly oral storytelling. Traditional storytelling, the telling of myths, folktales and fairytales, has become a significant part of the way I work as a therapist. (For a fuller exploration of myth and climate change see Deco 2015.)

Another important influence on my thinking about these themes has been the work of the Climate Psychology Alliance (CPA). This organization has created a forum in which to have conversations about how depth psychology can contribute to understanding the psychological and cultural causes of climate change. I feel a profound gratitude to this group of colleagues for stepping up to the challenge of trying to bridge the gap between psychotherapy and the environmental challenges that face us.

The nature of my therapeutic work has changed significantly as a result of these explorations. The arts have a crucial part to play, and storytelling an important and particular role. We live in a world of mass extinctions and warnings about the terrible consequences we face if we do not drastically and urgently reduce our carbon emissions. As well as taking action, it is important to identify the narratives that have led us into the precarious situation we find ourselves in. This task is both subtle and immense, local and global, as the threads run though the warp and weft of every part of our lives, economy and culture.

If we cultivate an ecological view, we see that the living world is a vast, interconnected web of relationships of which we are a part. We see straight away that 'the problems that are arising, are the result(s) of the fragmented way that we assess the world...the underlying metaphors of our culture hold true to the logic of industrial causation and mechanized interaction. Life is not like that' (Bateson 2016, p.31).

The discipline of ecology and the new developments in physics allow us to perceive a much more interconnected world, in which the relationships between things are where the important understanding lies. Although we may feel in the psychotherapy world that relationships are where we direct our attention, we rarely consider relationships with the larger than human world. Why this narrow scope of vision? We are of course children of our time, and our time and culture are shaped by Enlightenment values. And as philosopher Freya Mathews reminds us, the mechanistic point of view which has dominated science since the Enlightenment sees 'nature as consisting of matter, and matter is insensate, dead, drab, unvarying, devoid of interests and purposes' (Mathews 1991, p.31). The seeds of separation from nature are sown in the very way we are taught to think about the world. But more than this, we are, she says, a culture and an era without a 'cosmology'. A cosmology in the sense of something that 'serves to orient a community to its world, in the sense that it defines, for the community in question, the place of humankind in the cosmic scheme of things' (p.12). A cosmology is the ground from which the myths grow that shape a culture, and it seems we have dislodged ourselves from one, based on the religious certainties of the past, without providing ourselves with a new one. Does this matter? According to Mathews,

> a culture deprived of any symbolic representation of the universe and of its own relation to it will be a culture of non-plussed, unmotivated individuals, set down inescapably in a world that makes no sense to them, and which accordingly baffles their agency. (p.13)

Climate change and other 'large system' problems can elicit a response of helplessness. Indeed, these problems are so huge that it is hard to see how any one of us can make a difference. Although this is a real perception of the problem being one that has to be tackled collectively, perhaps there is also inertia related to the lack of a cosmology that

Mathews talks about? Has our sense of our own agency, as Mathews says, become 'baffled'?

Writing in *The Guardian*, Keenan Malik talks of a loss of faith in God, but also in reason. 'The world appears increasingly trapped between an atomized liberalism on the one hand and a sense of community created by fundamentalist religion or reactionary politics on the other' (Malik 2018); or to put it another way, our culture is characterized by both hyper-rationality and a widespread revolt against rationality (Lasch 1991).

Could it also be that we are affected by a 'learned helplessness'? A learned helplessness of the kind caused by complex chronic trauma. Van der Kolk (2015) describes an experiment by Maier and Seligman in which painful electric shocks were administered repeatedly to a group of dogs. Even when they were able to escape, the dogs did not attempt to get away from what was torturing them. Van der Kolk realized that in his traumatized human patients, something similar was happening. Their fight–flight response had been damaged. Continued unescapable trauma had undermined their capacity to take action to change the situation. 'Trauma robs you of the feeling that you are in charge of yourself, of what I will call self-leadership' (van der Kolk 2015, p.203).

So have we collectively had our capacity for self-leadership injured? Certainly it seems that many years have gone by since the dangers of 'global warming' were first flagged up by scientists and that remarkably little has happened. Climate scientists, and activists, have tried many ways to mobilize us to rise up in protest at what is happening to the delicate balance of our planet's atmosphere, with very limited success. Could it be that we are collectively suffering from the effects of a culture-wide version of long-term complex trauma? The result of which has diminished our psychological resilience and collectively left our state of mind less sound than it should be?

'The great thinning' described by Michael McCarthy (2012), the experience of sensing the abundance of nature, the quantities of insects, birds and other creatures diminishing does not perhaps justify description as a trauma, in the sense it is defined clinically. But it can and does create an ambient anxiety and a deep sense of loss that may be very hard to articulate. We just do not have the words. In her essay 'Elegy for a Country's Seasons' Zadie Smith (2018, p.14) points out that

> there is the scientific and ideological language for what is happening to the weather, but there are hardly any intimate words. Is that

surprising? People in mourning tend to use euphemism; likewise, the guilty and ashamed. The most melancholy of all the euphemisms: 'The new normal.' It's the new normal, I think, as a beloved pear tree, half drowned, loses its grip on the earth and falls over.

Robert McFarlane (2016, p.3) describes how words such as *bluebell* and *acorn* are being dropped from children's dictionaries and vocabularies in favour of words like *block-graph*, *blog* and *chatroom*. How can we find the words to locate ourselves as part of a world in which other species live if we do not have the words to describe them?

There is good evidence that unless we can find the words and create a coherent narrative, we have difficulty recovering from traumatic events (Amir et al. 1998). But there are thankfully attempts to create language to enable us to articulate the pains of this new situation. 'Solastalgia' is a term coined by the Australian philosopher Glenn Albrecht to describe existential distress caused by climate change. It is in fact included in The *Lancet* Commission's description of the impact of climate change on human health and wellbeing (Watts et al. 2015). It may become as much a common part of the language of psychiatry and psychotherapy as 'trauma' and 'personality disorder'.

The loss of diversity described by McCarthy is not just a feature of the natural world but is also present in our human ecosystem. As local high streets fail, and village pubs close, the idiosyncrasies of local cultures falter. As global chains take over town centres, there is a loss of the local varieties of vernacular visual language. As more and more of our communication with each other is through the homogenized language of the internet, there is a loss of local varieties of vernacular, verbal language. The loss of diversity and rich connection amongst communities, whether cultural or biological, impacts resilience and the capacity to survive traumatic events.

Harold Searles (1975, p.367) in his paper 'Unconscious processes in relation to the environmental crisis' postulates that

> an ecologically healthy relatedness to our non-human environment is essential to the development and maintenance of our sense of being human and that such a relatedness has become so undermined, disrupted and distorted, concomitant with the ecological deterioration, that it is inordinately difficult for us to integrate the feeling experiences, including the losses, inescapable to any full-fledged human living.

Distance from the natural world and its cycles of growth and decay diminishes our ability to tolerate the ordinary losses of life. If our capacity to cope with the normal losses of ordinary experience is diminished, then how much greater must be our deficit when it comes to the capacity to heal from trauma?

Bryant Welch (2008, p.7) proposes that the American mind is under an attack of a focused and intentional kind:

> As a country we have had a very hard time acknowledging the true role of trauma in our lives. It is, however, a paradoxical, colorless, odorless substance that now permeates all we experience, think, and do... Because of the pervasive trauma, our minds are already taxed when we begin participating in our liberal democracy.

The particular techniques used in American politics Welch identifies such as 'gaslighting' (i.e. creating situations in which people begin to doubt their own judgement) potentially re-traumatize a population already disconnected from the societal resources that could make them able to cope with this kind of mind manipulation.

Steffi Bednarek (2018, p.8) brings into personal experience how this state of disconnection might be affecting us:

> Refugees washed up on the shores of our rich countries make me blind and numb... In order to survive, I anaesthetize my human experience. I have forgotten how to connect with the land underneath my feet. I have killed off any notion that the Earth may be alive. I have banished God and the idea of the sacred. What I believe in is my individuality and the value of owning things. Matter is dead. I feel lost and empty. I live in a world and in a body that I no longer know how to inhabit.

This experience sounds so related to the experience of trauma. The numbing, the sense of emptiness and distance from the felt experience of the body. It is also a profound experience of abandonment and neglect. Distance from the natural world, its cycles of growth and decay, its reminder that we are part of a larger whole, is a loss we find hard to identify and articulate because it is related to preverbal experience. It is an experience of loss of containment and loss of safety at a fundamental level. 'If we broaden Winnicott's "holding environment" to include the holding environment of the earth, we can understand how realising the enormity of the crisis can threaten psychological disintegration and collapse' (Dodds 2011, p.123). This can evoke an unbearable anxiety, which we continually push out of view rather than threaten ourselves with the overwhelming fear and grief it might evoke. It is all the more unbearable because at some level we know we are all complicit in creating this loss. To deal with it we self-sooth with unnecessary consumption and in the process have become addicted and are perhaps unable to remember or recognize what true nourishment might feel like.

And so, we see that the very same problems that are creating our unsustainable use and abuse of the natural world may also be mirrored in the suffering of individuals who look for therapy.

Van der Kolk proposes that the way out of the chronic traumatized state is through the body, through awareness of how the body's alarm systems have been changed by repeated trauma:

> One of the clearest lessons from contemporary neuroscience is that our sense of ourselves is anchored in a vital connection with our bodies. We do not truly know ourselves unless we can feel and interpret our physical sensations; we need to register and act on these sensations to navigate safely through life… While numbing (or compensatory sensation seeking) may make life tolerable, the price you pay is that you lose awareness of what is going on inside your body and, with that, the sense of being fully, sensually alive. (van der Kolk 2015, p.272)

Much has been written on the importance of healing the body–mind split and how suffering must be understood as belonging to the 'body-self' (Frank 2013, p.169). What we are slow to acknowledge is the split between ourselves, or what we understand as ourselves and the non-human world. Perhaps the notion of a 'self' needs updating.

Living in us are communities of bacteria. Only one cell in ten that exists within the 'skin-bag' (Bateson 2016, p.28) we call ourselves is human. As we walk through the world, we are not single discrete beings, we are in fact microbiomes of trillions of creatures. Ecosystems interpenetrate each other, and we are part of many ecosystems whose health is also our health. A psychotherapy built on this understanding would have to hold as fundamental that the health of the biosphere in which we exist is essential to our own health and that the boundary between physical and mental health is a false one. This is one of many ways in which an ecological understanding might change our way of approaching a whole range of problems.

Concepts such as rewilding are also pointing the way to repairing the damage that's been done to ecosystems. Take for example the estate at Knepp in Sussex, a 3500-acre farm which over the last 12 years has seen species endangered in Britain, such as the nightingale and the turtle dove, return to nest (Tree 2018). The attitude has been to let nature do what it wishes. This approach has been so successful it is now inspiring conservation in many different parts of Britain and the world.

Could we not find an equivalent kind of rewilding for our human communities? Natural systems tend to be 'self-organizing', and as such are 'insensitive to perturbations or errors, and have a strong capacity to restore themselves, unlike most human designed systems' (Heylighen 2001, p.9).

Rather than endlessly implementing new managements strategies, perhaps just taking a hands-off approach might be more effective and less expensive. In the health service, for example, this might involve, rather than managing services and teams, allowing them to 'self-organize'. In the Netherlands home care provided by 'self-organizing' nursing teams has had multiple benefits:

> ...patients are highly satisfied. Moreover, surveys of employees over several years indicate the organization has the most satisfied workforce of any Dutch company with more than 1,000 employees. The model also appears to achieve savings. (Gray, Sarnak and Burgers 2015, p.1)

'Rewilding' human communities may involve relearning forgotten skills. Learning to repair, share and mend, but also remembering that each of us can contribute culturally, by making art, singing, creating theatre, etc. Much of our 'entertainment' makes us only consumers. We watch television and movies as passive receivers, whereas forgotten skills such as oral storytelling involve the audience in actively imagining.

Traditional stories (folktales, fairytales, myths and legends) give us a strand of connection to a past in which societies were less atomized and more able to navigate the area between the hyper-rationality that has been the dominant mind-set and the irrationality that seems to be surfacing in populist politics and conspiracy theories. Why does this matter? The manipulation of narrative has become so powerful with the wide reach of social media and its capacity to claim our attention and offer us both true and fake news. This means that story literacy is crucial in discriminating between toxic and constructive narratives. 'We think we tell stories, but stories often tell us, tell us to love or to hate, to see or to be blind… The task of learning to be free requires learning to hear them' (Solnit 2014, p.2).

The importance of finding and being able to share the narrative of traumatic events is, as I've already said, an important aspect to healing. Myths and legends do this on a collective scale and can help us to find a way of speaking about the immense global changes taking place.

Linking our own stories to traditional stories allows us to see that what may seem very lonely and solitary experiences are in fact part of our common human experience and shared across time and cultures. As our minds begin to be shaped by the intense use of technology, oral storytelling offers a chance to maintain and develop the old skills of memory and, more importantly, skills of imagination. In order to tell a story well it is necessary to visualize, to make something come alive in your mind. This is one of the natural resources of our species. In former times disciplines of the imagination such as 'memory theatres' and the bardic traditions of song and poetry added richness to local cultures and trained and developed the creative power of the imagination. This was often in the service of maintaining a community's connection with its past, strengthening its identity and making it more able to withstand difficulty and change.

In attempting to help individuals heal from trauma we need to see our efforts as existing in the context of the wider trauma landscape, one overarching aspect of which is our separation from the larger than human world. This will affect what we perceive in our clients. Where we might have seen a maladjustment, for example, a more connected way of seeing may perceive a grieving response, or an expression of existential terror.

Théogène Niwenshuti (2018), a survivor of the Rwandan genocide, in his paper 'A critique of embodiment', describes how he tried to find ways to heal this traumatic experience. His chosen art and healing form was dance performance. During a period he spent alone to try and process the experience he was trying to embody in his art, he describes how

> …during one night, I felt the need to move from the bed to sleep on the ground. I moved the bed away and slept on the floor for the rest of the process and even after, until I had submitted and presented the first part of my work. There was a very calming, comforting feeling when I moved to the ground – a sense of freshness, holding and full

contentment crossed my whole body. Every time I moved to the ground, I felt like I was going back into myself and into the ground; going into the ground was like going back into the soil, re-taking root in the whole of me, cells and soul feeding into a circulating, life-giving and renewal of energy. I could relate this feeling to another experience I had when one day, still during the war, an exhausted and feverish boy collapsed and, in an attempt, to save him I covered his body with soil and leaves. I had been lost with a group of children and women. Before dawn, the boy recovered, jumping around with energy, ready to continue the journey home with us. (p.123)

Although his paper is called 'A critique of embodiment', it is showing how attempts at 'embodiment' and healing coming from a split and un-embodied culture result in re-traumatization. It is only with an understanding of the interconnectedness of us all, with place, ground, planet, that we can begin to heal.

In other words, going back home could mean to (re)embody all within ourselves, the earth, the world, the other, and allow them to (re)embody us, not just in thought, superficial word, academic or political rhetoric, but in heart, feeling, emotion with an aim to achieve an integrated connection. Allowing this (re)embodiment, (re)claiming this connection, challenges the individualistic and survival logic that today's modern technological world seems to be promoting. (Niwenshuti 2018, p.123)

By trying to hold in mind both the cultural narratives and the individual struggle to be part of this culture and this society which forms each of our personal stories, we may, as Nora Bateson (2010) says, 'begin to stitch the world together again, from the inside'.

References

Amir, N., Stafford, J., Freshman, M.S. and Foa, E.B. (1998) 'Relationship between trauma narratives and trauma pathology.' *Journal of Trauma Stress 11*, 2, 385–392.

Bateson, N. (Writer/Director) (2010) *An Ecology of Mind: A Daughter's Portrait of Gregory Bateson* [Documentary film]. http://anecologyofmind.com/thefilm.html

Bateson, N. (2016) *Small Arcs of Larger Circles: Framing Through Other Patterns.* Axminster: Triarchy Press.

Bednarek, S. (2018) 'How wide is the field? Gestalt therapy, capitalism and the natural world.' *British Gestalt Journal 27*, 2, 8–17.

Deco, S. (2015) *Resilience and the Mythic*. Climate Psychology Alliance. Accessed on 3/9/2020 at www.climatepsychologyalliance.org/explorations/blogs/108-resilience-and-the-mythic

Dodds, J. (2011) 'The Ecology of Phantasy: Ecopsychoanalysis and the Three Ecologies.' In N. Totton and M.J. Rust (eds) *Vital Signs*. London: Routledge.

Frank, A. (2013) *The Wounded Storyteller* (2nd rev. edn). Chicago, IL: University of Chicago Press.

Lasch, C. (1991) *The Culture of Narcissism: American Life in an Age of Diminishing Expectations*. New York, NY: W.W. Norton.

Gray, B., Sarnak, D.O. and Burgers, J. (2015) *Home Care by Self-governing Nursing Teams: The Netherlands' Buurtzorg Model*. The Commonwealth Fund. Accessed on 3/9/2020 at www.commonwealthfund.org/publications/case-study/2015/may/home-care-self-governing-nursing-teams-netherlands-buurtzorg-model

Heylighen, F. (2001) 'The science of self-organization and adaptivity.' *The Encyclopedia of Life Support Systems 5*, 3, 253–280.

Malik, K. (2018, 1 April) 'Yes we've lost our faith in God, but we've lost our faith in reason too.' *The Guardian*, p.15.

Manley, J. and Holloway, W. (2019) 'Climate Change, Social Dreaming and Art: Thinking the Unthinkable.' In P. Hoggett (ed.) *Climate Psychology: On Indifference to Disaster*. Bristol: Palgrave Macmillan.

Mathews, F. (1991) *The Ecological Self*. London: Routledge.

McCarthy, M. (2012, 19 December) 'Nature studies: Our generation has seen a great thinning that we can't quite name.' *The Independent*.

McFarlane, R. (2016) *Landmarks*. London: Penguin.

Morton, T. (2013) *Hyperobjects: Philosophy and Ecology after the End of the World*. Minneapolis, MN: University of Minnesota Press.

Niwenshuti, T. (2018) 'A critique of embodiment.' *Strategic Review for Southern Africa 40*, 1, 117–133.

Searles, H.F. (1972) 'Unconscious processes in relation to the environmental crisis.' *Psychoanalytic Review 59*, 361–374.

Smith, Z. (2018) 'Elegy for a Country's Seasons.' In *Feel Free: Essays*. London: Penguin.

Solnit, R. (2014) *The Faraway Nearby*. London: Granta.

Tree, I. (2018) *Wilding*. London: Picador.

van der Kolk, B. (2015) *The Body Keeps the Score: Brain, Mind, and Body in the Healing of Trauma*. New York, NY: Penguin Random House.

Watts, N., Adger, N.A., Agnolucci, P., Blackstock, J. et al. (2015) 'Health and climate change: Policy responses to protect public health.' *The Lancet 386*, 1861–1914. doi:10.1016/S0140-6736(15)60854-6

Welch, B. (2008) *State of Confusion: Political Manipulation and the Assault on the American Mind*. New York, NY: Thomas Dunne Books, St. Martin's Press.

Postscript

A notable absence from the book is a chapter which may have been called 'Storying the Ending with Images and Narratives'. The chapter may have addressed the work of care homes, hospices, end-of-life care and the important work that goes on there in providing spaces to represent and reflect on mortality, grieving and the acceptance and welcoming of limits and threshold.

To meet this sense of what is missing and say goodbye for now I will quote part of a communication I received from Sarah Deco, the author of the last chapter, written in the light of the Covid-19 pandemic, which has suddenly created a deadly fringe around all our awarenesses.

> The pandemic has brought death right up into the foreground for us and a new relationship with mortality; both the possibility of personal death and the experience of how we are being collectively changed.
>
> For some the great mythic stories of mankind are in essence explorations of our relationship to death. We are now in the process of myth making. The narrative of this huge global experience can only exist on the scale of a myth and as we are living it, we are also composing it. We are both being told the story and we are telling it, forming it as we go along. With each act and decision we make day to day creating a picture of how this transition in human society will take shape. Awareness of our fragility has broken through our normal defences and death's presence pervades our parks and living rooms, our supermarket queues and hospitals. One thing already seems certain, we are entering into a new epoch and we have both the burden and the privilege of being alive as it is born. It may take many decades before we really see its shape.
>
> The startling imagery of healthcare workers in personal protective

equipment (PPE), the lines of beds containing patients plugged in to ventilators, the empty streets. These have become images that define this time and will presumable carry with them fearful associations for large numbers of people across the world. The separation of physical proximity from each other may make this harder to recover but we are also seeing how the appreciation of the natural world is burgeoning as a solace in troubled times. The sense of things being dismantled, broken down and apart only has meaning if we can re-build something more whole, vital and sustainable.

> the knowledge that all things must pass can soften or harden the human spirit. It can soften it, taking away its arrogance and its ignorance of human mortality; it can harden it, taking away its hope. (Dunne, *Time and Myth*, p.12)[1]

We have lost a lot though the experience of this pandemic. But the biggest loss is I think that of the naive belief in our safety from harm, a belief that everything would, pretty much, continue as it always has.

We can in the light of these chapters maybe have a greater sense of our human resilience, despite the disaster, and continue to wonder/wander where this story will now take us, still find some excitement in the unknown, and keep faith in our creativity in meeting these challenges yet with a wholehearted sense of what is at stake.

---

1   John Dunne (1973) *Time and Myth: A Meditation on Storytelling as an Exploration of Life and Death*. London: SCM Press.

About the Contributors

Tom Barber, MA, DProf, is an Integrative and Existential Psychotherapist, Supervisor, and Academic Mentor working in private practice for the last 25 years. Since the late 1990s he has been involved with running courses in counselling and psychotherapy, both in the UK and internationally, and was previously a director at a leading UK training institution, Contemporary College of Therapeutic Studies. Having completed his doctorate in Existential Psychotherapy and Counselling in 2017 through Middlesex University, he now divides his professional time between private practice, clinical supervision, student mentoring, and writing. He has authored and co-authored a number of published books, chapters and articles in various psychotherapeutic modalities, most recently in the areas of trauma and PTSD.

Charles Brown is an adult psychoanalytic psychotherapist, a member of the Guild of Psychotherapists and a UKCP Honorary Fellow. He is also a specialist addictions therapist. Charles lectures widely and is a training therapist and clinical supervisor. He is former Chair of Ethics Council for Psychoanalysis and Jungian Analysis (CPJA), which is a college of the UK Council for Psychotherapy, and he is current Chair of the British Association for Psychoanalytic and Psychodynamic Supervisors. In 2013 Charles founded BeMetherapy, an organization that provides low-cost long-term psychotherapy to visible minority ethnic people living in South London, where he also works in private practice.

Sheila Butler works as a Clinical Researcher and Coordinator of Projects in Mental Health Psychological Therapies and in specialist Personality Disorders Therapeutic Community Services in the NHS. She is a practising psychotherapist and a lecturer at the Open

University, developing courses on Research with Children and Young People, Childhood Studies and Child Development and Mental Health and Counselling. In addition, she contributes to development of the Open University schemes supporting students' learning with virtual and multimedia-based technologies and is involved with the Children's Research Centre (CRC) based at the Open University. She is the coordinator of the Practitioner Research Network (PRN) for the UKCP and a member of the Society for Psychotherapy Research (SPR). Her focus is on engaging research for practice, on the research–practice interface and on the potential of different methods of research to open up a space for new ideas and collective thinking on creativity and collaboration. She is currently developing a programme focusing on the interface between nature and wellbeing.

Sarah Deco is an art therapist who taught for several years on the Art Therapy training in Hertfordshire. She is also a Group Analyst and trained at the Institute of Group Analysis, London, where she was also Director of Training. She is on the advisory panel of the Climate Psychology Alliance. She is also a Storyteller, performing and running workshops in the oral tradition of traditional storytelling.

Tony Gammidge is an artist, filmmaker and freelance art therapist who specializes in using animation as a way of telling stories and exploring narrative. He has run animation projects in prisons, secure units and in psychiatric settings and with asylum seekers at Freedom From Torture in London. He is also a member of the Art Refuge team who provide art and art therapy to asylum seekers in Calais. He also runs Animated Tales, which provides training in animation, filmmaking and narrative in a therapeutic context. www.tonygammidge.com

Dominik Havsteen-Franklin completed his PhD in Psychoanalytic Studies at Essex University and an MSc in the Psychodynamics of Human Development. He has been a practising art therapist in mental health services for over 20 years, leading on arts and mentalization in health contexts. He also leads on evaluation, design and delivery of arts-based intervention development and training through the NHS training organization ICAPT. Further to this, he has also led or co-led clinical model development for arts therapists working with different clinical groups as part of different research teams. His published research to date has focused on practice development and defining clinical models from patient and clinician perspectives for a range of mental health contexts, including psycho education, complex depression, psychosis, personality disorder and responding to the Covid-19 pandemic.

Anthea Hendry is an art psychotherapist in independent and private practice, a supervisor, and a trainer. She lectured in further education and then qualified as a social worker before training as an art therapist. For many years she has specialized in working with both children and their parents and adults who experienced early complex trauma. She has worked with these client groups in various settings, including social services, the voluntary sector, the NHS, where she was Principle Art Psychotherapist, and now as a self-employed art psychotherapist. She has written articles and chapters about this work and is co-editor of the book *Creative Therapies for Complex Trauma: Helping Children and Families in Foster Care, Kinship Care or Adoption* (2017, Jessica Kingsley Publishers).

Emma Hollamby is Arts and Health Programme Manager at Ben Uri Gallery where she manages three core programmes under the Ben Uri Arts and Health Institute. Emma facilitates both art discussion and art-making sessions, also overseeing a programme of ongoing research and evaluation, disseminating evidence in support of this expanding field. Her keen interest in community-centred arts outreach with gallery collections has led to significant experience of working creatively with older adults in care settings.

Tania Kaczynski trained at Goldsmiths, University of London. She has many years' experience as an art psychotherapist in mainstream education working in a variety of schools. She emphasizes the need to 'normalize' and integrate psychotherapy. In addition she was a senior practitioner at The Studio Upstairs for over ten years, supervising students curating exhibitions and lecturing at Hatfield College. She has extensive experience of working with asylum seekers and refugees, firstly at Freedom From Torture, and in 2014 she co-founded the New Art Studio, where she is currently the Director.

Richard Kidgell has post-traumatic stress disorder resulting from experiences in the armed forces in the early 1980s. He was a client of Combat Stress for about 14 years from 2004, where he received art therapy from Janice Lobban. From 1985 until 2008, when he retired early for health reasons, he worked for GEC Marconi and BAE Systems as a professional systems-engineer, designing radar and communication systems. Since starting treatment at Combat Stress, he has become an enthusiastic amateur artist and amateur writer, and has twice given co-presentations to the British Association of Art Therapists with Janice Lobban.

Tania Korsak is a social anthropologist and Clean Language facilitator-trainer. She runs a private practice, in Brussels and online. By learning to pay close attention to people's subjective experience, her research with families facing severe chronic illness in their child has become an opportunity for rethinking ways in which carers and medical practitioners may work together for the benefit of all parties. Her work has given her an edge for working with midwives and the medical profession both individually and in groups. Clean Language in anthropological fieldwork, and vice versa, thus becomes a tool for paying attention to people's self-actualization in the continual becoming of this world.

Janice Lobban, art psychotherapist and Churchill Research Fellow, has specialized in veteran mental health since 2001 and has lectured on the subject in the UK and internationally. She edited and wrote chapters for *Art Therapy with Military Veterans: Trauma and the Image* (2017, Routledge). Currently, she is developing partnerships with museums and galleries to support socially avoidant or isolated veterans. She works privately and for a veterans' mental health charity.

Jon Martyn is an art psychotherapist and has worked with marginalized people, in group and therapeutic community settings, primarily working with borderline personality disorder, victims of torture and forced migration. Jon lectures on the MA in Art Psychotherapy at Goldsmiths, University of London, provides clinical supervision and is co-founder of the New Art Studio, a therapeutic art studio for asylum seekers and refugees (www.newartstudio.org.uk).

Dan Milne and **Jane Nash** are Directors of Narativ and are a married couple. Narativ's origins are multidisciplinary: Jane and Dan have backgrounds as theatre and filmmakers and they now combine coaching individuals and organizations in Narativ's Listening and Storytelling methodology with their own creative practice. This practice often takes the form of making work from their own stories.

Dominic T. Plant, DClinPsy, PhD is a Chartered Psychologist with a background in developmental and clinical psychology. He has worked at a specialist NHS CAMHS trauma clinic at the Maudsley Hospital, and held teaching positions at UCL and King's College London. Dominic presently runs a private clinical psychology practice in the City of London, alongside being a director and co-founder of TraumaPsychology (www.traumapsychology.co.uk), a bespoke education and training consultancy. Dominic identifies as a person of colour, and has grown up across Africa, Asia and Europe.

Carlotta Raby is a Chartered Clinical Psychologist, psychotherapist, and trauma specialist who has additionally studied human rights law, and held participation roles with UK mental health charities (such as YoungMinds, the Mental Health Foundation and the Evidence Based Practice Unit). Carlotta founded Luna Children's Charity (now Action for Child Trauma International: https://actinternational.org. uk) and is a director and co-founder of TraumaPsychology (www. traumapsychology.co.uk). Carlotta currently works as a clinical psychologist for the NHS full-time, as a consultant on trauma-informed practice to the Metropolitan Police Service, and as a volunteer psychologist with select charities.

Nili Sigal has a background in fine art and psychology. She has experience of working in mental health services, private practice and the voluntary and education sectors. She coordinated the monthly clinical meetings and wrote a blog for the London Art Therapy Centre for several years and was the founder and coordinator of the Complex Trauma, PTSD and Dissociation Special Interest Group for the British Association of Art Therapists. Nili works for the NHS, where she specializes in trauma-focused art therapy with adults. She is a supervisor and an approved EMDR therapist who has written about combining art therapy with EMDR. Previous publications include a chapter on working with children and families in *Art Therapy in Private Practice* (2018, Jessica Kingsley Publishers).

Gillian Solomon is a British-born art and cognitive behavioural psychotherapist with a BAFA from the University of Cape Town. She practised as an educational art therapist and artist during Apartheid in South Africa, with children traumatized by racist separate development, and in high-conflict families. She studied Family Law at Nelson Mandela University, and lectured family advocates at the Justice College Pretoria on attachment prior to the new SA Children's Act being passed in 2005. She documented the development of SA art therapy before and after democratic elections and highlighted the problems of post-colonial practice within the Health Professionals Council of South Africa in *Inscape* (2006). She completed an art psychotherapy master's at Derby University, as well as studies in cognitive behavioural therapy. She has worked for the NHS and has utilized the integrated use of imagery with CBT working with NGOs in SA. Since the onset of Covid-19 Gillian has focused on anxiety and its effects. She became a Diplomate of the Academy of Cognitive and Behavioral Therapies in 2017 and mentors CBT Nest. Gillian writes about the importance of imagery in evidence-based practice and its use in psychological change.

Martin Weegmann is a Clinical Psychologist and Group Analyst with 30 years' NHS experience. He has specialized in substance misuse, personality disorders and complex needs. Martin brought out *Psychodynamics of Addiction* (2002, Wiley) and has published five other books, his latest, *Psychodynamics of Writing* (2018, Routledge). He is busy at work on a new book, *Novel Connections – Between Literature and Psychotherapy*. He lives and works in London.

James D. West completed his first degree in Fine Art and Art History and then trained as an art psychotherapist. He was awarded his master's degree in Applied Psychoanalytic Theory in 1999. He has been a self-employed consultant within a number of organizations and in private practice since 1994, is a supervisor working in a wide variety of practice contexts and modalities, including addiction rehab, and is a registered clinical hypnotherapist and a master practitioner of NLP. He is a long-standing peer reviewer for the *International Journal of Art Therapy* and other journals. He was both an author and the editor of *Art Therapy in Private Practice* (2018, Jessica Kingsley Publishers) and is committed to the development of practitioner research.

Sandra Westland, MA, DProf, a former senior teacher in secondary education, is an Integrative Existential Psychotherapist, academic mentor and supervisor. She has worked in private practice for the last 20 years, which has included work with paramedics, ambulance technicians, emergency call handlers, prison officers and crisis teams. She was a director and tutor of a busy psychotherapy training college in London and has run Trauma Workshops in both the UK and internationally over the past three years. She completed her doctorate in Existential Psychotherapy and Counselling in 2017 through Middlesex University, and has authored a number of published books, chapters and research articles in psychotherapy. Sandra has a keen interest in examining various aspects of the human condition and the impact of trauma and recovery.

Subject Index

Author Index

CPI Antony Rowe
Eastbourne, UK
April 04, 2025